Charlotte

"Charlotte's Enterprises"
by Louise Barden and Helen Rishoi

Produced in cooperation
with the Charlotte Chamber of Commerce

Windsor Publications, Inc.
Chatsworth, California

Charlotte
City at the Crossroads

A Contemporary Portrait
by Bea Quirk

Windsor Publications, Inc.—Book Division
Managing Editor: Karen Story
Design Director: Alexander D'Anca
Photo Director: Susan Wells
Executive Editor: Pamela Schroeder

Staff for Charlotte: City at the Crossroads
Manuscript Editor: Douglas P. Lathrop
Photo Editor: Robin Mastrogeorge
Proofreader: Liz Reuben
Senior Editor, Corporate Profiles:
    Judith L. Hunter
Production Editor, Corporate Profiles: Una
    FitzSimons
Customer Service Manager: Phyllis Feldman-
    Schroeder
Editorial Assistants: Kim Kievman, Michael
    Nugwynne, Kathy B. Peyser, Priscilla
    Salazar, Theresa J. Solis
Publisher's Representatives, Corporate Profiles:
    Bob Berry, John Rosi, William Metcalfe
Layout Artist, Corporate Profiles:
    Mari Catherine Preimesberger
Designer: Ellen Ifrah
Layout Artist: Thomas McTighe

Library of Congress Cataloging-in-Publication
    Data
Quirk, Bea, 1954-
    Charlotte, city at the crossroads: a con-
    temporary portrait/by Bea Quirk.
        p.   cm.
    Bibliography: p. 282
    Includes index.
    ISBN 0-89781-315-4
    1. Industrial promotion—North Caroli-
    na—Charlotte. 2. Charlotte
    (N.C.)—Economic conditions. I. Title
HC108.C33Q57 1989
330.9756'76043—dc20   89-35792
                                   CIP

Windsor Publications, Inc.
Elliot Martin, Chairman of the Board
James L. Fish III, Chief Operating Officer
Michele Sylvestro, Vice President/Sales-
    Marketing

*Frontispiece: The city of Charlotte is alive with
refreshing spirit, economic opportunity, and community pride. The heart of this vibrant city, known as
uptown Charlotte, is pictured here rising over the
graceful trees and calm waters of Marshall Park.
Photo by Paul Epley*

Contents

Marshall Park and the Charlotte skyline produce a gleaming urban landscape during the city's cooler winter months.
Photo by Jim McGuire

Preface

In one of the many personal interviews I conducted with Charlotteans in the course of writing this book, the late Ben T. Craig, president of First Union Corporation, told me: "You've got to remember—Charlotte is a city that is politely on the make."

We both got a good chuckle over his observation, and it is one that is apropos in many ways. Charlotte is very much a city of contradictions. It is definitely a place of commerce where people make money, but it is also a genteel place where common courtesy and good manners are as important as how much you have in the bank.

Charlotte touts itself as a city of the New South, and as it has grown, it has taken on many of the trappings—both good and bad—of its Northern counterparts. Yet it remains very much a Southern city. Its people are friendly and generous to strangers and newcomers, yet it takes time to learn the ways of Charlotteans and to truly get to know them. The Queen City is a place of high culture—with an opera, symphony, and art museum—but it's also a place where tractor pulls and wrestling matches are big draws. It's a city of old-time wealth and proud natives, of newcomers from outside the region looking for new opportunities, and of rural North Carolinians who come here to seek their fortunes.

Somehow, their different backgrounds and cultures—even ways of speaking—mingle and rub off each other to create a city whose citizens seize opportunities and take actions to make the place they call home even better. Charlotteans are a proud people—maybe even to a fault—and they have a fierce love for their home city. This book attempts to grasp the reasons why and to show what that love and pride has accomplished here in the City at the Crossroads.

It is truly impossible to thank the innumerable people who have helped me make this book a reality. Some have provided facts and information, others have given me food for thought, and yet others have generously offered that all-important emotional support, love, and understanding.

I would, however, like to name a couple of special folks: M.S. Van Hecke, business editor of the *Charlotte Observer*; Jim Teat of McGuire Properties; and Dan Morrill, history professor at the University of North Carolina at Charlotte and consulting director of the Charlotte-Mecklenburg Historic Properties Commission. It was Dan who showed me how to look at Charlotte in new ways and with a sense of stewardship, and who provided me with inspiration when the Muses were quiet.

It is with this spirit that I dedicate this book to the people of Charlotte, past, present, and future. May they always remain stubborn and contradictory.

The setting sun casts a silhouette of St. Peter's Roman Catholic Church against the Wachovia Bank & Trust in uptown Charlotte. Photo by Mark Fortenberry

Uptown Charlotte glitters in the evening light.
Photo by Kelly Culpepper/Transparencies

Chapter 1

An Agreeable Village

The area that we today call Charlotte-Mecklenburg has always been an attractive place of pleasant beauty.

Spanish explorer Hernando de Soto is thought to have wandered through its thick forests and rolling terrain, but he did not tarry long. Other European explorers after him, however, recognized and appreciated the beauty of this bountiful land.

In 1700, with a small party of Catawba Indian guides who called the area home, English traveler John Lawson was moved to write that the Indians "had the finest part of Carolina while the English were enjoying only the fag end" in the east. It was, he said "delicious country" between the Catawba and Yadkin rivers.

In his travels here, Lawson followed a path taken by Indians for generations before him, one that other white explorers and settlers also followed: the Great Trading Path, which led from the Great Lakes to the Carolinas and points farther south. For countless years before the Indians traversed it, the path was probably a track used by migrating animals or a trail left by buffalo, which once were plentiful in the region.

This also was the path that settlers followed—south from Pennsylvania and Maryland and north from Charleston—to this virgin land of opportunity and freedom. The geography of the Carolinas was not conducive to the western migration from coastal

The Pineville birthplace of our 11th president, James K. Polk (the grandnephew of Thomas Polk, who was one of the area's first settlers), has been reconstructed and serves as a visual memorial to the early founding families of Charlotte. Photo by Mark Fortenberry

cities that had taken place in many of the other American colonies, and so the Piedmont (from the French, meaning "foothills") was settled by those hardy souls willing to make the long, onerous overland trek in Conestoga wagons.

Many of these folk were Scotch-Irish Presbyterians who, in search of liberty and religious freedom, had traveled from Scotland to Ulster in Ireland, then on to Pennsylvania in the New World, and from there to the Carolinas, where they had heard that land was cheap or free and full of rich potential. They brought with them a love of the land, a deep religious fervor, a respect for learning, an attitude of feisty and spirited independence, and a streak of shrewdness.

The first recorded settlers in what would become Mecklenburg County were Thomas Spratt and his family, who made their journey from Pennsylvania. They were soon followed by Thomas Polk of Cumberland, Pennsylvania, who came here, legend has it, to be close to Spratt's daughter Susannah, whom he married in 1755.

Polk might have journeyed for love, but he was also a practical and pragmatic man with a commonsense outlook toward the future. He chose to build a home for his new bride right on the Indians' trading path, where it intersected with another trade route that ran from east to west. That east-west route became modern-day Trade Street, and Polk named the Great Trading Path Tryon Street to curry favor with the colonial governor, William Tryon.

By starting this new settlement at the crossroads of two trading paths, Polk set the course for Charlotte's destiny, for the town would always be a center for trade and commerce. Today the intersection of Trade and Tryon (or simply, the Square) marks the center of Charlotte, serves as the focus for the entire Piedmont region with its more than five million inhabitants, and is where Charlotteans merge their dreams and visions of the future with a sharp eye and sturdy grasp of reality.

Polk and his neighbors knew what they wanted and how to get it. In 1762 they named their county Mecklenburg, after the German home of Queen Charlotte, the young, fragile-looking bride of King George III, and they named their settlement Charlotte Towne, hoping further to gain the good graces of the royal government.

Maybe it worked, maybe it didn't. But Polk wasn't taking any chances. After the town received its charter from the General Assembly of North Carolina in 1768, he and his neighbors began work on a political strategy to ensure that Charlotte was made the county seat instead of Rocky River, which was larger. At their own expense, they went ahead and built a courthouse—not on a corner of the crossroads, but smack-dab in the middle of the intersection. The strategy worked, for in 1774 the legislature made Charlotte the county seat because it already had a functioning courthouse (albeit a crude one).

The new county seat was located in the backwoods, on the frontier of the young colonial state where life was hard even by the standards of the time. But it was not completely isolated from the political goings-on of the 1770s. In fact, Charlotteans, in their own indomitable fashion, were on the fore-

FACING PAGE: The Hezekiah Alexander Homesite Rock House, which dates back to 1774, conjures up images of Charlotte's colonial years. Photo by Mark Fortenberry

ABOVE: Spirited pioneers in search of freedom and opportunity came to the area of Mecklenburg County by following previous generations of Indians, who had traveled the Great Trading Path from the Great Lakes region to the Carolinas. Photo by Mark Fortenberry

Thomas Polk came to the Charlotte area from Pennsylvania in the mid-1700s. Upon settling at the crossroads of the two great trading paths, Polk and his neighbors chose to name their new community Charlotte Towne, after Queen Charlotte, the wife of King George III. Pictured here is the home of Thomas Polk's grandnephew, James K. Polk. In this room one can imagine the lifestyle and activities of Charlotte's early settlers. Photo by Mark Fortenberry

front of the changes occurring.

The Scotch-Irish were stubborn and freedom-loving by nature, and they were no friends to the British crown or its government, which they perceived as tyrannical and despotic. This attitude was inflamed by orators and firebrand preachers such as Alexander Craighead. On May 19, 1775, when county militia delegates heard the news about the skirmish at Lexington and Concord a month earlier, they decided they had had enough.

Right there, at the crossroads of Trade and Tryon, the delegates declared Mecklenburg's independence from Great Britain, and the next day the Mecklenburg Declaration of Independence, as the document was called, was read amid loud cheers and the throwing of hats into the air. (It was because of this event that the intersection came to be called Independence Square.) But these rebellious frontier folk also recognized the need for order, and on May 31 they passed a list of "Resolves" setting up the structure for the county's operation.

A copy of the declaration was sent

by messenger to Philadelphia, where the Continental Congress was in session. But it was considered too radical at the time, and it was never introduced. In 1800 the original document was destroyed by fire. Consequently, the veracity of the declaration's existence is one of much debate among historians, although locals have been proudly touting and celebrating it for more than 200 years. No one questions the existence of the Resolves, however, as they were published in the *Cape Fear Mercury* in August 1775.

The Revolutionary War made the rugged life in Charlotte even harder for its citizens. That didn't stop them, however, from fighting courageously and gallantly for their new nation. And it was with their heroic determination and fighting spirit that they began the overall defeat of the British.

In 1780 Charleston fell to Lord Cornwallis, followed by the Americans' defeat at Camden, one of their worst of the war. The road to Charlotte lay open, and there was nothing the colonists could do about it except harass the advancing enemy troops.

This illustration detailed the elegance and charm of Charlotte's Central Hotel in the late 1800s. Courtesy, North Carolina Division of Archives and History

Late in the morning of September 26, 1780, the British entered the town on East Trade Street, and the Battle of Charlotte occurred. The Americans, under the leadership of Colonel William R. Davie, were badly outnumbered, and their only viable strategy was to use guerrilla tactics. The British took over the village easily, and Cornwallis settled into Tom Polk's house on the corner of the Square, where the battle took place. It was the first—and still the only— time the city has been invaded by enemy forces.

It was a bitter time for the City at the Crossroads, but it didn't stop the inhabitants from making life miserable for the occupying troops. Cornwallis' expected Loyalist support never materialized, his troops had great difficulty getting supplies and food from the countryside, and the troops were almost constantly barraged by snipers and ambushes.

Just one week after the battle, a foraging party of 300 men traveled to McIntyre's farm for supplies, only to be met by tenacious local farmers who shot at them seemingly from behind every tree and by ferocious attacks from the bees in McIntyre's hives. The incident became known as the Battle of the Bees. Afterward Cornwallis called Charlotte "a damned hornets' nest."

The stay was an unpleasant one for Cornwallis, who wrote, "Charlotte is

The Battle of Cowens Ford in the Revolutionary War is reenacted at historic Latta Place. Photo by Mark Fortenberry

This gold mining illustration shows the technique of boring used by miners in their quest for gold in the Charlotte area in the early 1800s. Courtesy, North Carolina Division of Archives and History

ing like a rooster in the Square.

Things settled down in Charlotte after the war, but two separate events occurred in the 1790s that changed the face and character of this little town and set it on its course of becoming a great center of trade and commerce. Yet no one saw the change coming, and when President George Washington visited Charlotte in 1791 (at a picnic supper held in the yard of Tom Polk's house on the Square), he wrote in his diary that the town was "a trifling place."

The first event, the invention of the cotton gin by Eli Whitney, occurred in 1793. With this new machine, growing cotton was highly profitable, and it became the area's first cash crop. Farmers could now produce cotton 12 times faster, yet its price declined by only 50 percent, making the farmers six times richer. The fertile land of the Piedmont was a perfect place to grow cotton, and farmers turned to it with a vengeance.

Charlotte quickly became the commercial center for this new industry. Banks appeared to serve the new needs of growers and buyers. In part, the city was considered a good place for the cotton trade because the intersection of Trade and Tryon was wide enough to allow an eight-mule cotton wagon to turn around, making it easier to get crops to buyers.

As a result of the growth of the cotton industry, farmers could no longer depend on their families to carry on all the labor the industry demanded. So they began buying more slaves. By 1830 there were about 5,000 slaves in Mecklenburg County, out of a total population of 25,000.

The other momentuous event of the 1790s was perhaps not as significant in the long run, but definitely more exciting: the discovery of gold in

an agreeable village, but in a damned rebellious country." The British defeat at Kings Mountain laid ruin to his plans to conquer the South—plans already in disarray due to the brave Mecklenburgers—and his troops left Charlotte in a panic just 16 days after their initial victory here. Cornwallis was defeated at Yorktown the next year, and a new nation was born amid a great celebration throughout the land. In Charlotte it was reported that one man showed his delight by crow-

1799 in what is today Cabarrus County. Young Conrad Reed was playing in Little Meadow Creek instead of attending Sunday school one morning, when he found a brightly colored rock that he brought home to his family, who used it as a doorstop. Three years later, it was discovered that this 17-pound rock was a golden nugget.

It was the first authenticated discovery of gold in this country, and it triggered its first gold rush. At the peak of the gold fever in the 1840s, there were about 75 to 100 mines within a 20-mile radius of the city, including shafts running beneath Tryon Street. But by 1850 only 10 mines were still open, and many gold miners had moved on to California.

Charlotte became a boomtown of sorts, further increasing the need for banks and businesses to serve the thriving economy. In 1835 Congress, after five years of lobbying by the tireless, undaunted Charlotteans, approved a U.S. mint for the city. No doubt contributing to the approval was the fact that both President Andrew Jackson and Senator James K. Polk, chairman of the Committee for Ways and Means, were native Mecklenburgers. (Polk, later president, was born near Pineville. Jackson was never quite sure where he was born, so both Mecklenburg County and Union County in South Carolina claim him as a son.)

The mint, then located on West Trade Street, was completed in 1837 and was designed by the famous Philadelphia architect William Strickland. Half-eagles and quarter-eagles minted here had a C over the date. Before it closed in 1861 (when North Carolina seceded from the Union), the mint produced over $10 million in coinage.

But Charlotte's growth was limited nonetheless, and its population did not grow between 1830 and 1850. Part of the problem was the decline of the gold mining industry, but another major factor was the lack of adequate transportation. There was no continuous water transportation to the coast, and travel by land was slow. In 1850, for example, it took eight days to travel to Cheraw, South Carolina, Charlotte's nearest market.

Charlotteans were aware of this problem, and as usual, they decided to do something about it. They lobbied and agitated the state government for some 25 years before the first railroad arrived in the city in 1852. The Charlotte & South Carolina Railroad connected Charlotte with Columbia and Charleston, beginning a new era in the city's history and setting the stage for it to become a commercial center for cotton, textiles, and other goods. When the first train arrived on October 14, some 20,000 people showed up to greet it.

Thus the City at the Crossroads became a railroad crossroads. In 1854 the North Carolina Railroad was opened—running from Charlotte to Goldsboro via Raleigh, Greensboro and Salisbury—followed six years later by the Statesville Line. The effect on the town was almost immediate. Between 1852 and 1860, Charlotte's population doubled to 2,265.

But Charlotte's march to prosperity was halted by events that touched upon the very heart and soul of the nation: the War Between the States—or, as it is also called, the Civil War.

Cotton was an important cash crop in the early years of Charlotte agriculture, and held a strong demand for many years. A wagon of cotton bales is shown here in 1898 being transported along one of Charlotte's new roads. Courtesy, North Carolina Division of Archives and History

On May 21, 1861, North Carolina became the last state to secede from the Union. Mecklenburg County contributed greatly to the cause, providing some 2,700 soldiers as well as cannonballs and iron products from the Mecklenburg Iron Works and cloth for uniforms from the Rock Island Woolen Mill. Charlotte—even though it was hundreds of miles from the sea—also became the site for the Confederate Navy Yard in 1862 when Norfolk was deemed too vulnerable. The yard never actually built any ships, but it did produce such military items as propeller shafting, wrought-iron rifle shot, and gun carriages.

Charlotte was spared any direct fighting, and General William Sherman passed east of the area. But the people were not unscathed by the conflict. For example, Abel Belk, father of William Henry Belk (founder of Belk Stores and grandfather of former Charlotte Mayor John Belk), was drowned by raiders from Sherman's army who were convinced he knew where the family gold had been hidden.

In April 1865 Jefferson Davis and his Confederate cabinet held their last meeting in Charlotte. There is still a marker on Tryon Street indicating where Davis was standing when he heard of President Lincoln's assassination. Mary Anna Morrison Jackson, widow of Stonewall Jackson, took up residence in Charlotte and reigned as first lady for many years after the war. Her home stood on what is now Stonewall Street.

Federal troops remained in Charlotte until 1872. Freed slaves voted and elected the city's first black aldermen. In 1866 Biddle Institute (later Biddle University, and then Johnson C. Smith University) was founded, with ambitions to become "the colored Princeton of the South." In 1888 Good Samaritan Hospital, the first hospital for blacks in the country, was opened.

But times were trying for farmers, both black and white. The land had been picked clean, money was scarce, and credit was unavailable. Many came to town looking for a better life. In 1869 Charlotte had a population of 4,400, 42 percent of it black. The city was bounded roughly by Morehead Street on the south, Twelfth Street on the north, McDowell Street on the east, and Cedar Street on the west.

Charlotte was a good place to start again after the war. It still had excellent railroad connections, its facilities had not been damaged or destroyed by the conflict, and there was a strong core of machinists and engineers who had worked at the iron works and naval yard. The city was primed for the industrialization that the South sorely needed to survive the destruction of its agrarian economy, and there were predictions it would become the "London of the South." But what the city needed most were leaders with a vision.

One such leader was D.A. (Daniel Augustus) Tompkins. His name is certainly not a household word in Charlotte today, but it was this South Carolina native whose vision and vitality forged the old Charlotte into a city of the New South. Tompkins epitomized the spirit and determination that made Charlotte the driving, ambitious city it has become, and he probably would be quite comfortable walking along Tryon Street today.

The widow of Stonewall Jackson, Mary Anna Morrison Jackson, moved to Charlotte after the Civil War and became a prominent citizen in the community. She is pictured here circa 1880. Courtesy, North Carolina Division of Archives and History

An engineer and industrialist who graduated from Rensselaer Polytechnic Institute in Troy, New York, Tompkins arrived in Charlotte in 1882 as a sales representative for Westinghouse. He spoke and wrote—passionately, zealously, and prolifically—about the South's need to turn away from agriculture and to industrialize, processing its own raw products rather than shipping them elsewhere.

Tompkins did more than preach, however, and he was tireless in his efforts to change the face of the South. He set up a system under which towns could build their own mills and then pay for them in installments. In Charlotte he started the Southern Cotton Oil Company and later, in 1893, the Atherton Mill.

He also was instrumental in getting the 12-story Independence Building, Charlotte's first skyscraper and tallest building in the state at the time, built in 1905 (It was torn down in 1981 to make room for the Independence Tower), and in 1892 he took over the faltering *Charlotte Chronicle*, turning it into a successful organ for the burgeoning business community. He renamed the paper the *Charlotte Daily Observer*, and it later became the *Charlotte Observer*. In 1894 Tompkins began the Southern Manufacturers' Club, the forerunner of the modern-day City Club.

Tompkins, of course, was not alone in his vision, and the industrialization of the area was viewed in moral terms by many. Mill owners were seen as saviors, providing employment for the poor, development for the community, and a source of pride for the region. Said one preacher of the day: "I personally believe it [industry] was God's way for the development of a forsaken people."

It certainly provided employment for those country folk leaving the land and pouring into the towns and cities. By 1904 there were some 300 mills within a 100-mile radius of Charlotte, with more than 85,000 looms and over three million spindles, about half the looms and spindles in all of the South. The first mill in Charlotte was built by the Oates family in 1881 with an initial investment of about $130,000. In 1904 there were 17 mills within the city limits.

Cheap waterpower made these mills possible, and most were built along rivers, notably the Catawba and South Fork. But again, men with vision stepped in. Cheap electricity could supply these mills even better and would further add to their proliferation.

The old 12-story Independence Building, which was Charlotte's first skyscraper, is pictured here in the 1920s. Note the Ivey's store down the way. Courtesy, North Carolina Division of Archives and History

A Southern Public Utilities trolley provided convenient transportation in uptown Charlotte in the 1920s. Courtesy, North Carolina Division of Archives and History

In 1904 James Buchanan Duke, president of the American Tobacco Company, invested $2 million and founded the Southern Power Company (later Duke Power Company). Building the plants and convincing skeptical mill owners was difficult at first, but by 1926 more than one-eighth of the cotton spindles in the nation were supplied with electricity from Southern Power. When Cannon Mills was founded at the turn of the century in Kannapolis, the supply of cheap electricity was a major factor in the decision to locate there.

Charlotte served as the commercial, service, and distribution center for the cotton and textile industries. It was to Charlotte that raw cotton was shipped to supply the area mills, and then from Charlotte that finished textile goods

were shipped to markets across the country. In 1888 four railroad depots served the city's freight traffic, and 20 passenger trains arrived and departed daily. To service the industry's financial needs—and those of other developing businesses—there were three banks: First National, Commercial National, and Merchants and Farmers National.

But although the railroads enabled Charlotte to grow economically, it was another form of transportation—the trolley—that made for the biggest change at the turn of the century. On May 18, 1891, the first electric streetcar left the Square at 3 P.M. for the suburb of Dilworth. Newspaper accounts described the "great and jolly crowd" that cheered its inaugural run and also noted that "bouquets were sent to adorn the car with, and every one was wild with joy."

The trolley system was just one project of the Charlotte Consolidated Construction Company, more commonly known as the "Four Cs." Its president was Edward Dilworth Latta, a haberdasher who came to Charlotte in 1876. A South Carolina native educated at Princeton University, Dilworth started a men's clothing store here, but his ambitions went far beyond fashion.

Latta and his partners, including Mayor F.B. McDowell, started the streetcar as a way to connect downtown Charlotte with their new 442-acre suburban development, called Dilworth. Their plan was to sell lots and homes to Charlotte's industrial work force, which was increasing rapidly as the city began realizing its manufacturing potential. It was a smart gamble—in 1892 Tompkins' Atherton Mill opened nearby, and he purchased 20 lots for workers. The Charlotte Trouser Company opened in Dilworth in 1894, and six more factories opened in the suburb in 1895, causing the *Daily Charlotte Observer* to call Dilworth the "Manchester of Charlotte."

Once Dilworth's survival was ensured with housing for industrial workers, Latta then turned to providing housing for the middle class. He even went so far as to contract with the Olmsted Brothers, who helped design Central Park in New York, to do the landscaping. But his favorite achievement, it is said, was the Latta Arcade, an elegantly styled downtown office center that opened in 1915 and which still stands today at 320 South Tryon Street.

Other suburbs also came into being at this time, notably Myers Park in 1910, developed by George Stephens on the 1,100-acre plantation owned by his father-in-law, John Springs Myers. Stephens called in city planner John Nolen and andscaper Earl Draper, both from Cambridge, Massachusetts, to design the community, which at the time was called the best development south of Baltimore.

As Charlotte grew, the trolley system was expanded several times. Its introduction was considered risky at the time, but Charlotte's city leaders were willing to take the chance in their efforts to modernize the city. Eventually, the system did pay off handsomely, as it enabled people to move out from "in town." This resulting sprawl made for a larger consumer base and created a larger demand for goods and services. The city's population grew from 11,551 in 1890 to 34,014 in 1910.

The city's economy—and population—got another large boost when the U.S. entered World War I. A war meant the need to train troops, and Charlotteans, sniffing a great opportunity, lobbied hard to get a base located here. They succeeded (as they often do), and Camp Greene opened in the summer of 1917. The camp housed between 30,000 and 60,000 men during its two-year existence and always had a larger population than the city itself. That influx pumped money into the economy and added excitement and vitality to the atmosphere.

Charlotteans opened their arms and their homes to the men in uniform, and so there was deep mourning when the influenza outbreak of 1918 killed

Leading citizen Edward Dilworth Latta, a major developer in Charlotte's history, founded the Dilworth housing development, established the city's first electric streetcar, and constructed the elegant Latta Arcade office center. Courtesy, North Carolina Division of Archives and History

many of the soldiers. They left Charlotte in wooden coffins amid torrential rains and red mud.

When the war ended in 1919, Camp Greene was dismantled in 90 days, vanishing almost without a trace. But the camp did have a lasting effect, as many of the men who served here returned to Charlotte to live and work.

Business boomed and there were good times aplenty in the years following the war and into the Roaring Twenties. The *Charlotte Post*, a black-owned newspaper, was founded in 1918, and it is still publishing today. In 1922 WBT, the South's first fully-licensed broadcasting station, signed on the air, and it was joined by WSOC in 1929. In 1926 a privately owned airport began operation, the precursor of today's city-run airport. A year later a branch of the U.S. Federal Reserve Bank opened in Charlotte.

Charlottean Cameron Morrison was elected governor in 1920, and his major accomplishment—winning a $65 million appropriation for the state's highway system—earned him the title, "The Good Roads Governor." The creation of this system helped Charlotte become a trucking crossroads, adding to its important role as a distribution center.

Morrison was also a friend to education, expanding the University of North Carolina at Chapel Hill, the University of North Carolina at Greensboro, and the North Carolina College for Negroes in Durham. His large working farm and mansion in Charlotte was once centered where SouthPark is today and encompassed much of the surrounding area.

The Great Depression hit Charlotte hard, as it did the rest of the country, but that didn't stop all progress or change in the city. In 1930 the first airmail was delivered, and 30,000 people

came out to the airport to see the first mail arrive. Although air travel was still for the brave, Mayor Ben Douglas, Sr., realized how important it would be to Charlotte's future. He was able to obtain funds for construction of a modern airport through the Works Progress Administration (WPA), pending approval of city bonds by the voters. In December 1935 voters approved $50,000 for the project. The facility officially opened on June 1, 1937.

Arts and culture also flourished. The old U.S. mint was moved brick-by-brick from downtown to the exclusive Eastover neighborhood to become, in 1936, the state's first art museum. The Little Theatre (now Theatre of Charlotte), the oldest community the-

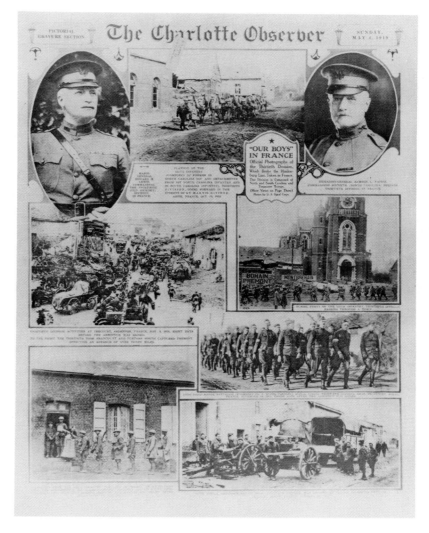

ABOVE: The Charlotte Observer *proudly ran a pictorial essay on May 4, 1919, featuring the soldiers of the Thirtieth Division who fought in World War I. The Thirtieth Division was composed of troops from North Carolina, South Carolina, and Tennessee. Courtesy, North Carolina Division of Archives and History*

FACING PAGE, TOP: *Drivers, mechanics, and enthusiastic spectators gathered on October 25, 1924 to participate in the inaugural race of the Charlotte Motor Speedway in Pineville. Courtesy, North Carolina Division of Archives and History*

FACING PAGE, BOTTOM: *The intersection of Trade and Tryon streets was photographed in the early 1900s, showing early model automobiles and a city trolley of that time. The old Independence Building, which stood 12 stories, can be seen to the right with its striped window awnings. Courtesy, North Carolina Division of Archives and History*

Cited as an outstanding example of the civil rights movement of the 1960s and 1970s, enlightened Charlotte residents continue to work together as a cooperative and supportive community. Photo by Mark Fortenberry

A prominent force in the community since the 1890s, the Charlotte Observer continues to be a strong source of news, information, and commentary. Photo by Ernest H. Robl

ater in North Carolina, began its operations in 1927, and the Charlotte Symphony was founded in 1932.

When World War II began, Charlotte had a population of approximately 100,000. There were shortages, of course, and Charlotte men once again went off to fight for their country. But this war didn't cause as much upheaval in Charlotteans' life-styles as previous conflicts. During the war, however, the military did take over part of the city's airport for a training center, renaming it Morris Field.

Life in postwar Charlotte, like in the rest of the nation, was heady as the troops returned home with dreams of getting back to work, starting families, and recreating prosperity. It didn't take long for changes to occur.

Along with the returning soldiers came numerous immigrants. Many Greeks came to Charlotte, and today they make up the largest ethnic community in the area. The Jewish community was also growing, and in 1942 Harry Golden started the *Carolina Israelite*, which pricked the city's—and the nation's—conscience during the turbulent 1960s. New colleges sprang up to meet the growing demand of men furthering their education through the GI Bill. Charlotte College was founded in 1949, and in 1965 became the University of North Carolina at Charlotte, the fourth campus in the state's university system. Also in 1949, Carver College, a two-year program for blacks, was begun. In 1963, it became Central Piedmont Community

College, today the flagship of the state's community college system.

Also in 1949 WBTV went on the air, becoming the first television station in the Carolinas. It portended other changes ahead in the next two decades—the construction of Independence Boulevard, the Charlotte Coliseum, Ovens Auditorium, and Charlottetown Mall (today Midtown Square), the city's first indoor mall. In 1954 the *Charlotte Observer* became part of the Knight-Ridder Chain, which in 1959 also purchased the evening daily, the *Charlotte News*, originally founded in 1888. And the county kept growing, from a population of 197,052 in 1950 to 272,111 in 1960.

One of the biggest changes to hit Charlotte—as well as the rest of the

South—in the 1960s and 1970s (and continuing even into the 1980s) was in race relations, a result of the civil rights movement. Although there were demonstrations and marches in Charlotte, change here was not marred by the intense violence seen in so many other Southern cities.

In 1963 there were sit-ins and demonstrations in cities throughout North Carolina. Here, in a move motivated by a combination of social conscience, community pride, and economic concerns, the board of the Charlotte Chamber of Commerce passed a resolution on May 23 of that year calling for the desegregation of Charlotte's businesses. Mayor Stan Brookshire and Chamber president J. Ed Burnside were the driving forces

In 1964 Charlotte became the first major Southern city to desegregate, and in 1974 began a successful program of school busing that continues today. Photo by Jane Faircloth/Transparencies

31

ABOVE: *Office workers gather for lunch in revital-*
ized uptown Charlotte. Photo by Diane Davis/
Transparencies

FACING PAGE: *One of the developments which*
helped breath life into the uptown district and eased
the growing crush of traffic was the creation of Tryon
Street Mall. Photo by Matt Bradley

PAGES 32-33: *Discovery Place is a great*
educational treat for the entire family. Photo by
Paul Epley

behind both the resolution and its
implementation.

During that summer, the city's
restaurants and public accommodations
were integrated by white business leaders taking blacks to lunch at previously
all-white establishments. The idea was
young restauranteur "Slug" Claiborne's,
and the process was started on May 29
when, by prearrangement, Brookshire
and Dr. John Cunningham took Fred
Alexander (the first black elected to
Charlotte's city council in the twentieth century) and the Reverend Moses
Belton to lunch at the Manger Inn.

With this, Charlotte became the
first major Southern city to desegregate, a year before passage of the Civil
Rights Act in August 1964. The city
received international attention for its
efforts.

But that didn't mean all was peace-
ful. Brookshire received threatening
phone calls, and a cross was burned in
his yard. In 1965 the homes of Fred
Alexander, his brother Kelly Alexander, Sr. (president of the state's

NAACP chapter and later chairman of
the national organization), civil rights
leader Dr. Reginald Hawkins, and
lawyer Julius Chambers were bombed.
Fortunately, there were no serious
injuries. In a solid show of unity, both
blacks and whites met at Ovens Auditorium to protest the bombings, and
the city remained calm.

Charlotte was to stand out in other
areas of race relations as well. In 1969
black parents sued the school board in
the case of *Swann v. Charlotte-Mecklen-*
burg Board of Education. U.S. District
Court Judge James B. McMillan ruled
that the school board must use busing
to racially integrate the school system,
and his ruling was unanimously upheld
in 1971 by the U.S. Supreme Court.
There was much opposition to the ruling, but by using the determination,
grit, and common sense that had been
their strengths for so many years,
Charlotteans banded together and
began court-ordered busing in September 1974.

Even into the late 1980s, the Char-

ABOVE: *Celebrations and events for all ages are held throughout the year, including the annual Festival in the Park, where this young boy discovered the joys of painting. Photo by Mark Fortenberry*

FACING PAGE: *As the fifth largest urban region in the nation, Charlotte has developed into a leading center of business and commerce. Photo by Mark Fortenberry*

PAGES 36-37: *Finance and banking provide a central focus to Charlotte's business community. Photo by Jane Faircloth/Transparencies*

lotte-Mecklenburg system has been used as a national example of how busing can work successfully. Within the community, however, the debate continues to this day. Nevertheless, white flight from the schools has been minimal, and enrollment is still over 50 percent white. In 1983 voters elected architect Harvey Gantt as the city's first black mayor, and he was reelected in 1985.

While Charlotte was changing socially at this time, it also was changing physically. Much of the change occurred in the downtown central business district.

The foundation for the growth and expansion that this area experienced in the 1970s and 1980s was laid in the 1960s. In December 1961, as part of a federal urban renewal project, 238 acres of land were cleared east and south of the Square in an area known as Brooklyn. Forty acres were used to expand the government plaza, and Marshall Park was created. The project also provided room for the downtown to expand. But it also destroyed inner-city neighborhoods and much of Charlotte's black heritage. Helping to reclaim that heritage was the formation in 1974 of the Afro-American Cultural Center.

Also during the 1960s, an agreement was reached between the city and Southern Railway to clear 25 acres of obsolete warehouses and spur lines, which created room for the Charlotte Convention Center, completed in 1973 under Mayor John Belk.

Belk was just one of a group of community and business leaders who, in the 1970s, recognized the need to revitalize the declining downtown area. Much of the activity was practical and concrete, such as the construction of the Radisson Plaza Hotel on the Square; the opening of Spirit Square Center for the Arts in the renovated First Baptist Church; the rebuilding and rehabbing of Fourth Ward, a residential neighborhood bordering downtown; and the creation of the Charlotte Uptown Development Corporation by the Charlotte City Council to promote growth in the area. Also contributing to a new atmosphere all over the city was the legalization of liquor by the drink in 1978.

But Belk—and others—also recognized the importance of symbolism. In 1974 he officially designated the central business district as "uptown" to generate positive, upbeat feelings about the area. It took time, but the name stuck and has become part of the general usage in the city.

As successful and exciting as the 1970s were, the next decade topped even those earlier accomplishments. For example, Discovery Place, rated one of the top 10 hands-on science museums in the country, opened its doors in 1981; in 1984 a transit mall was completed that facilitates the flow

of public transportation and provides a beckoning streetscape for pedestrians; the construction of office buildings reached an all-time high; and a performing arts center was announced in 1988 as part of a retail-office complex on the Square. Uptown also became the place to party and celebrate, with the introduction of such festivities as SpringFest (every April) and First Night Charlotte (on New Year's Eve).

A major driving force in the growth of uptown has been Charlotte's banks. Two of the country's strongest super-regionals, NCNB National Bank and First Union National Bank, are head-quartered in the city, and both made a commitment to uptown development early on. Theirs are the skyscrapers that rise the highest in the city, and their growing presence fuels the need for additional services and businesses. They also attract other financial institutions, both large and small, national and international, making Charlotte one of the country's largest financial centers.

Although much of the focus has been on uptown, it has not been the only place where economic growth has been occurring at a dizzying pace. SouthPark, which started as a mall, added business parks, office complexes, and its first skyscraper. If the area were a municipality, its commercial activity would make it one of the 10 largest cities in North Carolina. Out by UNCC, University Research Park, a high-tech business park that opened in the early 1970s, began a big expansion. The area has grown into University City, with a satellite hospital, lots of new homes, and University Place, a 250-acre mixed-use development planned in the European style and which opened in September 1985.

The airport became a hub for Piedmont Airlines when deregulation went into effect in the late 1970s, and a major expansion followed. In 1982 a new terminal opened, and the facility became the Charlotte/Douglas International Airport. Every year since 1981, the airport has been among the country's fastest growing and will probably become one of the nation's 10 busiest sometime in the 1990s. The introduction of a nonstop flight to London in 1987 further added to the excitement. Piedmont merged into USAir in 1989, but that is not expected to halt or slow down the airport's growth.

The 25,000-seat Coliseum opened in 1988, just in time for Charlotte's NBA team, the Hornets, to begin its first season. The Mint Museum of Art nearly doubled its size in 1985 and hosted the "Ramesses the Great" exhibit from Egypt in 1988 and 1989, attracting more than 600,000 people in its four-month run.

Charlotte was—and still is—being transformed from a midsized Southern town into a major U.S. city. Commerce and trade have always been Charlotte's lifeblood. But today, as a national distribution center, a retail and service center for the country's fifth largest urban region and among the top eight financial centers in the U.S., Charlotte has truly fulfilled the destiny laid out for it more than 200 years ago by Tom Polk when he built his house at the crossroads of two trading paths.

Charlotte today is at a new crossroads facing a new challenge. Having met its destiny, the city must decide where it will go from here and what life in this "agreeable village" will become in the future. If what its citizens have done in the past is any indication, it will certainly remain pleasant yet challenging, businesslike yet warm and friendly, and above all, an agreeable place to live the good life.

A Convenient Place for Trade

Right from the start, Charlotte has been a center for trade and commerce. When the General Assembly of North Carolina designated it the Mecklenburg County seat in 1768, it noted that the town was "a convenient place for trade."

Located at the intersection of two Indian trading paths, Charlotte has been, throughout its history, a crossroads town: a place where people stopped on their way to somewhere else, and a place where goods were stored before being shipped off to their ultimate destination.

The nature of the crossroads has changed and grown with the times, beginning with the slow, onerous wagon routes and then followed by the railroads. Modern, paved interstates

later replaced the Indian paths, and I-77 and I-85 became the modern crossroads for truckers. The city's first airport began operations in the 1920s, and the modern facility has grown into another transportation hub, bringing people, goods and services through the Queen City's gates.

With its hustle and bustle and commercial activity, Charlotte also became a place to make money. Here is where rural folks and people from other states came—and still come—to seek their fortune, either in the trading activity itself or as part of the activities that service it, such as banking, accounting, law, retail, entertainment, and communications.

Charlotte's citizens have not only been ambitious for themselves, but for

Alive with trade and commerce, Charlotte is now the largest city between Atlanta and Washington, D.C. Photo by Matt Bradley

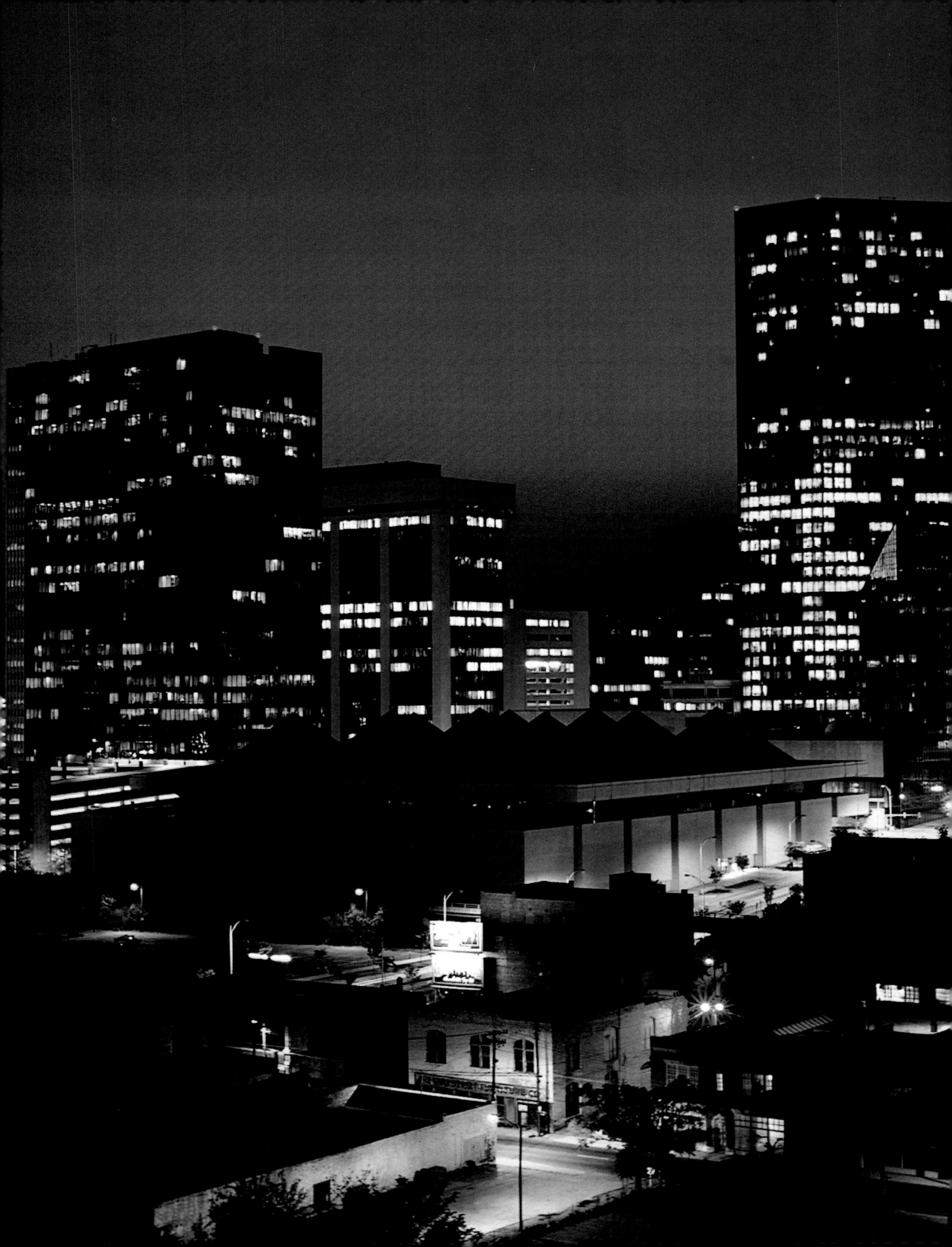

Enthusiastic Charlotte residents have helped to build a city of which they can be proud. Photo by Matt Bradley

their city as well. By cannily blending vision and creativity with pragmatism and shrewdness, they have transformed their city from a midsized Southern town into a rising star of the New South with a growing national and international reputation.

In a very real sense, Charlotte has no natural features going for it to make it successful—it's not an ocean or river port, it has no mountains—nothing to make it stand out or to give it an edge. Except its people. Charlotte is truly a

self-made city, brought into being and maturing through the spirit of its citizens. Whether pushing for a railroad or a branch of the Federal Reserve Bank, for an NBA franchise or a performing arts center, Charlotteans have shown a knack for setting ambitious goals for themselves and then achieving them.

This has made Charlotte a brassy city, a characteristic not always admired by its neighbors. In fact, it has been said of Charlotte that if it could suck as well as it could blow, the

Looking east over Highway 74 and Interstate 277, commuters make their way into the heart of Charlotte's business district. Photo by Paul Epley

Catawba River would be the Atlantic Ocean! A little arrogance notwithstanding, however, Charlotteans have a great love for and pride in their city, which makes it a special place to live.

That pride is demonstrated not just in business accomplishments and civic projects, but also in the caring, warm, and friendly atmosphere which adds so much to the quality of life.

But Charlotte is, above all, a business town, and it is the wheels of commerce—primarily in the form of transportation and banking—that have driven the city's transformation and success. The numbers amply illustrate that success.

With a population of approximately 385,000, Charlotte is the largest city between Atlanta and Washington, D.C. Mecklenburg County is approaching 500,000 residents, and there are more than 5.2 million people living within a 100-mile radius of Charlotte, more than any other city in the Southeast. More than a million people live within a 50-mile radius, which encompasses the seven-county region known as the Charlotte-Gastonia-Rock Hill Metropolitan Statistical Area. There are 70 towns and cities within a 40-mile radius.

These figures make Charlotte the hub of the nation's fifth largest urban area, generally known as the Piedmont, which extends through both Carolinas.

Tree-filled neighborhoods seem to encircle uptown Charlotte in this northwest autumn view. Photo by Paul Epley

With the city's location in the southwest corner of North Carolina near the South Carolina border, it is well situated to serve both states. The North Carolina part of the Piedmont makes up 31 percent of the state's land but has more than half of its population.

That population is dispersed through numerous small towns, giving the Piedmont an unusual urban character. With an excellent road system connecting these towns with Charlotte, the Queen City is able to serve as the financial, service, and commercial center for the area. This enables Charlotte

to achieve levels of business growth and economic development much greater than expected for a city of its size. In 1987, for example, it ranked 10th in the nation in terms of wholesale sales. This can also be traced back to Charlotte's location, which puts one-half of the country's population within one hour's flight time or a day's drive by truck.

Consequently, warehouses abound in Charlotte, and thousands of salespeople use the city as their base as they travel through the Carolinas and the rest of the Southeast. If you live in the Carolinas, chances are the products you use passed through Charlotte. Apple Computer has its East Coast distribution center here, which means that every computer used east of the Mississippi comes through the Queen City.

More and more companies are locating regional operations and headquarters here, including Allstate Insurance Company, IBM, The Travelers Insurance Companies, and CIGNA Insurance Company. Okuma Machine Tools, a Japanese firm, located its U.S. headquarters here in 1988.

In addition to its excellent road network, Charlotte also boasts of one of the fastest growing airports in the country, Charlotte/Douglas International Airport. Many call the airport the single most important factor contributing to Charlotte's economic

vitality. Ranked among the 25 busiest in the U.S. and among the top 35 worldwide, the airport became a hub for Piedmont Airlines with the advent of deregulation in the late 1970s. Today it remains a major point in the network of USAir, which merged with Piedmont in 1989. Trucking is still important to the area as well, with almost 200 trucking firms located in the county. Nearly 300 trains roll through the area each week.

Charlotte not only provides services for a large population base, but also draws upon the resources of that popu-lation when needed. For example, about 16 percent of the jobs in Meck-lenburg County are filled by people liv-ing in neighboring counties, a figure expected to jump to 24 percent by 2005. This expanded work force is an especially attractive feature in bringing large companies and corporate head-quarters to the city.

That's something Charlotte does quite well. More than 300 Fortune 500 firms have a presence, such as IBM, Westinghouse, and Celanese, and there are well over 400 companies with headquarters in the city, such as Gold

A variety of neighborhoods and towns are home to the more than one million people who have settled within a 50-mile radius of Charlotte. Photo by Jane Faircloth/Transparencies

Bond Building Products, Nucor, Duke Power Company, Belk Stores, and Piedmont Natural Gas. About 200 foreign firms have offices or facilities here, attracted by a foreign trade zone and a local customs office.

In 1988, 462 firms expanded or opened offices, creating 6,031 new jobs and investing $440 million into the local economy. That followed the record year of 1987 when 649 firms

all have AAA bond ratings.

The reasons for Charlotte's growth are many: the airport and other transportation amenities; an efficient, well-educated work force; an array of educational institutions that work with business and industry to provide job training and higher education; a clean, well-run local government; an attractive tax rate; a sound business environment; a high quality of life; a low cost of living; a mild climate; and a good location between the mountains and the ocean and between the Northeastern U.S. and Florida.

Among all these factors, however, one other does stand out along with the airport: the banking industry. In 1988, with more than $57 billion in assets headquartered here, Charlotte was the seventh largest financial center in the U.S., making it the largest such center between Pittsburgh and Los Angeles.

This ranking is a result of Charlotte's

Employees of Harold M. Pittman Company utilize the latest in computer technology to maintain inventories and expedite customer orders. Pittman is a national supplier of graphic-arts supplies and equipment. Photo by Paul Epley

expanded or opened offices, creating nearly 11,000 jobs with $1.017 billion worth of investment. Between 1978 and 1987 there were a total of 2,295 new or expanded businesses, 137,961 new jobs created, and more than $2.5 billion invested.

Industry publications have called Charlotte the "Sun Belt overachiever of the 1980s" in the growth of office markets. Charlotteans are also proud that Charlotte is one of the few U.S. cities where the city, county, and state

being the home for First Union National Bank and NCNB National Bank, two of the country's most aggressive super-regionals and among the 40 largest banks in the U.S. Among other roles, they have been key players in the revitalization of Charlotte's central business district, known as uptown. Their "friendly" rivalry and growth, fueled by deregulation of the banking industry, have spurred new heights of construction there, and today uptown is Charlotte's centerpiece, exemplifying the city's ambitions and accomplishments with both soaring skyscrapers and pedestrian walkways.

But First Union and NCNB are not the only major financial institutions in the city. The Federal Reserve Bank of Richmond has had a branch here since 1927. First Wachovia, also among the top 40 banks in the U.S., has a major presence in the area. Such finance-related firms as Barclays American Corporation, a diversified financial services company and a subsidiary of Barclays Bank PLC, and Royal Insurance, among the country's 25 largest insurance companies, have their headquarters here. Home Savings of America, the second largest savings and loan in the U.S., has its East Coast operations center in Charlotte.

Their presence has attracted others.

Many new jobs are being created in the Charlotte business community as firms continue to open offices in the area and continue to invest in the local economy. Photo by Mark Fortenberry

Two new banks have been started in Charlotte in recent years, First Charlotte Bank in 1983 and Bank of Mecklenburg in 1988. In 1988 Charlotte had offices of five of the country's largest banks, 69 companies dealing with financing and factoring, 58 firms offering capital for transportation and equipment, 139 mortgage banks and 11 savings and loan associations (five of which had headquarters here).

All this means that both business and consumers have a wide array of financial and banking services to draw upon. Banking is convenient, too; in 1988, 115 banks had 163 branches throughout Mecklenburg County, giving the area one of the country's highest ratios of bank branches to population. No point in the city is more than 2 1/2 miles from a bank office.

Yet there's more to Charlotte's economy than transportation and banking. For example, travel and tourism are making increasingly important contributions to the area, bringing in more than $1 billion in revenues in 1988. Almost one out of every 10 workers in Mecklenburg County is involved in the travel industry. Tourism got a big boost in 1988, when the 25,000-seat Charlotte Coliseum opened in August, followed by the premier season of the Charlotte Hornets, the city's NBA franchise.

High-tech industries are also on the rise. University Research Park (URP), a 2,500-acre high-tech, research-oriented complex in the northeast part of the county, is the second largest of its kind in the state. It was begun in the

1960s, and today boasts of such tenants as IBM, Verbatim, Dow Jones, Southern Bell, and AT&T. The firms at URP, which employ nearly 10,000 people, have developed close working relationships with the University of North Carolina at Charlotte (UNCC). These two facilities—along with University Place, a 250-acre mixed-use development, and University Memorial Hospital—make up the central focus of University City, one of the fastest growing parts of Mecklenburg County.

University City, however, is not the

area's only "hot" growth spot. South-Park, in southeast Charlotte, is quickly becoming an urban center in its own right. Along I-77's southwest corridor, more than $600 million of development is under way as a result of the opening of the $47-million Charlotte Coliseum.

Such national developers as Carley Capital Group and Trammell Crow are involved in the Charlotte market, along with such real-estate giants as Merrill Lynch, Coldwell Banker, and Cushman & Wakefield. The city is also

FACING PAGE: Emphasis on banking as a major industry has established Charlotte as one of the nation's largest financial centers. Photo by Billy E. Barnes

ABOVE: One First Union Center, a new Charlotte skyscraper, is pictured here during its grand opening in 1988. Photo by Mark Fortenberry

home for two of the largest general contractors in the U.S., the Jones Group and McDevitt & Street. Construction costs are approximately 83 percent of the national average of 183 cities surveyed by the Dodge Building Costs Survey.

The city's ties to its past economic achievements also remain strong. Although the textile industry as a whole has declined in surrounding counties in recent years, the yarn segment of the industry remains strong, and about one-third of the U.S. producers are located in North and South Carolina. Charlotte remains the service center for these mills, and the fact that its wholesale sales of chemicals and allied products ranks among the top 10 cities in the country is a result of this role.

Although the North Carolina Piedmont has about two-thirds of the state's manufacturing jobs, manufacturing in Charlotte remains small, employing about 16 percent of the work force. Manufacturers still locate here, however, and two of the biggest new additions include Otto Industries, a German firm manufacturing large trash containers, and Okuma Machine Tools, considered the worldwide leader in the machine tools industry. Other major manufacturers in the county are IBM, Lance, and General Tire.

Yet all of Charlotte's industries owe their strength and vitality to the city's transportation network. It's always been that way, and Charlotte's leaders have been wise enough to recognize that fact and to take advantage of it.

For example, Charlotte officials and businessmen agreed heartily with the *North Carolina Whig* when a September 22, 1852 editorial said of the impending completion of the city's first railway line: "The future prosperity of Charlotte will soon be placed upon a solid foundation."

The first freight train arrived rather quietly on October 14 of that year at the depot off South College Street, but the city went wild when the first passenger trains arrived on Thursday, October 28, carrying folks from Chester, Winnsboro, and Columbia, South Carolina. The president of the Charlotte and South Carolina Railroad was among those welcomed by some 20,000 people, and everyone celebrated with a barbecue and fireworks—both still big favorites in the Queen City.

A reporter was so carried away by these festivities that he wrote: "Thus passed away the most brilliant and glorious day that the history of Charlotte has furnished for seventy-odd years."

The reporter may have overstated the excitement of the celebration, but there was no way of downplaying the importance the railroad played in Charlotte's development. During the railroad's first three months of operation, it carried 38,645 bales of cotton out of the Charlotte Depot.

For more than 100 years the depot was a center of activity, the hub around which life in Charlotte revolved, as goods were shipped in and out, warehouses were filled and emptied, people came and went, and business and personal lives intertwined. In a 1976 *Charlotte Observer* editorial, Jack Claiborne wrote of the railroads: "People set their clocks and scheduled their lives in keeping with the arrivals and departures of trains."

BELOW: Steam turbine testing takes place at the Westinghouse Steam Turbine plant in Charlotte. Photo by Paul Epley

FACING PAGE, TOP: A Norfolk & Southern freight train pulls out of the railway yard in the early morning hours. Photo by Kelly Culpepper/Transparencies

FACING PAGE, BOTTOM: A supervisor at one of the Mercedes-Freightliner plants in the Charlotte area makes a quality-control check on one of the company's many precision-made truck parts. Photo by Paul Epley

ABOVE: Approximately 30 percent of the nation's largest trucking companies operate in Charlotte. Photo by Diane Davis/Transparencies

FACING PAGE: The trucking industry provides employment for nearly 14,000 people in the Charlotte area. Photo by Mark Fortenberry

In 1949 about 95,000 carloads of freight came in or out of the city, or about 200 carloads a day, and approximately 254,000 passengers arrived or departed. Four lines accounted for the service: the Southern, Seaboard, Norfolk & Southern, and Piedmont & Northern. In an annual overview of the industry that year, an article in the *Observer* noted, "Atlanta was known as the distributing center of the South. Today, though, Charlotte's position is not exceeded by Atlanta."

But the railroad's moment of glory passed on into history. The peak of passenger travel was reached in the 1920s, when there were between 25 and 30 trains serving travelers daily. Only two companies serve Charlotte today, Southern and Family Lines, and Amtrak's Southern Crescent, which connects New Orleans and New York City, is the only passenger train serving the city.

Still, about 300 freight trains move

through Charlotte each week, and they continue to play a vital—albeit smaller—role in the city's economy. It is the railroad which makes Charlotte an inland port facility, through a system in which containerized cargo is transported via rail to such North Carolina ports as Wilmington and Morehead City, or to Charleston, South Carolina and Norfolk, Virginia for loading onto oceangoing tankers.

But the railroad's mark remains. I-85 was built near the rail lines, and along its route through Mecklenburg County are bulk warehouses, trucking terminals, and heavy equipment facilities. I-77, on the other hand, is geared toward people instead of cargo, with business parks and facilities stressing landscaping, sleek architectural design, and amenities such as parking.

The truck and the automobile were major reasons for the decline of the railroad, but their development did not occur overnight. In 1919 C.H. "Char-

lie" Fredrickson became the first to offer "store door pick-up and delivery service" between Charlotte and Statesville, and his company, Fredrickson Express, still holds state certificate number C-1. During the Great Depression, Doc Thurston, although he held an engineering degree, got tired of looking for a job, bought a truck for $300, and started hauling peaches and other freight. His company, Thurston Motor Lines, is among eight trucking firms—including Fredrickson's—currently headquartered in Charlotte, each with a net worth of $5 million or more.

For many years Charlotte was touted as the second largest trucking center in the U.S., second only to Chicago. For years no one—not even Chamber of Commerce officials—seemed to know where this "fact" came from or even if it was true, but people used the figure all the time anyway. (You'll still hear it in some quarters.) Then, in a September 1975 column, *Observer* business editor Roy Covington dug up the figure it was based on: the number of over-the-road runs that started or ended in the city during the 1950s.

Today about one-third of the country's 100 largest trucking firms operate in Charlotte, including nine of the top 10. There are almost 14,000 people employed in the industry.

But when you talk of transportation in the Queen City today, you mean the airport. Ben Douglas, Sr., truly the father of air travel in Charlotte, would be beside himself with joy at the facility that now bears his name. One of the fastest growing airports in the country over the last decade, and expected to be among the 20 busiest in the U.S. by 1995, Charlotte/Douglas International boasts of a passenger terminal with more than 600,000 square feet of

enclosed space, three runways, four concourses with 39 gates, and more than 350 daily flights by eight major airlines and two commuter lines. The facility also accounts for more than 17,000 jobs, adding nearly $400 million to the local economy each year, and is a major drawing card in the city's economic development efforts. In 1988 it served more than 14 million passengers.

The first airplane flight in Charlotte occurred in 1912 when Thornwell "Thorny" Andrews took off from the fairgrounds in Dilworth (now the area around Dilworth Road East and Dilworth Road West) as part of the Mecklenburg Declaration Day festivities. Three other attempts had already failed, so he was awarded a gold watch for his successful efforts. Later, an airstrip was added to Lakewood Park, the popular amusement park located in the Glenwood neighborhood, and air shows became a big attraction.

Charlotte's first airport (if it could really be called that) was a dirt runway in Myers Park, near what is today Selwyn Avenue and Queens Road West. The Charlotte Polo Club also used it as a playing field, and it was not not uncommon for play to stop so a plane could land. Pilot Johnny Crowell began airport operations there in 1922. A few years later, a group of investors began Charlotte Airport, located on what is today the Golden Circle Store at Freedom Mall. It was run by a series of managers, including Crowell, but it rarely showed a profit. The first airmail arrived in Charlotte on April 1, 1930 (before a roaring crowd of 30,000), and Eastern Airlines began passenger service in December of that year, but the facility's operations remained poor even for that time period.

This bothered Charlotteans' pride. It also rankled Douglas, who was elect-

FACING PAGE: *Once responsible for more than 80 percent of the airport's flights, Piedmont Airlines has now merged with USAir. Photo by Kelly Culpepper/Transparencies*

ed mayor in a political upset in 1935, and who felt air transportation was a key to Charlotte's future development. In August 1935 the Chamber of Commerce asked the city council to provide adequate air services to meet the city's needs, and the next month Douglas applied for funds from the Works Progress Administration (WPA) for airport construction.

The WPA funds, ultimately totaling $339,231.85, were awarded pending passage of a $50,000 bond, which voters approved in December. The facility, named after Douglas, began operations on June 1, 1937, with Eastern providing two flights daily. In 1938 one of the runways was extended, and in 1939 the other two were lengthened, and Eastern had six daily flights.

The official dedication took place on April 21, 1941, when 10,000 people heard the keynote address by New York City Mayor Fiorello La Guardia. At that time, the facilities included an administration building, one hangar, three gravel runways, and a complete lighting system.

During World War II a portion of the airport was taken over by the U.S. Army and used for training purposes. Known as Morris Field, it was turned over to the city when the war was over.

The airport continued its expansion after the war, and in July 1954 a $5-million capital improvement program was completed, culminating in a new runway and a terminal building. In 1968 outside consultants developed a 17-year master plan calling for such new amenities as a longer runway and an enlarged terminal.

The expansions didn't always come on schedule, but the major parts of that plan did come to pass. Bonds for the new runway were passed in 1972, although, due to legal complications, it was not completed until 1979. Charlotteans also found it difficult to believe growth predictions for the airport, and bonds for the new terminal were defeated in 1975. Nevertheless, Piedmont Airlines made Charlotte one of its major hubs in 1978 when deregulation went into effect.

In that same year the bond issue for a new terminal passed by a two-to-one ratio, and it opened its doors on May 2, 1982. By this time Piedmont's and Charlotte's futures were bound together closely. In 1987 they were awarded the London Gateway, and nonstop flights to London began that June. By 1988, before Piedmont's merger with USAir, the airline accounted for more than 80 percent of the flights out of Charlotte/Douglas, and USAir announced its intention to keep Charlotte as a major hub. Both the city and the airline look forward to a continued strong working relationship, and Charlotte is the site for a flight crew training facility for USAir.

To accommodate all this growth, the airport is continuing to physically expand, funded by $184 million in bonds approved by voters in 1985 and 1987. This money is being used for such projects as a terminal expansion, two added parking areas, extended runways, additional gates, and an international concourse.

The airport is run as a department of city government, and its management continues to look to the future. The facility's master plan is reevaluated and updated on a regular basis. The nine-member Airport Advisory Committee, which acts as an advisory board for the city, includes members from surrounding neighborhoods in order to keep lines of communication open and to involve them in the growth process.

Feeding the airport's growth, but also feeding upon it, is Charlotte's

First Union National bank, originally founded in 1908 as Union National, has achieved unparalleled growth along with its friendly rival NCNB. The new One First Union Center, pictured here, can perhaps be described as the culmination of recent growth and prosperity for First Union National. Photo by Ernest H. Robl

financial community. Although banking has been around much longer than airplanes, it was also in the Depression years that Charlotte's banking community took its first steps to become what it is today. Like the airport, it too has been able to benefit and grow due to deregulation.

Actually, one of the first recorded banking transactions in Charlotte took place some time between 1818 and 1823, when town commissioners borrowed money from the Charlotte branch of the Bank of New Bern to build a church. In 1834 a branch of the North Carolina Bank opened in the town, followed by the Bank of Charlotte, the first bank here to be locally owned.

When Charlotte grew as a commercial center, so did its banking community. After all, trade means money, and buyers and sellers not only need a place to keep it, but they also need institu-

tions to handle and finance their transactions and activities. Then, as now, banking required such support services as lawyers and accountants, adding even more to Charlotte's status as a commercial and service hub for the region.

But it was the opening of a branch of the Federal Reserve Bank of Richmond in 1927 that gave Charlotte a big boost in becoming a banking center. Because the Fed branch was located here, smaller community banks in surrounding towns turned to Charlotte banks for check clearing and other services. This enabled the banks here to expand their income base, making many of them big enough and strong enough to open after the 1933 "Bank Holiday" and survive the Depression. A lot of the smaller community banks weren't so lucky.

Even without the knowledge of what was to come, Charlotteans were excited and proud of the new Fed branch, and more than 650 bankers and dignitaries attended a banquet to celebrate its opening. More than 20 people moved to Charlotte from Richmond to operate the branch, and on its first day of operations, December 1, 1927, the branch cleared some 15,000 checks worth more than $3 million—all by hand!

North Carolina, unlike many other states, has always allowed branch banking. Its first state-chartered bank, the Bank of Cape Fear, had branches as far back as 1804. More than 100 years later, Charlotte's two homegrown banking giants, First Union and NCNB, took advantage of these banking laws to grow and expand, putting them in an excellent position to take advantage of the liberalized interstate banking laws of the 1980s.

Their beginnings, of course, were small. NCNB got its start in 1874

when several Charlotte investors began Commercial National Bank with $50,000 of capital. After nine months of operation, it paid its first cash dividend and remained a major Charlotte bank through the Panic of 1893, the Crisis of 1907, and the Great Depression.

Its rival down the street, First Union, began in 1908 as Union National Bank, founded by H.M. Victor with $100,000 of capital raised by selling stock at $100 per share. In 1947 it became the first Charlotte bank to open a branch office in the city.

The 1950s and 1960s saw in-state merger activity on the scale of the interstate merger mania of the 1980s as true statewide banking networks began to emerge. In 1957 Commercial National merged with American Trust (formed in Charlotte in 1901) to create American Commercial Bank. Two years later American Commercial

The growing need for office space and services to support the banking industry has resulted in a flourish of construction activity and employment opportunities for the Charlotte area. Photo by Paul Epley

merged with First National of Raleigh, and in 1960 merged with Security National Bank of Greensboro to form North Carolina National Bank. The new bank continued to acquire banks throughout the state during the 1960s and 1970s. The name was shortened to NCNB National Bank in 1982.

Union National Bank, meanwhile, merged with Asheville-based First National Bank and Trust in 1958, changing its name to First Union National Bank. From 1958 to 1973, it acquired 28 community banks across North Carolina. Its in-state growth was culminated in March 1985 when it merged with Greensboro-based North-western Financial Corp.

The banks' rivalry moved from in-state to interstate when a 1985 U.S. Supreme Court ruling opened the door for out-of-state acquisitions, and both institutions experienced unprecedented growth. NCNB got a head start when it was able to enter the Florida market in 1982 due to a grandfather clause in the state's banking laws. First Union fol-lowed suit as fast as it could, making its first out-of-state move in November 1985 when it acquired Florida's Atlantic Bancorporation.

At the end of 1988 First Union had assets of $29 billion, and as of April 1989 had completed a series of mergers with 21 banking organizations in the Carolinas, Georgia, Florida, and Ten-nessee. Also at that time, the bank announced its agreement to acquire Florida National Banks of Florida. When completed, the merger will cre-ate the second largest bank in Florida.

Between 1982 and mid-April 1989 NCNB had completed 16 mergers in Maryland, Virginia, Georgia, Florida, and South Carolina, as well as several intrastate mergers within North Caroli-na, giving it assets of $29.6 billion. That figure did not include its interest

in NCNB Texas, which NCNB began managing for the FDIC in July 1988. By April NCNB had acquired 49 per-cent of the Texas institution, with an option to acquire the rest within five years. When that acquisition is com-pleted, NCNB's assets will be about $50 billion, putting it among the 10 largest bank holding companies in the nation.

North Carolina banks have been well-suited to become regional banking powers. They have in-depth experience in merging operations and in branch banking, and by surviving—and grow-ing—in their home state's highly com-petitive market, they have become aggressive and innovative. These are the corporate skills and abilities required to become a super-regional in today's new banking environment.

But First Union and NCNB are not alone in Charlotte. The state's third largest bank, Wachovia Bank & Trust, although based in Winston-Salem, has a major presence and long history in Charlotte. It has been able to claim a place in the city since 1897, when Charlotte National Bank was formed. Wachovia merged with Charlotte National in 1939, and also joined the interstate merger frenzy in 1985 by acquiring First Atlanta Corporation in Georgia.

As First Union and NCNB have grown, so has their need for office space, for workers, and for support ser-vices—from lawyers to restaurants, and from computer programmers to paper suppliers. They have fueled Charlotte's construction boom and the influx of well-educated workers, have attracted other firms to the area, and gained international attention for the city. All of this will continue as the banks keep expanding in the future.

First Union and NCNB have also set the standards for being good corpo-

FACING PAGE: From glass-adorned skyscrapers to the improved quality of life, Charlotte's business community has made a major impact on the future development and prosperity of this thriving city. Photo by Mark Fortenberry

rate citizens in Charlotte. Both have been generous in supporting such community organizations as the United Way and the Arts and Science Council, as well as educational and literacy programs, health and human welfare projects, capital campaigns, and civic undertakings such as the performing arts center. That support has come in the form of money, leadership, and volunteers.

Just as being a crossroads town means transportation and money, however, it also means travel and tourism. The first known inn in Charlotte was located at 209 West Trade Street and was owned by Patrick Jack. The next one established, Cook's Inn, at 20 West Trade Street, was honored by a visit from George Washington during his 1791 visit to Charlotte. He shared a characteristic of many modern travelers today, leaving in such

haste that he left his powder box behind.

Charlotte's modern-day hotels (which run the gamut from top-of-the-line to budget to bed-and-breakfast inns) are a far cry from the inns of old. There also are a lot more of them. In March 1988 more than 15,000 rooms (including those planned or under construction) were available in about 100 facilities.

All this travel business is a relatively new phenomenon. Back in 1981, for example, the Charlotte area had just over 7,000 hotel rooms. The growth has intensified in recent years. In 1987 Mecklenburg County earned $968 million from travel and tourism, a 20.4-percent increase over 1986 and a 153 percent increase over six years. That figure accounted for nearly 17 percent of the state's total travel revenues, up from 15.8 percent in 1986.

ABOVE: The plush Marriott City Center hotel is situated in the heart of uptown Charlotte. Photo by Mark Fortenberry

FACING PAGE: Luxurious Adam's Mark Hotel in uptown Charlotte offers about 600 guest rooms, pool facilities, a choice of fine restaurants, and live entertainment. Photo by Mark Fortenberry

In 1988 the county's travel and tourism revenues topped $1 billion.

That growth can be traced to a variety of factors: the business climate, the increasing number of new firms, Charlotte's status as a distribution center, its location, and an airport and transportation network that make it easily accessible by plane and auto. But, as is often the case in Charlotte, its citizens also took some very definite actions to encourage and enhance that growth.

The first step was the approval by voters of liquor by the drink in 1978, followed by the creation in 1984 of a convention and visitors bureau, first as part of the Chamber of Commerce,

then as an independent bureau. Charlotte took a statewide leadership role in all of these actions. It was also among the first North Carolina cities to approve a room occupancy tax to fund the bureau and other travel and tourism programs after the General Assembly made such a tax a local option.

The Charlotte Convention & Visitors Bureau (CCVB), with an annual budget of about $1.5 million, not only supplies help and information for business travelers and tourists, but also actively promotes the city as a meeting and convention site. The 134,000-square-foot Charlotte Convention Center in uptown hosts numerous

ABOVE: Promoted as an ideal trade show and convention site, Charlotte has developed some major convention facilities, including the Charlotte Apparel Mart, which features 60,000 square feet of available show space. Photo by Billy E. Barnes

FACING PAGE: Exciting Carowinds amusement park is located just 10 miles from uptown Charlotte. Photo by Mark Fortenberry

trade and consumer shows, and talk of expanding the facility has recently gained intensity. Another show site, the Merchandise Mart, is being expanded from 120,000 to 220,000 square feet, and the newly opened Charlotte Apparel Mart has 60,000 square feet of convention space. Visitors can also enjoy such attractions as the Mint Museum of Art; Discovery Place, rated among the top 10 hands-on science museums in the U.S.; Carowinds and Heritage U.S.A., two nearby amusement parks; the Charlotte Motor Speedway; and NBA games featuring the Charlotte Hornets.

Just as the boom in the travel industry came about because of calculated, well-planned actions, so has much of Charlotte's economic growth. Many of those actions have come about as a

result of local government and the business community working together, and cooperation between the public and private sectors is an established tradition in the city.

One of the major voices for the business community is the Charlotte Chamber, which can trace its history back to 1880 when dry-goods merchant Samuel Wittkowsky served as its first president. The modern-day organization was formally incorporated in 1915 as the Charlotte Chamber of Commerce, was renamed the Greater Charlotte Chamber of Commerce in 1976 and then became simply the Charlotte Chamber in 1984. Today it ranks among the 12 largest chambers of commerce in the nation.

The chamber has been touting Charlotte as a place for business since its

inception, and that spirit was exemplified by Clarence Kuester, who was also known in the 1920s as "Booster" Kuester for his tireless efforts to promote the city in any way he could wherever he went.

Over the years the chamber has championed the cause of highways in North Carolina and paved streets within the city; hired the first city planner to recommend the best spot for the state's first skyscraper, the Independence Building; promoted the construction of Ovens Auditorium and the Charlotte Coliseum; worked for the revitalization of uptown; helped promote the city as a convention site; encouraged international trade; and helped push for passage of a myriad of bonds for public facilities and infrastructure, education, and an improved quality of life.

Under the direction of president Carroll D. Gray, who joined the chamber in 1984, the Charlotte Chamber has intensified its economic development efforts. In 1986 it began a three-year national marketing campaign, funded through both private and public sector monies, to attract new firms to the area. The original goal was to generate 6,000 inquiries in three years; that figure was exceeded within two years.

Yes, a crossroads town is an exciting place, filled with infectious enthusiasm, a dynamic hustle and bustle, a wealth of activities and goings-on. Trade, money, and travel are its driving forces. Its people are ambitious and work hard, but they also know how to play. They are friendly and outgoing, and no one is ever truly a stranger for long.

Charlotte is truly the epitome of a city growing up at the crossroads.

Charlotte begins to waken as morning dawns over the heart of the city's business and commercial district. Photo by Matt Bradley

The City's Front Porch

When Charlotte is talked about as a crossroads city, it is not meant merely symbolically, nor is it a futile attempt to recapture a dead past.

You can still see and walk through the crossroads which served as the catalyst for Charlotte's birth and which remains its essence today. (Unless it's the middle of the night, though, you'll have to dodge the traffic.) The crossroads of Charlotte's past, where two ancient Indian trading paths met, is now a vital and integral part of the city's economy, life-style, and vigor, as well as of its self-image, dreams and ambitions for the future.

That crossroads is the intersection of Tryon Street, running from north to south, and Trade Street, running from east to west. Called Independence Square, or simply the Square, it is the focal point of the city's central business district. It is also still the heart of the city's transportation network, with 41 lanes of traffic leading into the area and 42 leading out. It is also the point at which the mass-transit bus system converges.

Although that central core is no longer the geographic center of Charlotte, it is the very heart of the city, pumping prosperity through the region, acting as a driving force behind the area's economic development, and providing a focus for the city as it defines itself and what it wants to become. It is where visions and dreams merge with concrete and steel, where visionaries' grand schemes meet with the banker's eye for the bottom line, where art and

Once the crossroads of two ancient Indian trading paths, the intersection of Trade and Tryon streets is now the vital center of Charlotte's central business district. Photo by Paul Epley

ABOVE: *Office workers relax in the warm sunshine during their lunchtime break. Photo by Mark Fortenberry*

PAGES 72-73: *Uptown Charlotte shines in the evening light. Photo by Kelly Culpepper/Transparencies; Inset: Shining glass towers climb into the sky over Charlotte's central district. Photo by Jim McGuire*

culture coexist with commerce, where both trees and office towers line the streets, and where Charlotteans are at their most lighthearted and free-spirited, but also where they are at their most deadly serious, doing what they do best—making deals and doing business.

There is something unique about Charlotte's central district. But it takes some time to figure out what that is. After all, with its gleaming skyscrapers proudly penetrating the Carolina blue sky, office workers filling its streets every workday, cultural and entertainment offerings, shopping, restaurants, hotels, and residential sections, it provides the excitement, glamour, and glitz of any sophisticated urban center. And with new construction occurring on almost every major street, the district is a major selling point in the city's economic development efforts. The area sizzles with optimism, vitality,

and success, coming not just from the attractive physical environment, but also from the people who work, live, and play there.

The relationship between Charlotteans and their center city is a special one, one that permeates the atmosphere and which creates the uniqueness of which they are so proud. To them it is their front porch, the place where they put their best face forward to visitors, where they welcome guests, and where they put out a giant welcome mat to all who pass by. And many do pass directly through here, as there are more than 2,500 hotel rooms within one mile of the Square.

To begin with, Charlotteans don't refer to the area by such mundane terms as *center city* or *downtown* Charlotte's entire central business district is called "uptown." That name not only communicates Charlotteans' pride and upbeat attitude about the place, but also demonstrates a tie to the past, something very valuable and important in this time of great change at the crossroads.

For most of its existence, uptown—today encompassing about three square miles—*was* Charlotte. This is where the first settlers built their homes and where they put up their courthouse. For much of its history, the city proper included only this area, and everything else around it was part of the county. In 1869, for example, the city comprised roughly the area between Twelfth and Morehead streets and McDowell and Cedar streets, and reports say that it was about a half-hour walk from one side of town to the other. Beyond those boundaries were farms and woods.

Slowly but surely, the city grew geographically as it annexed surrounding areas, but the sense that the essence of Charlotte was uptown remained. Until the 1950s, when Northerners began their influx to Charlotte-Mecklenburg, the center city was always referred to as uptown. Many local historians believe this was because no matter where you were coming from, you had to go uphill to reach the district.

Although downtown became the general usage during the 1950s, the term uptown was never actually forgotten. Yet as the area declined in the 1960s— like urban centers across the U.S.—it didn't really seem appropriate either. When Charlotteans came together a decade later to save and revitalize their downtown, they decided the old name was the one that truly exemplified their hopes and aspirations

for the future.

In 1974 Mayor John Belk made it official: Charlotte's central business district was to be known as "uptown." It has taken time for the name to be accepted and widely used—and the ongoing flow of newcomers must be continually educated about it—but the name "uptown" has stuck. And be sure to note the pride in a Charlottean's voice when he or she mentions it.

The pride isn't new, however—only rediscovered. In the first half of the twentieth century, area residents in the county and beyond took the train into uptown Charlotte to do their shopping. Such a daylong trek was quite an adventure, often including shopping for clothes at Belk, drinking a cola at the Woolworth lunch counter, or taking in a show at the Carolina Theater.

From about 1945 to 1955, while the post-World War II boom was under way and before mass use of the automobile made suburbs and shopping malls possible, uptown was in its heyday. About half the workers employed uptown commuted by bus, and it was a

Independence Square in uptown Charlotte features the golden "Grand Disco" sculpture. Photo by Mark Fortenberry

mob scene at the end of the day as people scurried around trying to catch one. Buses often were filled to standing-room-only capacity. The stores were always packed on the weekends, and during the Christmas season, it was elbow to elbow. Doctors had their offices here, there were movie houses and hotels, and all the fine restaurants were located uptown.

But such an urban flowering was not to last. People moved farther and farther out to the suburbs. In 1956 Charlotte's first suburban shopping center, Park Road Shopping Center, opened, followed by its first covered mall, Charlottetowne Mall (now Midtown Square), in 1959. People no longer came to shop or play uptown—those amenities were now closer to home—and both businesses and residents left the area, further intensifying the cycle of decay.

The cycle did not progress as far in Charlotte as in other American cities. One factor that helped was the building war between the city's two big banking rivals, First Union and NCNB, which began in 1954 and which continues to this day. In 1954 First Union erected what is now the First Union Bank Building, the first new structure built uptown in 25 years. In 1961 NCNB built what is now the BB&T Center, followed by First Union's 32-story First Union Center in 1971. Three years later NCNB followed with its 40-story building at Trade and Tryon. In 1988, First Union completed its 42-story office tower on South College Street, and NCNB plans to top that in 1992 with a 60-story building.

But the banks were not the only ones working for a revitalized uptown. By the early 1970s a strong enough consensus had been reached so that effective action began to take place,

slowly building momentum and bearing fruit. The clearing out of 238 acres in the inner-city neighborhood of Brooklyn in the 1960s made possible the creation of the government center complex and Marshall Park. Large employees, such as Belk, Ivey's, and Duke Power, along with the banks, made a commitment to keep uptown as a major employment base.

In 1973 the Civic Center opened (now the Charlotte Convention Center), followed by the Radisson Hotel and the Overstreet Shopping Mall. Spirit Square, the city's arts center, opened its doors in 1976 in the renovated 1909 First Baptist Church. City government, recognizing the importance of a revitalized uptown, created the nonprofit Charlotte Uptown Development Corporation (CUDC) in 1978 to help foster and promote the area. From 1981 to 1985, CUDC provided $30 million worth of financing at below-market rates through local banks to rehabilitate and refurbish some 20 uptown buildings.

Not all the efforts were strictly business, however. Uptown supporters recognized that for the heart of the city to thrive, it needed residential sections as well. There was already a place to start: Fourth Ward, originally a voting district and once one of the city's finest neighborhoods. By the early 1970s, however, it was in shambles, with many of its beautiful homes neglected and decaying.

A group of committed citizens—scoffed at as silly dreamers by many—decided that Fourth Ward shouldn't die. Consultants were called in. Groups as diverse as the Junior League and the Charlotte-Mecklenburg Planning Commission began putting in time and committing funds. A consortium of local banks lent money to the city, which then made

ABOVE: *Renovation of the Fourth Ward has once again produced a neighborhood full of charm and grace. Photo by Billy E. Barnes*

FACING PAGE: *Marriott City Center is conveniently located just one block from the Charlotte Convention Center. Photo by Matt Bradley*

mortgage loans at below-market rates to those willing to renovate or buy in Fourth Ward.

It was a risky venture, and those that arrived early were true urban pioneers, sticking out both their necks and their pocketbooks. It was slow going at first, but eventually the area turned around. Today Fourth Ward is again one of the finest of Charlotte's neighborhoods, with elegant, tree-lined streets, wide brick sidewalks, old-fashioned street lamps and charming renovated Victorian houses, along with newly built multifamily dwellings. The neighborhood has been designated an historic district by the city government, and the Charlotte-Mecklenburg Historic Properties Commission has designated some dozen sites as historic properties. Similar efforts are now coming to fruition in Third and First wards, where there is a greater mix of commercial and residential activity. Between 1974 and 1986 local banks

committed more than $65 million of financing at below-market rates for the redevelopment of these three neighborhoods.

This revitalizing activity of the 1970s laid the groundwork for the transformation of the 1980s. As Charlotte matures, the crossroads at its core is changing, symbolic of what is occurring throughout the city and outlying region. In the early part of the decade, there was the opening of Discovery Place, ranked among the top 10 hands-on science museums in the country; the construction of the Charlotte Plaza, Independence Center, and the Marriott Hotel; the completion of the Tryon Street Mall to facilitate the flow of public transportation and encourage pedestrian activity; the opening of the Afro-American Cultural Center; and the addition of art galleries, restaurants, and other entertainment facilities. All these changes made uptown the center for cultural activities and celebrations of all kinds, such as SpringFest, the city's salute to the visual arts; JazzCharlotte in the fall; and First Night, a family-oriented New Year's Eve party that is also a showcase for the area's performing arts groups.

The biggest changes, however, occurred as the decade came to a close. Fall 1988 saw the opening of One First Union Center, the headquarters for First Union Corporation, with 1.2 million square feet, and at 42 stories the tallest structure between Atlanta and Washington, D.C. Also in 1988 the Charlotte-Mecklenburg Gov-

The opening of Cityfair in uptown Charlotte has helped to establish the area as a major retail center. Photo by Mark Fortenberry

ernment Center opened, as well as the 10-story Gateway Center, the first structure in a six-block development that will include an urban park and several other office buildings. The second building of that development, the 187-room Compri Hotel, opened in spring 1989.

Also at the end of 1988, the 120,000-square-foot Cityfair opened in time for the Christmas season, with a variety of specialty shops and eateries, making uptown's position as the largest retail center in the Carolinas even stronger. A new hotel, The Dunhill, opened as well.

Also in 1989 the enlarged, redesigned main branch of the Charlotte-Mecklenburg Public Library had its grand reopening; the Federal Reserve Branch moved into a new home; the Charlotte Apparel Mart, with showrooms for women's apparel sales reps and hosting five trade shows annually, opened its doors; and a renovated, expanded Spirit Square reopened.

The 1990s also promise to be exciting. For example, the 31-story Interstate Tower, located just off the Square, is expected to be completed in 1990. And in a project that will be difficult to top, NCNB is expected to open its new corporate headquarters in 1992. At 60 stories, it will be the tallest building in the Southeast and will feature a major hotel, retail space, and the North Carolina Performing Arts Center at Charlotte, all located right at the Square.

All that construction means big bucks. Total uptown development from 1972 to 1987 topped $1.27 billion, and in 1988 uptown property was valued at more than $1.4 billion. The ratio between private and public investment in uptown from 1971 to 1987 was 16.5 to 1, well above the national average. The entire city has benefited from these investments. In 1987 the average revenue generated per square mile in Charlotte was $618,000, compared to the $3 million generated per square mile in the central business district.

Charlotte has been prepared for its uptown growth, and long-range plans have been implemented to facilitate the flow of traffic caused by the 100,000 people expected to work here by the end of the century. For example, the city's goal is for 16 percent of the uptown work force to use mass transit by 1994. (The 1988 figure was nine percent.)

The first major step in meeting this

goal was the construction of the $8.4-million Tryon Street Mall (funded by a bond referendum) in 1984. Before the mall was built the transit system had about 80 buses running at peak hours; in 1988 that number was 133, a rate that could not have been reached without the mall. Other programs include monthly passes and express buses during rush hours.

The Tryon Street Mall also transformed uptown from a dowdy-looking area, where bus riders crowded together in one spot, to an attractive place with wide, welcoming sidewalks and trees lining the streets and with bus stops all along its 11-block area. During daytime hours on weekdays, people can ride any bus in the uptown area for free. Still, city planners recognize that cars will continue to be a major source of transportation for many years, and new parking facilities are added with each new major project.

Although uptown may be described as the heart of Charlotte, it is not the only area in Mecklenburg County where growth is occurring at a rapid rate. SouthPark is becoming known as Charlotte's second downtown, and

University City is literally emerging from cow pastures to become a satellite mini-city. The I-77 corridor, particularly near the new Coliseum and the airport in the southwest, is another focus of building activity.

SouthPark is rapidly becoming the retail, commercial and service center for the city's southeast, where much of Charlotte's residential growth has occurred in recent years. Just some two decades ago, the area was farmland, the site of a dairy and where the grandchildren of the owner, North Carolina Governor Cameron Morrison (known as "The Good Roads Governor" during his administration in the 1920s), hunted quail and watched deer play.

Today SouthPark is the focus for one of the wealthiest neighborhoods in the Southeastern U.S., with an annual median household income of around $45,000. If it were a separate municipality, it would have the third largest central business district in North Carolina. About three million square feet of office space provide work space for approximately 25,000 white-collar workers and house the corporate and regional headquarters of such firms as

Cityfair offers 120,000 square feet of specialty shops, restaurants, and attractions. Photo by Ernest H. Robl

The shaded benches and roomy sidewalks of Tryon Street Mall create a comfortable atmosphere for commuters. Photo by Kelly Culpepper/ Transparencies

Gold Bond Building Products, Equitable Life Assurance Society, Coca-Cola Consolidated, (fifth largest bottler in the U.S.), Piedmont Natural Gas, IRM, and CIGNA Company.

SouthPark also boasts of a 1.4 million-square-foot shopping mall (after which the entire area is named and which once served as the anchor for development), plus more than another 60,000 square feet of retail space, mostly high-end specialty shops. Among those shops is the prototype store for noted fashion designer Alexander Julian, an alumnus of the University of North Carolina at Chapel Hill.

When SouthPark Mall opened in 1970, newspaper accounts reported that its air-conditioning system was large enough to cool 400 homes. It is the largest shopping center in the area, and in 1988 it was enlarged by 434,000 square feet to include a food court and

the city's first Thalhimer's. The original anchor tenants, Belk and Ivey's, both recently upgraded and redesigned their stores, making them the flagships of their chains. A fifth large department store will also be added to the mall in the future.

The SouthPark area is marked by the intersection of Sharon and Fairview roads, one of the city's busiest. It boasts of 111 stores, 30 restaurants, 16 bank branches, 53 office buildings, seven churches, a three-theater movie complex, and four hotels: the all-suite Guest Quarters, a Hyatt (the second in the state), Marriott Courtyard, and the Park Hotel, one of only 196 hotels worldwide with a Preferred Hotel rating. In May 1988 SouthPark's first skyscraper opened—the 13-story 6100 Fairview Road Building. The area even has its own magazine, *Update*, a four-color quarterly with a circulation of

built in 1973, was the first structure in Charlotte to feature gold reflective glass, and the Equitable Building, designed by former Charlotte architect Harry Wolfe, received the prestigious Honor Award from the American Institute of Architects.

The brothers-in-law, however, are not yet finished changing the face of Morrison's farm. Work began in 1988 on Morrocroft, a 178-acre mixed-use development that will include single-family luxury homes, condominiums overlooking a man-made lake, 240,000 square feet of retail space, 240,000 square feet of office space, a 20,000-square-foot library, and a day-care facility for up to 250 children. More than $5 million will be spent on landscaping and infrastructure, nearly a quarter of the development will be open space, and there will be strict architectural controls.

Sunlight glints off the reflective gold glass of the Morrison Building. Photo by Paul Epley

more than 20,000.

Much of this development is the result of the hard work and business savvy of two of the heirs of Governor Morrison, grandson John W. "Johnny" Harris and H.C. "Smoky" Bissell, Jr., who is married to Harris' sister Sara. By the end of 1988 their firm, The Bissel Companies, had developed in South-Park 22 office buildings with 1.7 million square feet, more than half the total in the area. Most of those buildings are located in two suburban corporate office parks, the 65-acre Park and the 90-acre Carnegie, started in 1987. The showcase of Carnegie is the 250,000-square-foot Rotunda, named for its distinctive shape and which features a water display with 50 waterfalls running the length of the building.

Both centers are known for their high-quality building design and lavish landscaping. The Morrison Building,

ABOVE: *Waterfront shops and restaurants line the man-made lake of University Place. Photo by Matt Bradley*

FACING PAGE: *The stylish Lakefront Shoppes at University Place have been recognized as being one of the finest commercial developments produced in recent years. Photo by Mark Fortenberry*

PAGES 86-87: *The landmark Rotunda building, with its lavish display of waterfalls, is situated at the heart of the Carnegie corporate center in SouthPark. Photo by Jane Faircloth/Transparencies*

PAGE 87 (insets, clockwise from top left): *The Coca-Cola Consolidated offices create a stunning composition of water and light. Photo by Jane Faircloth/Transparencies; The fashionable Belk department store in SouthPark Mall features a wide range of merchandise for the area's shoppers. Photo by Mark Fortenberry; A pleasing design of flowering trees and green foliage lends an appealing landscape to the SouthPark area. Photo by Jane Faircloth/Transparencies*

Charlotte's southeast is not the only area that has developed its own commercial, retail and service center. University City, in the county's northeast section, is anchored by four institutions that serve a growing community of more than 70,000 people in a 25-mile radius, including Cabarrus County. They are the University of North Carolina at Charlotte (UNCC), the fourth largest university in the state's university system; University Research Park (URP), a 2,600-acre high-tech research-oriented park, the second largest of its kind in the state; the 130-bed University Memorial Hospital; and University Place, a 250-acre, mixed-use planned development.

University City is a direct result of smart urban planning, and once again, is a story that starts with farmland and cows. Even as recently as the late 1960s, there were more cows living in the area than people, and the most common sounds were their gentle mooing and birds chirping. But the cows

moved aside, and the sound of bulldozers started making way for the sounds of people and business when UNCC and the Charlotte Chamber worked together to create University Research Park in 1972. URP's growth was slow at first, but when IBM opened its facility there in 1978, things began to take shape.

That same year, the Charlotte-Mecklenburg Planning Commission asked UNCC officials to develop a plan by which growth could be redirected from the city's Southeast to the North and Northeast, where resources were underutilized. The study, completed the next year under the direction of Dr. Jim Clay, then director of UNCC's Urban Institute, called for the creation of a focus, or catalyst, to redirect the growth.

That focus was University Place, and UNCC was the driving force behind its creation. The university still oversees implementation of the development's master plan, which UNCC faculty orginally developed. Coming up with innovative ways to deal with government red tape, UNCC was able to make the land available for commercial use (and increase its endowment by $4 million), choosing Carley Capital Group of Madison, Wisconsin, to develop the site. In 1987 UNCC received national recognition from the American Association of State Colleges and Universities for its work with University Place. The project remains a prototype for a joint-venture college-area development, and visitors come from as far away as the Soviet Union and Thailand to learn how it was done.

University Place had its grand opening in September 1985, and by the close of 1988 the planned $400-million community was about one-third completed, with the area's only

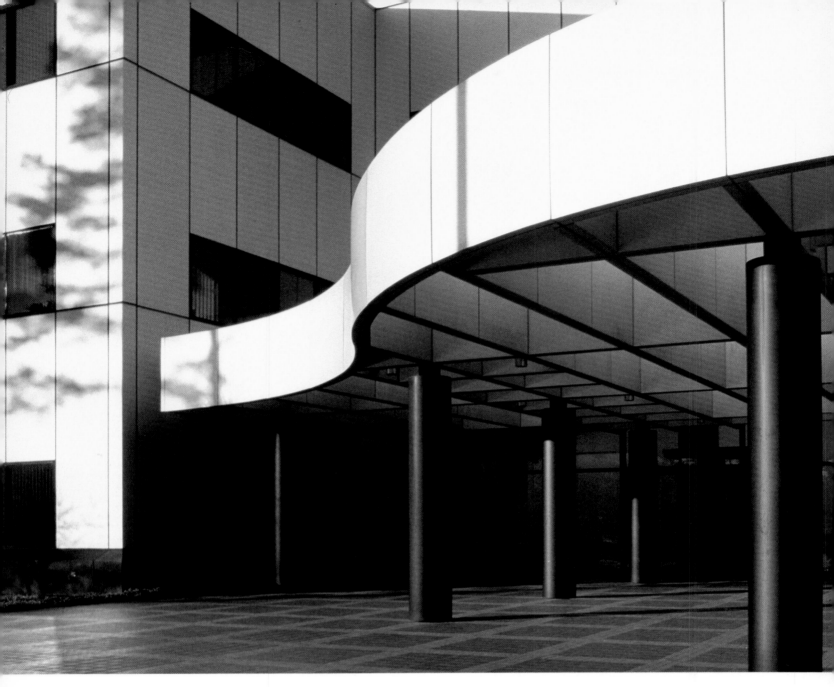

Southern Bell's corporate data center is located in University Research Park. Photo by Kelly Culpepper/Transparencies

Hilton Hotel; the state headquarters for the Oasis Shrine; One University Place, a 93,000-square-foot office building; about 30,000 square feet of other office space; nearly 200,000 square feet of retail and restaurant space; a six-screen movie theater complex; four bank branches; a Montessori school; and four residential neighborhoods. Coming on line are a regional shopping mall, a conference center adjoining the hotel, and an office park.

The community has been designed to merge the visual appeal of a pedestrian mall with a European flair, along with the convenience of an automobile-oriented shopping center. With a

fountain and man-made lake at the center and lots of paths, it's very much a warm "people place" where walking is encouraged. In 1986 the Lakefront Shoppes that border the lake were named "best commercial development" by the Charlotte Board of Realtors.

But University Place couldn't stand alone, and it's the synergy among the major components that gives University City its strength and appeal. UNCC helped create the development, and now its students and faculty play, work, and live there. Both UNCC and University Place provide services for the companies and employees at URP and are major selling points as the park

The need for single-family homes in the University City area is increasing with the recent growth of the neighborhood's business community. Photo by Kelly Culpepper/Transparencies

works to attract more. In turn, the park's firms are generous supporters of the university.

For example, UNCC faculty does research for park members, students complete internships at URP, and the school provides a variety of training programs for the firms' employees, from graduate degree programs to specially designed courses. UNCC's resources were a major reason Verbatim Corporation, a subsidiary of Eastman Kodak, decided in 1987 to manufacture its optical disks at the park.

Land at URP is primarily available for research complexes, data processing centers, and corporate headquarters, and sites are heavily landscaped with lots of trees and greenery. In early 1989, 12 firms with approximately 10,000 employees were located at the Park: Allstate, AT&T, Clarke Checks, Collins & Aikman, Dow Jones, EDS, EPRI, IBM, Home Savings of America, Southern Bell, Union Oil, and Verbatim. Many of them have expanded their facilities since coming to the park. They have been attracted here not only by the university and the area's residential and recreational amenities, but also by its proximity to the airport (a 20-minute drive) and uptown (15 minutes) and easy accessibility to interstates I-85 and I-77. Recreational activities on Lake Norman are also nearby.

These blue-chip firms have attracted numerous smaller companies, many of them high-tech in nature, to the University City area, and commercial developments inside and outside the park and University Place have cropped up to meet their needs for space. The Bissell Companies, Charter

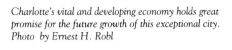

Charlotte's vital and developing economy holds great promise for the future growth of this exceptional city. Photo by Ernest H. Robl

Properties, Carolina Fairfax Properties, and Pizagalli are just some of the developers with projects either completed or planned.

With all this business activity comes the need for homes. In addition to the 1,000 units planned for within University Place, some 25 developers are planning about 2,500 single-family homes. Some workers, however, are choosing to live in the southwest region of the county, particularly along the I-77 corridor and in the lower Steele Creek area.

But business is booming in this area, too. The construction of the new

$47.4-million Charlotte Coliseum, which opened in August 1988, has been a catalyst for about $600 million worth of development in the area, such as Lakepointe, home of regional centers for Southern Bell, Digital Equipment Company, and National Cash Register, and the corporate headquarters for Belk Stores; the 125-acre Coliseum Center; Coffey Creek Park; and Arrowpoint, where Royal Insurance has its corporate headquarters.

The area had been primed for growth even without the Coliseum. It's close to the airport and has an excellent road network, which includes the

Billy Graham Parkway connecting I-77 and I-85, and is conveniently located to the residential neighborhoods of the southeast. The York Road Landfill, once a block to development, has been reclaimed and turned into Renaissance Park, a 450-acre recreation complex with a golf course and tennis and equestrian facilities. There are also nearly 6,000 hotel rooms in the corridor.

Arrowood Southern Industrial Park, the state's largest industrial park, is located along I-77, and its tenants include Frito-Lay and General Tire. South Point, another office park,

boasts a foreign trade zone. It is predicted that this southwest section of the county will rank second, behind uptown, in new job creation by 2005.

So although uptown is the front porch of the city where Charlotte puts on the razzle-dazzle, Charlotteans haven't forgotten the rest of the house. A vibrant central city extends its wealth throughout the area, as amply demonstrated in Charlotte by the success of SouthPark, University City and the I-77 corridor. Their dynamic interplay creates a synergy that is making Charlotte a great city, not just of the South, but of the nation.

A Can-Do Spirit of Caring

Charlotte is first and foremost a city of commerce and a city of business, but it is also a city of caring, where civic responsibility and citizen participation are taken very seriously. Part of that spirit comes from the business community's recognition that improving the quality of life also improves the climate for commerce. But it also comes from a firm belief that you should give something back to the community where you make your money. Home-grown companies have been putting that belief into action for years, and firms new to the area have quickly followed suit. It's a commitment that comes at the personal level, too.

One example of this caring and commitment is the United Way. The local organization has met its annual fund-raising goal on time without extensions since 1954, one of the best records in the country.

The group can trace its roots back to 1931, when the community raised more than $139,000 for emergency relief in response to people's needs during the Great Depression. A Community Chest, and later a War Chest, were formed to raise funds, and in 1952 United Community Services (UCS) was formed, made up of 22 agencies and programs. Its fund drive, called the United Appeal Campaign, raised nearly $745,000 that year. A capital funds board was created in 1957 to schedule agencies' capital fund drives to ensure their success.

In 1969 the United Appeal campaign topped the $2-million mark for

The generous cooperation and support among the people of Charlotte is evident in the many activities concerning community welfare, such as the Habitat for Humanity project. Photo by Kelly Culpepper/Transparencies

FACING PAGE: *The Boy Scouts of America are supported by the United Way of Central Carolinas, helping to promote a sense of self-reliance and discovery in the young men of today.* Courtesy, United Way of Central Carolinas

LEFT: *Supported by the United Way of Central Carolinas, the neighboring Carrabus County L.I.F.E Center provides enriching experiences for older adults.* Courtesy, United Way of Central Carolinas

the first time, and UCS moved into new headquarters at 301 South Brevard Street, where the United Way is still located today. The United Appeal became the United Way in 1971.

The organization has continued to expand its services, as well as the size of the community it serves. In 1973 Mecklenburg and Union counties began conducting their United Way drives together, and in 1987 Cabarrus County joined the combined efforts. Today the local United Way is known as the United Way of Central Carolinas, which raised more than $15 million in 1988 with the help of about 5,000 volunteers. Approximately a quarter of a million people were helped in the three counties by 60 agencies. About one-fourth of the budget goes for services that strengthen and enrich individuals and families; nearly 20 percent is used for youth development services.

The United Way has left its legacy in many other ways, especially through the creation of such organizations as the Foundation for the Carolinas, a community foundation started in 1958. In 1989 the foundation managed some

450 funds, including a scholarship fund for children at housing projects.

Over the years the foundation has provided seed money for new groups in the city, including the Mecklenburg Council on Adolescent Pregnancy; Metrolina Food Bank; Friendship Trays; Child Care Resources, a clearinghouse and advocacy group for day care; and International House, a support group for internationals living in and visiting Charlotte. In the mid-1980s, through a grant from the Charles Stewart Mott Foundation of Flint, Michigan, the local foundation also began working directly with low-income neighborhood groups, efforts it has continued since the Mott funding ended in 1989.

Local government also is progressive and compassionate—but efficiently run. Charlotte is one of the few U.S. cities of its size that has a triple-AAA bond rating—in other words, the city, county, and state all have that top-rated status, as rated by Moody's and Standard and Poors. In 1988 a productivity task force chaired by Hugh McColl, chairman and chief executive officer of NCNB Corporation, analyzed

ABOVE: *The stately Mecklenburg County Courthouse, located in uptown Charlotte on Fourth Street, recalls the many years of city government history. Photo by Mark Fortenberry*

city government's operations and generally gave it good grades. Its specific recommendations were acted upon by staff.

The community also prides itself that its local governments seem to have perfected the art of getting everyone involved in the act while still getting some action. This can make for some cantankerous goings-on at times, but it's always been done with good Southern manners. Such open debate and discussion yields a community consensus that enables everyone to move forward on a given problem. It's a philosophy of "moving slow to go fast."

There is some concern, however, that as Mecklenburg County faces increasingly complex urban challenges, that sense of consensus will be harder to reach because of the myriad of interests clamoring to be heard, and that a shared loyalty to the community as a whole will be lost. The Civic Index

Project is just one group looking at ways to make sure that doesn't happen. Leadership Charlotte, a community leadership development program run by the University of North Carolina at Charlotte's Urban Institute, also works to instill a sense of communitywide awareness in its participants.

One way for citizens to get involved in local government is through citizens' advisory boards and commissions. There are about 100 such city, county, and joint bodies—some standing and some ad hoc—to which citizens can be appointed by the city council, the board of county commissioners, or the mayor. Approximately 1,000 volunteers serve on these bodies, which run the gamut from the Planning Commission and Airport Advisory Board to the Tree Commission and Sister Cities Committee. Volunteers also organize and serve on committees that work toward the passage of bond referen-

dums. In large part this grassroots support is why few bond referendums fail in Charlotte-Mecklenburg.

One outstanding example of government and citizens working together successfully for the benefit of all is the $47.4-million, 25,000-seat Charlotte Coliseum—often called the city's crown jewel—which opened on time and within budget in August 1988.

Charlotteans began talking about the need for a new Coliseum in the early 1970s when the Atlantic Coast Conference (ACC) basketball tournament left Charlotte (then with a 10,000-seat arena) for bigger facilities. In 1980 a Charlotte Chamber of Commerce task force concluded that the city had a definite need for a 25,000-seat facility. In 1982 Mayor Eddie Knox appointed the Committee of 100 to determine the parameters of the facility and what amenities were needed, as well as to find a location. In

1983 the committee recommended a site on the Billy Graham Parkway.

Even after that, the possibility of an uptown site continued to be explored, making the process the most thorough and broad-based of any other recent community project. But it was the Billy Graham site that was presented to voters in 1984 when they approved the $47.4 million for the project, the largest bond ever approved by city voters at the time.

Mecklenburg County citizens are served by a city-county government. The county includes the city of Charlotte, six small towns (Pineville, Matthews, and Mint Hill in the south, and Huntersville, Cornelius, and Davidson in the north), and unincorporated parts of the county. These unincorporated areas—mostly located in the rural parts of the county—are quickly disappearing, however, as Charlotte and the other towns move to

annex them into their borders.

Generally, the county government provides human services, such as health and education, and serves the unincorporated areas. The city—or towns, each of which has its own town council—provides such urban services as trash pickup, water, and sewage disposal. Consolidating city and county governments has been the subject of debate for years, and although such consolidation is still probably years in coming, the issue is no longer laughed at or lightly dismissed.

The city of Charlotte has used a managerial form of government since 1928. A mayor is chosen in a partisan election every odd-numbered year. Institutionally, the position of mayor has little power, with no voting authority except in some zoning decisions and in case of a tie on the city council. But the mayor does possess great symbolic and persuasive power (more or less, depending on his or her political skills) and, as the city's main public representative and spokesperson, can set the general direction for where it is headed.

The city council is made up of 11

ABOVE: *The federal government maintains a presence in Charlotte in the form of the United States Post Office and Courthouse on Mint Street. Photo by Mark Fortenberry*

LEFT: *Mecklenburg County residents are served by a city-county government, in which the city provides the daily urban services such as water, power, and sanitation, while the county provides human services to meet the needs of education, health, and general welfare. Photo by Mark Fortenberry*

in 1986. The elections are partisan and held in even-numbered years. The chair is generally the top vote-getter of the majority party.

District representation also is used to elect representatives and senators to the North Carolina General Assembly. The system began in 1984 after a federal court order. The county sends eight representatives and (together with Cabarrus County) four state senators to the legislature. Elections for the school board are nonpartisan and held in even-numbered years. All nine members are elected at-large for staggered four-year terms.

Among many other efforts, the city of Charlotte has received high marks nationally for its work in providing low- and moderate-income housing. Government, along with the business community and private citizens, has created innovative programs and come up with a variety of ways to deal with this problem afflicting all of America

The Charlotte Housing Authority is an independent city agency governed by a seven-member board appointed by the mayor and city council. Its main responsibility is to provide safe and adequate housing for low-income groups, and as such it builds public housing with funds from city government and works with other groups who provide low-income housing. In early 1989 it owned or managed housing for about 12,300 people and provided rent subsidies for about 4,000 more.

The agency has received national attention for continuing to build low-income housing (at the rate of 50 units per year) without federal support. In 1988, through the creation of the Innovative Housing Fund, the city council committed several million dollars to continuing these efforts, and as the name of the fund implies, they are seeking new ways to do it. For exam-

members, seven elected from districts and four elected at-large in partisan elections held the same year as the mayoral election. The mayor pro tem, elected by the council, traditionally has been the top vote-getter of the majority party. The elections became partisan in 1975, and district representation was introduced in 1977.

Mecklenburg County also uses a managerial system, which it has employed since 1962. There are seven members on the board of county commissioners—three elected at-large and four from districts, a system introduced

The nationwide nonprofit organization, Habitat for Humanity, builds much-needed housing through the help of local volunteers. Charlotte boasts the largest affiliate of this organization and has constructed more than 50 homes in the area since 1984. Photo by Kelly Culpepper/Transparencies

ple, the Charlotte-Mecklenburg Housing Partnership was formed late in 1988 to complement the Housing Authority and to enable new partnerships and coalitions to address the problem.

The Housing Authority also has gained national national attention for its programs dealing with crime prevention and upward mobility. Its Gateway Program is designed to provide residents of public housing (with incomes of under $12,500) with the skills and job training needed to get better jobs, then to help them save the funds so they can move out of the projects into a home or apartment. This is done by taking part of their rent and putting it into an escrow account. The

program is unique in the country, and legislation had to be passed in Congress before the authority could implement it. The enabling legislation allows the residents to keep such benefits as food stamps while enrolled in the program. Stepping Stone is a five-year progam with similar goals for families with annual incomes over $12,500. Both programs got under way in 1989, and about 100 families are enrolled in each one.

Many of these actions are the result of the city council's adoption in 1987 of a formal housing policy. It has three main components. The first recognizes the need to keep the current housing stock up to standards, and so the city is aggressively enforcing the building code and, through the Community Development Program, supplying financial resources to help landlords comply with them.

The second component recognizes that housing needs do not exist in a vacuum, but rather are part of the whole cycle of poverty. The Gateway and Stepping Stone programs are indicative of this approach.

The third component seeks to involve private money to help build low-income housing. Two such joint public-private ventures were started in 1989, Stone Haven and the rehabilitation of Hoskins Mill.

The community as a whole also recognizes the need for emergency shelter for the homeless. In 1988 and 1989

the businesses and private citizens of Charlotte joined the local government in raising $1.5 million for a shelter for homeless men on North Tryon Street and for expansion of Charlotte Emergency Housing, which provides shelter for homeless women and children in a house in front of the Park Road YWCA. (About 90 percent of the women have a job and a place to live when they leave the program.) The building for the men's shelter, which opened in 1988, was purchased by the city with help from the United Way, the Charlotte Home Builders Association and its auxiliary, and Charlotte Pipe and Foundry. In addition, George Shinn, majority owner of the Charlotte Hornets, was asked by Mayor Sue

The availability of low-income housing is a primary concern of Charlotte's government, and it has succeeded in building homes without the support of federal aid. One such home is pictured here under construction near Johnson C. Smith University. Photo by Kelly Culpepper/Transparencies

PREVIOUS PAGE: *Religion plays a major role in Charlotte, with more than 600 houses of worship representing a spectrum of denominations. Photo by Jane Faircloth/Transparencies*

Myrick to raise the rest of the funds, and he did so by turning to the corporate community, churches, and individual citizens, as well as through fund-raising efforts involving the Hornets. Donated labor and in-kind gifts also made the shelter possible.

churches among the volunteers—built more than 50 homes, most of them in Optimist Park. Fourteen of those were built in five days in the summer of 1987, when 300 volunteers from 12 states and Canada (including former President Jimmy Carter and his wife Rosalyn) came together for a successful project that attracted extensive media attention.

Charlotte-Mecklenburg has also received national attention and acclaim for its work in the area of recycling. In 1984 the city of Charlotte and Mecklenburg County signed an interlocal agreement giving the city responsibility for solid waste collection and the county responsibility for disposal. In response, the county has developed a 20-year solid waste management plan with three major objectives: to recycle 15 percent of the county's waste stream by 1994 and 30 percent by 2006 (an increase from one percent in 1988); to incinerate, through resource recovery, 40 percent (up from zero percent in 1988); and to landfill 30 percent (down from 99 percent in 1988).

ABOVE: *Working in cooperation with local and city government, the residential and corporate communities have banded together to institute major recycling programs in the Charlotte area. Photo by Diane Davis/Transparencies*

Other groups also are responding to Charlotte's housing problems. The Council for Children, an advocacy group, made housing one of its priorities in 1989. So did Mecklenburg Ministries, a council of churches, synagogues, and other religious bodies that works for economic and social justice.

Charlotte also is home to the country's largest affiliate of Habitat for Humanity, a nonprofit building company that works with volunteers and families in building homes together—a concept commonly referred to as "sweat equity." From 1984 to 1989 the affiliate—with some 35 crews from 20

As part of these efforts, the county's waste-to-energy facility in the University City area went on-line in the summer of 1989. Steam produced by the facility is sold to the University of North Carolina at Charlotte (UNCC) while electricity goes to Duke Power Company. The county also is exploring the possibility of building a second such facility in the Arrowood area.

In addition, Mecklenburg County

introduced a pilot recycling program with curbside pickup for consumer households in 1987. By early 1989 some 16,000 households were involved in the Curb It! program, and approximately 70 percent of them actually participated by recycling newspapers, glass, aluminum cans, and plastic soft-drink bottles. All of Charlotte's single-family households will be included in the program by 1990.

In addition, there are nine drop-off recycling centers located throughout Mecklenburg County. At the Harrisburg Road Landfill, the county recovers cardboard, salvages scrap metal, and recycles yard waste by converting it into mulch. In all county offices, computer and office paper is recovered for recycling.

Business support for recycling efforts has been strong and has contributed to its success. Coca-Cola, for example, has donated consultation and some equipment for the Curb It! program, and Pepsi-Cola and the glass industry also have contributed help. The National Association for Plastic Container Recovery is headquartered in Charlotte, and in the fall of 1989 the city will host the National Recycling Conference.

Although Charlotte is very much a secular city, the influence of religion is quite strong even for a city located in the heart of the Bible Belt. There are more than 600 houses of worship in Charlotte, with practically every denomination and a growing number of international churches represented. In 1953 there were 240 churches, or

BELOW: Greek Orthodox is one of the many religions represented in Charlotte. Photo by Jane Faircloth/Transparencies

one for every 556 people. A writer at the time waxed eloquent: "Charlotte is recognized as the greatest church-going city in the world next to Edinburgh, Scotland."

As in the rest of the South, the Bap-

ABOVE: A Pentecostal celebration is observed at the Myers Park Presbyterian Church. Photo by Jane Faircloth/Transparencies

tist Church is a major Protestant denomination, but in Charlotte the Presbyterians also have a longstanding and strongly-felt influence. When the area was first settled by the Scotch-Irish in the mid-eighteenth century, it was to the Presbyterian Church—originally in the form of traveling preachers—that settlers turned for a civilizing influence in this rough frontier land. Many of the oldest churches in Mecklenburg were Presbyterian, among them Sugaw Creek (founded in 1755), Steele Creek (1760), Hopewell (1762), Poplar Tent (1764), Center (1765), Providence (1767), and Philadelphia (1770).

The Sabbath was strictly enforced in those days, and even cooking had to be done the day before. Attending church was no short commitment; the service often began at 10 in the morning and lasted until sunset, with only about an hour's break for lunch.

During Charlotte's history, members of the Presbyterian Church began such educational institutions as Davidson College, Queens College, and Johnson C. Smith University, as well as Presbyterian Hospital and Alexander Children's Center (originally an orphanage, and now serving emotionally disturbed children). During the 1950s author James Baldwin described Charlotte as "Presbyterian pretty." At one point in the 1970s, all the members of the county commission were not only Presbyterians, but members of the same church as well. In 1989 the Presbytery of Charlotte included 142 churches with 45,000 communicants in seven North Carolina counties.

There has always been an evangelical streak in Charlotteans. Alexander Craighead, founder of Hopewell Presbyterian, belonged to the New Side movement, which found a focus in the evangelical aspects of the church's

teachings. Charlotte also was the home for A.G. Garr, who in the 1930s bought the old city auditorium and moved it to the intersection of Tuckaseegee and Dilworth as a site for his popular revivals.

During the 1940s, the annual Charlotte visit of Bishop C.M. "Daddy" Grace—who loved to display the wealth he acquired from his loyal, enthusiastic followers—was marked by parades, welcome signs, and outdoor baptisms at the House of Prayer pool. A crowd of 25,000 greeted his arrival in 1947.

World-famous evangelist Billy Graham was born and raised in Charlotte. His father's dairy farm was located where Park Road Shopping Center now stands. The worldwide ministry of Graham's brother-in-law, Leighton Ford, is based in the Queen City. Although the PTL Ministry founded by Jim and Tammy Bakker is located in nearby Fort Mill, South Carolina, many Charlotteans have been followers of this electronic church. And in 1985 Charlotte was where Bhagwan Shree Rajneesh, the Indian holy man who had a commune in Oregon, was nabbed trying to flee the country.

Although Protestant Christianity has been by far the dominant faith practiced in Charlotte, others also have worshipped here. St. Peter's Roman Catholic Church, located on Tryon Street, was dedicated in 1852. In 1988 there were 10 Roman Catholic parishes in Mecklenburg County with nearly 25,000 members. Membership in the diocese, which covers 26 counties, is expected to double by the year 2000.

In 1850 there were nine Jewish fam-

FACING PAGE: St. Peter's Roman Catholic Church, built in the mid-1800s, is located in the heart of Charlotte, and houses one of the 10 Roman Catholic parishes in Mecklenburg County. Photo by Ernest H. Robl

ABOVE: The new Little Rock AME Zion Church has served the community of Charlotte since 1981. Photo by Mark Fortenberry

ilies living in the county, and the first orthodox congregation met in 1895. Today in Mecklenburg there are about 5,000 Jews and two congregations, plus a Jewish Community Center located on Providence Road.

The church has always played an important role in the lives of American blacks as well, acting as a source of comfort and unity, expressing blacks' needs and concerns, and providing a place for black leadership to develop. Charlotte is no exception.

Although predominantly black congregations exist in most every denomination, it is the African Methodist Episcopal (AME) Zion Church that has had the biggest effect on Charlotte's black community. The church has approximately 1.5 million members, 75,000 of which are in North Carolina, giving the state the largest population of AME Zion Church members in the country. Mecklenburg County alone has 34,000 members.

The AME Zion Church was founded in 1796 by blacks who wanted a Christian church to express their unique culture and experience. In 1864 the church formed its first congregation in Charlotte (also the first black church here) at the Clinton Chapel, located in Third Ward on South Mint Street.

The second AME Zion congregation in Charlotte was the Little Rock AME Church. Originally located in Third Ward, the church moved to First Ward, where it became a cornerstone of the black community there. When the congregation built its church, members decided to turn to an architect for its design rather than ordering ready-made blueprints from the church organization. They hired James M. McMichaels, one of the city's leading architects (he also designed the church

that now houses the Spirit Square Center for the Arts), and raised $20,000 for construction—an amazing sum of money at the time.

In the late 1970s it appeared that the 1911 structure would become a victim of urban renewal. But the efforts of the congregation and the Charlotte-Mecklenburg Historic Properties Commission saved it from demolition, and today the renovated building serves as the home for the Afro-American Cultural Center. The new Little Rock AME Zion Church opened in 1981, literally only steps away from its first home.

Charlotte has also played a major role in the church's history nationwide. In 1896, under the guidance of Bishop T.H. Lomax, the church brought its publishing house and offices to the city. The publishing house is still here, located at 401 East Second Street, and it continues to publish the church newspaper, *Star of Zion*, as well as church school literature. With the home missions, records, relief, pension, and finance offices located in the Queen City, Charlotte is considered the headquarters for AME Zion. In July 1988 some 10,000 delegates came to Charlotte for the church's 43rd Quadrennial Session of the General Conference.

Even as the city as a whole comes together for the common good, so does its churches. Ecumenical efforts have created such organizations as Crisis Assistance Ministry, which provides emergency resources for the poor, and Loaves and Fishes, which provides food to hungry families.

It is Charlotteans' commitment to each other—whether through the efforts of their church or through secular efforts—which makes the city special and which creates such a fierce sense of loyalty in its people.

FACING PAGE: Cooperation between the different religious denominations has helped to create community assistance programs for those in need. Photo by Bill Gleasner/Transparencies

Chapter 5

Quality Services for the Good Life

For a city truly to offer the good life to its residents, it must provide attractive, warm places to live, education that prepares its youth and gives adults ongoing training so they both can meet the challenges of the future, and health care that is efficient and caring. Charlotte has a long history of serving its citizens well in these areas and continues that tradition today, working to make sure all of them have the same access to the good life.

Providing a warm, attractive place to live, however, means more than a varied housing stock of quality construction, good design, and reasonable cost. The homes—whether single family dwellings, apartments, or condominiums—need to be located in neighborhoods where people feel a sense of place and belonging.

Mecklenburg County takes great pride in its neighborhoods. The Charlotte-Mecklenburg Planning Commission has identified 130 of them within the county, and in early 1989 there were more than 400 neighborhood organizations on file in its office—running the gamut from social groups and crime watchers and those tackling community issues such as youth unemployment and economic development to longstanding groups with citywide visibility and political clout. Although many of these organizations are from middle- and upper-class neighborhoods, an increasing number of low-income groups are becoming more active and are beginning to serve as forceful agents of change.

Comfortable homes, strong educational opportunities, and a wide range of medical services help to create a happy, healthy, and well-educated way of life for Charlotte residents. Photo by Paul Epley

ABOVE: *The vital spirit of Charlotte's many neighborhoods creates a special environment in which to live and work. Photo by Mark Fortenberry*

RIGHT: *Preservation of historic structures is a prime concern in the Charlotte area, providing the community with an entertaining and educational link with the past. Latta Place is one such successful historical site, recreating the life and activity of an 1800s plantation. Photo by Mark Fortenberry*

The neighborhood movement in Charlotte reached its peak strength in the early 1980s, and one of its long-lasting achievements was the introduction of district representation to the Charlotte City Council in 1977. Today neighborhood groups remain a force to be reckoned with, especially in terms of growth and new development. Developers often contact and work with neighborhood activists before applying for zoning changes or announcing a project so that a consensus can be reached before the official process begins. Often done with the help of the Planning Commission, this consensus building often means more

years with input from government, business, and the general public. Even as the plan changes and is fine-tuned in response to new trends and situations, its basic commitment is to balancing growth with preservation.

Charlotte's oldest neighborhoods are the 23 located within the inner city. For these communities, preservation of their historic homes, churches, and other structures is an integral part of keeping their spirit and integrity. Two local government boards help these neighborhoods—and groups all over the county—work for historic preservation. The Historic Properties Commission is a joint city-county board that identifies and safeguards historic structures, helps to find resources for the adaptive reuse of historic structures, and educates the public about the history of the community. The city also has a Historic Districts Commission, which does the same work for collections of historic buildings in neighborhoods and commercial districts.

For those interested in local history, the Hezekiah Alexander Homesite and History Museum focuses on North Carolina and Mecklenburg history with changing exhibits and tours of the home, the oldest building in the county. In 1986 the Historic Properties Commission put together walking tours of six of Charlotte's oldest neighborhoods—Biddleville, Dilworth, Elizabeth, Fourth Ward, Myers Park, and Plaza-Midwood. The brochures, with maps, are still available from the Historic Properties Commission.

The history of these neighborhoods is rich and multifaceted, providing a fascinating look at Charlotte's roots. Biddleville, for example, took its name from Biddle Institute (now Johnson C. Smith University), named after Major Henry Jonathan Biddle, whose widow

preparatory work for developers but less time and money spent down the road dealing with the concerns of area residents.

Even as Charlotte grows and becomes more urban, the strength and vitality of its neighborhoods are sure to remain. Protecting their integrity and preserving the special fabric they create is a basic tenet of the Planning Commission's 2005 Plan. This land-use plan, a blueprint for the county's growth, is actively used as a guide when elected and appointed officials make decisions concerning these issues. It is not a stagnant document, however; it is updated and rewritten every five

ABOVE: Colorful details of restored Victorian homes in the Fourth Ward highlight the turning autumn leaves. Photo by Kelly Culpepper/Transparencies

FACING PAGE: Uptown Charlotte rises over the green trees of Dilworth, looking northwest over Kenilworth Avenue. Photo by Paul Epley

donated a large sum of money to establish a college for blacks in Charlotte after the Civil War. The university's Biddle Hall, with its soaring clock tower, has been a symbol of liberation and learning for area blacks since its completion in 1883. Today the hall is on the National Register of Historic Places.

From 1891 to 1909 Dilworth, the city's first suburb, was also the home for Latta Park, a 90-acre amusement park. Professional baseball teams played there, as did football squads from Davidson College and the University of North Carolina. The park also included a pavilion, a theater, and a lily pond with walking paths encircling it. Among the many entertainers who thrilled visitors there was Buffalo Bill and his Wild West Show. (Today's Lat-

ta Park encompasses what was once the pond.)

Elizabeth is the only Charlotte neighborhood named for a woman. In 1897 the area became the site for Elizabeth College, named after Anne Elizabeth Watts, whose husband, Gerard Snowden Watts, provided most of the funds to begin the institution. The college moved out of Charlotte to Salem, Virginia in 1915. In 1917 Presbyterian Hospital moved to the area from West Trade Street, dramatically altering the neighborhood's personality. The college's main building has been demolished, but the home of William Henry Belk (founder of Belk stores), dating back to the turn of the century, is still standing and now houses administrative offices.

In its heyday at the beginning of

ABOVE: *The historic Overcarsh House, located on West Eighth Street in the Fourth Ward, offers elegant bed-and-breakfast lodging in a gracious Victorian atmosphere. Photo by Matt Bradley*

FACING PAGE, TOP: *The affluent Myers Park neighborhood features luxurious tree-lined avenues. Photo by Kelly Culpepper/Transparencies*

FACING PAGE, BOTTOM: *The prolific housing boom of northeast Mecklenburg County is illustrated by this new development in the University City area. Photo by Kelly Culpepper/ Transparencies*

the twentieth century, Fourth Ward was full of large homes complete with gardens—as well as horses, cats, dogs, goats, and pigs. Also located there were the Charlotte Cotton Mill, the city's first; St. Peter's Hospital and the North Carolina Medical College (still standing at Poplar and Sixth streets and now an office building that houses the Charlotte Convention & Visitors Bureau), which made the neighborhood the city's first medical center; and the Berryhill Store, the community's center for political as well as social and commercial activity (After all, Fourth Ward began as a voting district).

Today the Berryhill Store is home for Alexander Michael's, a neighborhood bar and restaurant that follows in the proud social tradition of the original business. The neighborhood has been designated a local historic district with 10 historic structures. Two buildings, the Overcarsh House and the Liddell-McNinch House, are on the National Register of Historic Places.

Myers Park can date its opening to precisely September 1, 1912, when the first trolley car passed through the gateway on Queens Road. Although not the oldest of Charlotte's neighborhoods, it is certainly considered the grande dame. Many of Charlotte's old-time families still live here, and it remains a symbol of old-time wealth and power. It features wide, meandering streets and a lovely canopy of trees, and in the spring the azaleas and dogwoods bloom and flourish in a dizzying array of color and scent. The Myers Park Foundation was formed in 1978 to further the preservation efforts of the Myers Park Homeowners Association, and in 1986 the foundation published a history of the neighborhood, *Legacy: the Myers Park Story* by Mary Norton Kratt and

Thomas W. Hanchett.

What is today called Plaza-Mid-wood actually was once a collection of neighborhoods, and among the most notable was Chatham Estates, developed by a local wealthy textile family. The community was the only one in Charlotte with its own trolley line, completely unconnected to any others. But because of the inconvenience this caused in traveling to and from the area, Plaza-Midwood never became as popular as other neighborhoods such

older homes in such neighborhoods as Chantilly. In addition, custom-built homes are gaining in popularity, and a growing number of builders are now serving this demand.

Those who prefer a small-town atmosphere choose to live in one of Mecklenburg County's six towns—Matthews, Mint Hill, and Pineville in the south, and Davidson, Huntersville, and Cornelius in the north. Each town has a separate government, and children attend the consolidated Charlotte-Mecklenburg school system. More and more people who work in Charlotte are also choosing to live in surrounding counties that are more rural and less developed, such as Cabarrus, Gaston, Lincoln, Rowan, Union, and York (in South Carolina).

Most of Mecklenburg's workers, however, still choose to live there, and the county makes up 48 percent of the home market for the seven-county area. Within Mecklenburg, single-family homes make up about 50 percent of the housing stock, with 30 percent apartments and 20 percent condominiums.

ABOVE: *New residential construction in Charlotte has maintained a record level of activity since 1985. Photo by Mark Fortenberry*

as Myers Park and Dilworth.

Charlotte's neighborhoods—both old and new—currently offer a variety of housing options and life-styles. Area residents can choose from lake-front condominiums on Lake Norman and Lake Wylie, luxury apartment communities, and rambling old farmhouses in the still-rural areas of Mecklenburg and surrounding counties. The area also offers other single-family houses, such as restored Victorian homes in Fourth Ward, brand new homes featuring traditional or transitional architectural styles in the southeast and northeast, and refurbished

In the third quarter of 1988, the average price for a new home was $116,000 and $94,000 for a resale. Housing remains affordable, however, as homeowners generally get more house for their money than in other U.S. cities. For example, construction costs in Charlotte have remained at about 80 percent of the national average for the last several years, and the ratio of the average housing cost to family income is 2.15 to 1, compared to the national average of 2.4 to 1.

Since 1985 housing

permits—which generally mirror actual construction in Charlotte—have stayed at record levels. There were 3,593 permits issued for single-family homes in 1985, 3,709 in 1986, 3,888 in 1987, and 4,210 in 1988.

Housing trends are beginning to show some geographic changes, however. In 1987 the southern part of the county was still the area of greatest new home construction, as it had been for several years (accounting for 47 percent of all new construction), but the growth rate was decreasing, with only a three-percent increase. The southeastern area accounted for 21 percent of the new home market, but closings were down by five percent that year.

The northeast is by far the hottest growth spot, with its share of new homes jumping to 21 percent in just a few years. Permits increased by 25 percent in 1987 alone, and that trend is expected to continue with the ongoing development of University Place and University Research Park. The Lake Norman area is beginning to see more single-family construction in addition to the traditional lakeside condominiums of recent years.

The remaining five percent of new home construction in 1987 occurred in the northwest and southwest, and the southwest is a definite place to watch for future growth. Permits increased there by nine percent in 1987.

Apartment construction in Charlotte, as in most markets, has fluctuated greatly in the last decade. Growth has been the general direction, however, with almost half of the total rental market being built between 1980 and 1988. At the end of 1988, there were 44,500 apartments in complexes with 50 or more units. As of November 1988 the average one-bedroom apartment measured 684 square feet and rented for $383 a month, a two-bedroom unit averaged 949 square feet in

Condominiums comprise approximately 20 percent of the available housing space in Charlotte. Here, springtime blossoms adorn the exterior of an Eastover condominium complex. Photo by Jane Faircloth/Transparencies

size and $435 in monthly rent, and a three-bedroom apartment was an average of 1,262 square feet in size and rented for $507 per month.

One fast-growing segment of the multifamily market has been retirement communities, and there are many reasons for this trend. A growing number of the working adults moving to Charlotte bring along their retired parents, who often seek a separate place to live. Senior citizens also are attracted to the area because of its four distinct seasons with a mild winter, and its convenient location—between Florida and the Northeast, as well as between the mountains and the shore.

More national and out-of-state firms are entering the Charlotte housing market. For example, in 1987 the county's two largest homebuilders, the John Crosland Company and Ralph Squires Homes, were purchased by out-of-state firms. Crosland was acquired by Dallas-based Centex Real Estate Corporation and Squires by Beazer Homes, a British firm. UDC Homes, Ryan Homes, and Ryland Homes have been in Charlotte for some time and each have significant market shares. Other recent newcomers to the area include M/I Schottenstein of Ohio, Pulte Homes from Michigan, and U.S. Home, Ken Lokey Homes, and Weekly Homes, all out of Texas.

But a community needs more than good homes in pleasant neighborhoods in order to be a good place to live. Educating its people is another important aspect of a good quality of life, and Mecklenburg County is facing

FACING PAGE: Children gather to board their school bus at the Merry Oaks Elementary School. Photo by Diane Davis/Transparencies

ABOVE: A school crossing guard safely guides children as they cross the street on their way to school. Photo by Jane Faircloth/Transparencies

today's education challenges head-on through its public school system, a variety of private schools, and several top-notch institutions of higher learning.

Mecklenburg boasts of five colleges and universities—the University of North Carolina at Charlotte (UNCC), Central Piedmont Community College (CPCC), Davidson College, Queens College, and Johnson C. Smith University. All of them are members of a 10-member consortium of area colleges that work together for quality education. The other members are Barber-Scotia College, Belmont Abbey College, Gaston College, Wingate College, and Winthrop College.

Of all these institutions, however, the Charlotte-Mecklenburg School System (CMS) has the most far-reaching impact on residents' education. The consolidated city-county system is the 30th largest school system in the country, and in the 1988-89 school year had an enrollment of approximately 75,000 students. During that year it was made up of 101 schools and six special programs with an annual budget exceeding $318 million, 75 percent of which went directly into instructional programs. Its per-pupil expenditure of nearly $4,000 was one of the highest in North Carolina and the South. Students who graduated in 1988 received more than $3 million in academic scholarships. In 1987 voters approved $31 million in bonds for new schools and for renovation and improvement of existing ones.

CMS uses busing to achieve racial integration under a 1969 court order that was upheld by the U.S. Supreme Court in 1971 and implemented in September 1974. Although not marred by the intense outbreaks of violence that occurred in many other American cities, the Charlotte experi-

ence was nevertheless a tense and traumatic one that tested the city's ability to deal with conflict and create consensus.

Passions cooled as communitywide support and cooperation helped the system work. In 1979 the *Wall Street Journal* explored what had occurred in Charlotte and reported, "After nine years, Charlotte has one of the most thoroughly integrated school systems in the country and the turmoil normally surrounding busing has faded into general acceptance. Blacks now share equal resources."

Although Charlotte continues to gain national attention as a model for successful school integration, there remains an ongoing debate within the community over the use of busing to achieve it. In 1988 about 12,000 CMS students were bused to achieve integration, and the average trip for an elementary school student took 20 minutes; the average trip for secondary school students was 22 minutes. White flight has been minimal, and in 1988 enrollment in the system was 57.5 percent white. About 35 private schools in Mecklenburg County offer a variety of educational options to a student population of approximately 9,000.

CMS has gained national attention in other areas as well. It rates above the U.S. average in such areas as daily attendance (94.2 percent in the 1987-88 school year) and students who plan to continue their education after graduation (78 percent in 1987-88). In 1988 the system's Cities in Schools program was cited as North Carolina's most outstanding dropout prevention program, and the system was one of four in the country selected to participate in a pilot program for the Challenger Foundation to benefit space study.

CMS's career development program

for teachers is considered a model for other school systems in the state and throughout the U.S., as is its annual financial report. The CMS Finance Department has received the Certificate of Achievement for Excellence in Financial Reporting from the Government Finance Officers every year since 1977.

Individual schools and staff members within CMS have also received national recognition. In 1988 First Ward School, located uptown, was honored by the Outstanding School Recognition Program sponsored by the U.S. Department of Education (Previous CMS winners have been Myers Park High School and Carmel Junior High). That same year the library and media program at East Mecklenburg High was one of 62 recognized by the U.S. Department of Education, and Gail Morse, a teacher at Alexander Junior High, received the National Christa McAuliffe Educator Award, presented to five teachers in the nation for innovative use of technology in the classroom.

Central Piedmont Community College (CPCC) also has received national acclaim, having been recognized as one of the top five community colleges in the U.S. by the American Association of Community and Junior Colleges. CPCC is considered the flagship of the 58-member North Carolina community college system, and its more than 200 classroom sites throughout the county serve about 50,000 students each year with vocational and technical training, literacy classes, certification programs, and associate degrees.

CPCC was officially formed in 1963 when North Carolina began its community college system, but its roots date back to 1949, when Carver College was founded to provide a two-year

FACING PAGE: The remarkable Belk Tower pierces the evening sky over the campus at the University of North Carolina at Charlotte (UNCC). Photo by Kelly Culpepper/Transparencies

FACING PAGE (inset): Located just 19 miles north of Charlotte, Davidson College is considered to be one of the nation's leading liberal-arts colleges. Photo by Mark Fortenberry

Art students leave the classroom to take advantage of natural daylight during a Queens College art class. Photo by Mark Fortenberry

program for blacks. It was later combined with the Industrial Education Center to become CPCC, which has its main campus on Elizabeth Avenue just outside of uptown Charlotte.

CPCC is known for providing education services and for meeting vocational and training needs that are not handled by other area institutions. Its responsiveness to the community has enabled it to help people who have not made it in the educational system their first time around, who need additional or upgraded skills, who want to step up the job ladder or change careers, or who simply want to take courses for personal enrichment in such areas as theater, art, music, foreign languages, sports and cooking.

Many of CPCC's activities are linked to economic development. It works closely with the Charlotte Chamber to help new and expanding businesses with training and courses specifically designed to meet their labor needs, and is often involved in the chamber's business recruiting efforts. Duke Power Company, Verbatim, Home Savings of America, Royal Insurance Company, and Okuma Machine Tools are just some of the companies the college has worked with.

In 1990 a new technology center is scheduled to open at CPCC that will expand its capabilities into retraining of low-skilled workers for jobs in high-tech industries such as electro-optics. In addition, CPCC has an International Business Center, which acts as a resource for firms that want to export and for individuals interested in international trade as a career, as well as a Small Business Center, which helps emerging small-business owners and entrepreneurs.

CPCC has also gained national recognition for its Adult Basic Literacy Education (ABLE) program, started in 1983. ABLE was one of the first programs in the U.S. to use computers to teach illiterate adults, and in its first five years it had reached some 5,000 people in seven locations, including one in Freedom Mall. CPCC still offers traditional classroom instruction in reading and writing for adults.

The University of North Carolina at Charlotte (UNCC) has a far-reaching influence throughout the community and has received national and international attention for its achievements. The university—now with an enrollment of 13,000, one of the largest and fastest-growing in the state university system—had its beginnings in 1947, as one of 12 college centers set up in North Carolina to meet the educational needs of returning World War II veterans. Bonnie Cole, who was to become a driving force behind the institution's expansion, was named president that first year and also taught engineering math.

Then housed in the old Central High School, the center officially became Charlotte College in 1949 and became a four-year institution in 1963. In 1965 it became UNCC, the fourth school in the state university system. By then the campus had moved to northeast Mecklenburg County off

Highway 49, and although it had been founded with an urban mission, there was nothing much surrounding it at the time except pastures and grazing cows.

Today, however, the fields and the cows have pretty much disappeared, thanks in large part to the efforts of UNCC. The university was instrumental in the creation of University Research Park (URP), the state's second largest high-tech industrial park, and was the impetus for the development of University Place, a 250-acre mixed-use development that has been a catalyst for economic growth in the area. The university has drawn national accolades for these endeavors and in 1987 received the national award for institutional innovation from the American Association of State Colleges and Universities.

UNCC retains close working relationships with tenants at URP, such as IBM, AT&T, and Verbatim, a subsidiary of Eastman Kodak. Verbatim decided to relocate its optical disk operations to Charlotte in 1987, and one of the factors leading to that decision was UNCC's $8.3-million applied research building, scheduled to open in 1990. There, UNCC and Verbatim will work together on optical disk technology. This new industry—intended to make magnetic disks obsolete—is expected to grow tenfold by the end of the century, and UNCC officials have said the partnership gives Charlotte the potential to become the next Silicon Valley.

UNCC excels in other areas as well. In 1987 and 1988 *U.S. News and World Report* rated it one of the 10 best comprehensive universities in the South. The 1988 book, *How to Get an Ivy League Education at a State University,* named UNCC one of the top 115 state universities in the U.S. Its engineering school is the second largest in North

Carolina, and its accounting graduates have one of the best track records in the state for success on the certified public accountants' examination. Its architecture school is one of two in the state.

While CPCC and UNCC are relative newcomers to Charlotte, three others—Davidson, Queens, and Johnson C. Smith—have long traditions. Yet they too are changing with the times.

For example, Presbyterian-affiliated Davidson, located 19 miles north of Charlotte, was founded in 1837 as a

ABOVE: *As the fourth school to be included in the state university system in 1965, the University of North Carolina at Charlotte (UNCC) now enrolls some 13,000 students and continues to grow at a rapid pace. Photo by Ned Swift/Transparencies*

TOP: *A leading manufacturer of floppy disks, University Research Park tenant Verbatim will be working closely with the University of North Carolina at Charlotte (UNCC) on optical disk technology when UNCC's planned applied research center opens in 1990. Photo by Kelly Culpepper/Transparencies*

Founded in 1867 as an institution to educate freed slaves, Johnson C. Smith University currently enrolls more than 1,000 students at its Charlotte campus. Photo by Mark Fortenberry

men's college, but went coed in 1973. At first women were to make up no more than 40 percent of an entering class, but in 1988 the percentage of men and women accepted became based on the number of applications received from each sex.

Davidson, with an enrollment of about 1,400, is considered one of the top liberal-arts colleges in the U.S. and ranks fifth nationally in the number of Rhodes Scholarships and second in Rockefeller Fellowships awarded. Among its graduates is former Secretary of State Dean Rusk, for whom the school's international studies program is named. In addition to its campus activities, the program sponsors an annual conference for the public on

world themes, as well as a summer program for Charlotte-Mecklenburg teachers.

In a way, Queens College is a mirror image of Davidson. It was founded in 1857 as the Charlotte Female Institute and was located in uptown Charlotte (which is how College Street got its name). From 1896 to 1910 the school was called Presbyterian Female College. It then took on its present name to honor the first school in Mecklenburg County (for young men only), which was known as the Queen's Museum. Queens moved to its current location in Myers Park in 1913 and began admitting men to its newly instituted graduate programs in 1979. Men were accepted as undergraduates for the first time in 1988.

In the late 1970s Queens faced serious problems, and the way it handled them gained national media attention. With enrollment dropping and the endowment shrinking, new president Billy O. Wireman responded, not by asking how the college could survive, but by asking how it could better serve the community. And then the college went about doing it.

Queens now has several different programs in addition to its traditional four-year, liberal-arts curriculum, all geared toward serving women of varying ages and backgrounds. The New College and Graduate School are designed for working men and women, offering undergraduate and graduate degrees (including an MBA), while the Queens Instititute for Lifelong Learning (QUILL) provides noncredit personal and career development courses. Queens COMPUTE offers hands-on computer training for individuals and companies, and Women in Management is a specially designed program for women executives. New Dimensions is for women aged 23 and older who are returning to college. In 1988 enrollment increased to 1,400, and the endowment grew to $10 million.

Johnson C. Smith University (JCSU) traces its history back to 1867, when it was founded as the Biddle Institute (later Biddle University) to educate freed slaves, making it one of the country's first historically black colleges. Its goal was to become "the colored Princeton of the South." Local Presbyterian churches were the instigating force behind its establishment on 97 acres just north of uptown Charlotte, but it was a $1,900 contribution from Mrs. Henry Biddle of Philadelphia which made the dream come true, and so the college was named in her husband's honor.

The early presidents were white Presbyterian ministers. In 1891 Dr. Daniel J. Sanders became the first black president, and black faculty members soon followed. The first Biddle alumnus to become president was the Reverend Henry L. McCrorey in 1907. He was a friend of Jane Berry, a wealthy white woman from Pennsylvania who was looking for a way to memorialize her late husband, Johnson C. Smith. She gave the school more than $700,000 between 1921 and 1929, and in honor of her contributions, the school was renamed Johnson C. Smith University.

JCSU is now a four-year liberal-arts school with an enrollment of approximately 1,200 students. It recently added four new academic programs, known as Centers of Excellence—in freshman studies, honors college, banking and finance education, and natural sciences—which are providing models for other U.S. colleges. A major fund-raising effort in 1984-85 garnered $5 million, adding greatly to the university's continuing development.

But just as a community needs educated citizens, it also needs healthy ones, and Charlotte has long cared for the medical needs of its people. One woman, in particular, played a leading role in organizing and structuring that care.

Jane Wilkes and her husband, Captain John Wilkes, were both New Yorkers but were living in Charlotte when the Civil War broke out. Captain

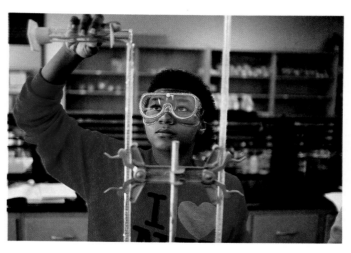

Johnson C. Smith University offers a wide variety of liberal arts programs from the sciences and literature to banking and finance. Photo by Mark Fortenberry

Wilkes, a graduate of the U.S. Navy Academy, helped with the war effort of his adopted South in many ways: supplying flour to the army, helping develop rail lines, and producing the rails in his Mecklenburg Iron Works. He later founded the First National Bank.

Mrs. Wilkes also contributed to the war effort. She worked to convert D.H. Hill's Military Institute into a military hospital, where she cared for Confederate soldiers. After the war, in 1878, she was instrumental in the opening of St. Peter's Hospital, the first civilian hospital in the state. The building that first housed the hospital, still standing at Sixth and Poplar, has been converted into condominiums.

Mrs. Wilkes often visited New York to raise money for the hospital, including funds for one of North Carolina's first x-ray machines. In 1888 she raised money from Northern friends to start Good Samaritan Hospital, the first hospital for blacks in the country. Because of her tireless efforts, she was often called the "Godmother of Charlotte Hospitals."

In 1940 St. Peter's was merged with Charlotte Memorial Hospital, which had been built with city and federal funds. Three years later the North Carolina legislature created the Charlotte Memorial Hospital Authority to govern the facility. The governing body's name was changed to the Charlotte-Mecklenburg Hospital Authority in 1961, and the facility became the Charlotte-Memorial Hospital and Medical Center in 1974. In 1985 the 130-bed University Memorial Hospital opened in the northeast part of the county, and today the authority is responsible for 15 different facilities throughout the county. The main hospital, with more than 800 beds, is located near the intersection of East Morehead Street and Kings Drive.

Cardiac care is Memorial's strongest specialty, and it is also a center for organ procurement and transplants. The organ program was begun in 1970, and the success rate of its kidney transplants is above the national average. Memorial also has the only hospital-based helicopter ambulance service in the area

Memorial is the newest of three general hospitals in modern Charlotte (two with satellite facilities) with a total of about 2,000 acute-care beds. Presbyterian Hospital traces its roots back to 1898, when three local physicians founded the Charlotte Private Hospital. In 1902, 10 doctors bought the hospital and gave it to the six churches of the Presbytery in Charlotte. The hospital board met for the first time the following year, and the new facility began operations out of the former Arlington Hotel located at West Trade and Mint streets in uptown Charlotte. The hospital moved to its present location on Hawthorne Avenue in 1917.

Today Presbyterian has about 650 beds, and its specialties include cardiac care at the Belk Heart Center, delivering babies (about 6,000 annually, making it one of the 50 largest maternity centers in the nation), and cancer care. It is the first hospital in the area to apply for designation from the American College of Surgeons' Commission on Cancer as a comprehensive community cancer program, and is one of the few hospitals in the Southeast to receive funding for national cancer research studies under the National Cancer Institute's Community Oncology Program. In 1987 the hospital opened Presbyterian Specialty Hospital, which offers care and surgery for the eye, ear, nose, and throat, as well as plastic surgery.

In 1906 Mercy Hospital was found-

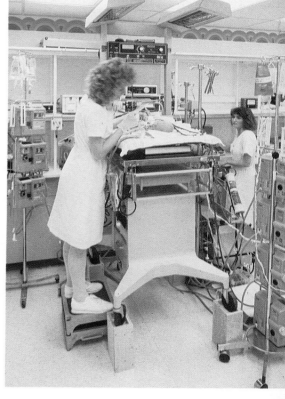

ABOVE: *Nurses at the Neonatal Intensive Care Unit in Charlotte Memorial Hospital and Medical Center tend to their newborn patient. Courtesy, Charlotte-Mecklenburg Hospital Authority*

FACING PAGE, ABOVE: *The Charlotte medical community provides an extensive variety of services, meeting the health-care needs of its patients. Photo by Mark Fortenberry*

FACING PAGE, BELOW: *The Charlotte Memorial Hospital and Medical Center has been serving the Charlotte community from its current facility since 1974. Photo by Mark Fortenberry*

ed in uptown, on East First Street behind St. Peter's Catholic Church, by the Sisters of Mercy from nearby Belmont. The facility was moved to its present location on East Fifth Street in 1916. In 1987 it opened a satellite facility, the 85-bed Mercy Hospital South, in southeast Mecklenburg County. The hospital has about 400 beds and offers cardiac care and home health-care services, as well as housing Charlotte's Poison Control Center.

Mecklenburg County serves as a regional medical center and consequently has a wide diversity of services. There are more than 800 practicing physicians representing nearly every

specialty and subspecialty, as well as more than 250 dentists. In addition to the three general hospitals, there are seven specialty hospitals with about 600 beds that offer such services as orthopedic and psychiatric care. Patients can turn to these facilities for such advanced services as organ (including heart) transplants, genetic and infertility counseling, in vitro fertilization, laser eye surgery, and a lithotripter (a machine that destroys kidney stones without surgery).

The hospitals also offer specialized care centers for heart disease, cancer, breast disease, diabetes, back problems, bone disorders, pain management, and

Not only is Mecklenburg County a center for medical care, it is also a center for medical education. Memorial is a major teaching hospital, and with about 125 residents receiving training in nine areas, it is one of the largest graduate medical educational programs in the U.S. not located on a university campus. Nursing programs are offered at Presbyterian and Mercy hospitals, as well as at Queens College, UNCC, and CPCC. Certificate programs in medical, radiologic, laboratory, and surgical technologies are available at these institutions as well. In addition, Charlotte serves as a regional center for the North Carolina Area Health Education Centers (AHEC) program. AHEC is a statewide system that provides primary and continuing education for health professionals in a variety of fields.

But Charlotte's medical hallmark is clearly cardiac care. Open-heart surgery is performed at three facilities—Memorial, Presbyterian, and Mercy—unusual for a city of Charlotte's size. The largest of the three is Memorial, home to the Carolinas Heart Institute, a 75,000-square-foot facility that specializes in cardiac care, surgery, and research. The five-story structure opened in March 1988 with six operating rooms, 14 cardiovascular recovery stations, 20 coronary intensive care rooms, a cardiac diagnostic laboratory, and other support areas. It is also here that a special team of surgeons, led by Dr. Francis Robicsek, performs heart transplants. The doctors completed their first human heart transplant on 31-year-old Sandra Collier of Forest City on January 6, 1986.

Charlotte's reputation for cardiovascular research is an international one, and much of that research has occurred at the Heineman Medical Research Center, established in 1940 by Char-

The 400-bed Mercy Hospital houses the city's Poison Control Center and offers home health-care services as well as cardiac care. Photo by Mark Fortenberry

sleep disorders, among others. Mothers-to-be can choose from a variety of birthing options. Charlotte was one of the first U.S. cities to have the technology for magnetic resonance imaging, and its hospitals were among the first to pioneer outpatient surgery.

Yet the cost for these services is reasonable. According to the American Chamber of Commerce Researchers Association, Charlotte's health-care costs in 1987 ranked only slightly above average for 242 midsized American cities. Furthermore, they were well below the costs in such cities as Atlanta, Baltimore, Dallas, Denver, and Houston.

lotte native Dannie Heineman. The center has been on the cutting edge in new techniques and technology in cardiac care since the 1950s, when its researchers developed the country's first seamless artificial arteries. In 1985 Dr. Robert Svenson and a group of physicians performed the first open-heart surgery using only a new laser beam technology they had developed. Work is continuing on improving laser technology to treat clogged arteries.

Specialty hospitals also play an important role in the health of the area The Charlotte Rehabilitation Hospital provides chronic long-term care for stroke victims and patients with spinal cord and brain injuries, while the nationally recognized Orthopaedic Hospital of Charlotte features one of the country's few metabolic bone labs.

These specialty hospitals also care for mental health. Three private facilities—the Charlotte Treatment Center, Charter Pines Hospital, and CPC Cedar Springs Hospital—provide inpatient and outpatient services for both children and adults for chemical dependency and psychiatric problems, plus free educational programs for the entire community. A variety of programs also is offered by the county's Mental Health, Mental Retardation, and Substance Abuse Department.

In sum, Charlotte recognizes that the good life means more than commerce, bustling streets, and towering skyscrapers. Its people must also be well-educated, their health well-cared-for, and their homes pleasant and affordable in order for them to achieve their dreams and work together for a bright future for all.

ABOVE: Charlotte retirees enjoy the area's temperate climate, participating in many outdoor activities. Photo by Paul Epley

FACING PAGE: This linear accelerator is used in radiation therapy in the treatment of cancer. Courtesy, Charlotte-Mecklenburg Hospital Authority

When to Play Is the Thing

In our previous chapters, we have looked at Charlotte's history, its commercial and business accomplishments, the workings of its government, and the friendliness and caring of its people.

Now, in our last chapter, we get to look at the playfulness of Charlotteans and their love of a good time. Leisure activities of all kinds abound—from walking through a tree-filled park to browsing through art galleries, from playing rugby to exploring the world of science at Discovery Place, from listening to the symphony or local jazz groups to celebrating the rites of spring uptown at SpringFest, and from attending summer theater at Central Piedmont Community College to cheering on the city's NBA franchise, the Hornets, at the Charlotte Coliseum.

To be sure, Charlotte-Mecklenburg is an urban community (although you can still find rural areas, especially in the northern part of the county). The community, however, has not lost sight of the need for green space. A canopy of some 60,000 trees graces the city's streets, especially in Myers Park and Eastover, and a city arborist is on staff to oversee the care of these trees and the planting of new ones. Within its city limits, Charlotte also has a bird sanctuary, Wing Haven, where more than 137 species of birds have been sighted on its three acres.

Another example of the local citizenry's commitment to trees and green space is the fact that both the city of Charlotte and Mecklenburg County have their own park systems. The bulk

From an exhilarating day of waterskiing on Lake Norman to an evening of music with Opera Carolina, Charlotte is brimming with an abundance of leisure activities. Photo by Mark Fortenberry

ABOVE: The McAlpine Greenway will eventually cover about 5,000 acres of untouched land, creating an extensive park system for outdoor enjoyment, as well as a natural habitat for local wildlife. Photo by Paul Epley

of the county's system is made up of nine parks encompassing approximately 2,300 acres, most of which are nature-oriented and geared toward passive recreational activities. (There is, however, a public golf course at Harrisburg Road Park, built on portions of an old landfill.) The system also includes two historical sites: Alexandiana, where the Mecklenburg Declaration was signed, and the McIntyre Cabin Site, where the Battle of the Bees took place. A community center, the David

B. Waymer complex, is included as well.

Two of the county's parks—McDowell on Lake Wylie, and Latta Plantation on Mountain Island Lake (the county's major source of drinking water)—have nature preserves. McDowell Park is 800 acres in size, and among its unique offerings are paddleboats, which the park makes available to rent. Latta Plantation Park, 760 acres in size, also features an historic plantation, an equestrian center, and a

raptor center that cares for injured birds of prey (some of which may be viewed by the public). The park is also the site of a folk music festival every June.

The Mecklenburg County Park and Recreation Department is also in the process of creating a greenway system around the county's streams and creeks that will encircle all of Mecklenburg in a "green necklace." By early 1989 the county had acquired approximately 1,200 acres, more than half of it donat-

ed, primarily from developers. When completed early in the next century, the greenway will cover about 5,000 acres encircling some 20 creeks. The first leg of the greenway, McAlpine Greenway Park, opened in 1979, and three other segments—Walden, Campbell Creek, and Mallard Creek—are expected to open by the end of 1990.

The purposes of the greenway are many. The linear parks will provide a trail system for biking, walking, and jogging, connecting neighborhoods to schools and neighborhoods to parks, thereby reducing the need for cars. It also will contribute to flood control, act as a filter for water runoff and air pollution, and be a habitat for birds, small animals and other wildlife, trees, and plants. It is one of the most extensive countywide park systems being planned in the nation.

Lake Norman, 20 miles north of Charlotte, and Lake Wylie, 13 miles to the south, offer lots of opportunities for boating enthusiasts, and an increasing number of people are living on the lakes year-round and commuting to Charlotte to work. Both the mountains and the beaches are just a few hours' drive away by car.

The city's parks number about 125, ranging in size from less than an acre to almost 500 acres, and the Parks and Recreation Department also runs 16 recreation centers that offer year-round programs, including arts and crafts. The Marion Diehl Center has facilities and offers programs specifically designed for senior citizens, the physically disabled, and the mentally retarded.

The city also runs a variety of sports leagues for both children and adults in soccer, softball, volleyball, and basketball. During the summer about 400 softball teams are enrolled in city leagues, and during the two-month fall

ABOVE: Spectacular sunsets can be seen over the region's many waterways. Photo Bill Gleasner/ Transparencies

ABOVE LEFT: Lake Norman and Lake Wylie abound with sailing opportunities for boating fans. Photo by Kelly Culpepper/Transparencies

PAGES 138-139: Springtime blossoms in vivid color throughout the city's many parks. Photo by Mark Fortenberry

A few friends take a moment to converse in the lush surroundings of this Fourth Ward park. Photo by Matt Bradley

grounds. When completed, the park also will have a recreation center, a swimming pool, and an outdoor amphitheater.

The city and county parks are just two of the resources available to those wishing to participate in sports and other recreational activities. The YMCA has eight branches, all of which have women's locker rooms and shower facilities. The YWCA has one center for health, physical education, and recreational activities, seven scattered sites for after-school programs, and two day-care centers. (A third day-care center, located uptown, opens in 1990.) The Jewish Community Center also provides a variety of programs for children and adults regardless of religious affiliation. In addition, Central Piedmont Community College offers a diversity of classes each quarter in outdoor activities and sports.

Neighborhood athletic associations offer another outlet for children, and a number of neighborhoods also have swim clubs for both children and adults. The city has five public pools, and the county has plans to open its $6-million aquatic center during the next decade.

In addition, there are hundreds of public and private tennis courts and more than 20 golf courses in Mecklenburg County. There also are plenty of clubs and leagues to meet most anyone's needs for participatory sports, including bowling, cycling, fencing, gymnastics, hockey, karate, orienteering, rugby, and skydiving.

If watching sports is more your style, Charlotte still has plenty to offer. Historically the area has been—and will continue to be—a hotbed for college basketball, particularly that played by the eight-team Atlantic Coast Conference, referred to simply as the ACC. None of the teams are from Charlotte,

season, another 150 teams compete. Volleyball leagues play nine months a year.

The showpiece of the city's park system is the 470-acre York Road Renaissance Park, which opened in the summer of 1988. Once the site of a city-owned landfill, Renaissance has an 18-hole golf course, a tennis complex, a five-field softball complex, two lighted soccer fields, picnic areas, and play-

but four of them makes their homes in North Carolina (Duke, N.C. State, the University of North Carolina at Chapel Hill, and Wake Forest), and enough alumni from the remaining colleges (Clemson, Georgia Tech, Maryland, and Virginia) live in Charlotte to create lots of rivalries among basketball fans in the Queen City.

With the opening of the 25,000-seat Charlotte Coliseum in August 1988, the ACC Championship Tournament returned to Charlotte on a rotating basis. The city will host the tournament in 1990 and 1991, and there are hopes that Charlotte will become its permanent home. In addition, negotiations have produced plans for Charlotte to host the NCAA Final Four Tournament in 1994.

The Coliseum also is the site of the Tournament of Champions, which debuted in December 1988. This four-team clash features N.C. State or UNC-Chapel Hill (which play on a rotating basis) plus three nationally prominent teams.

But the big news in Charlotte basketball history in 1988—and for many years to come—was the much-heralded arrival of the Charlotte Hornets, the city's NBA franchise and the first major-league pro sports team in the Carolinas.

The team was brought to Charlotte through the efforts of many people, but they all were led by the vision, chutzpah, and determination of one man—entrepreneur George Shinn. He and his partners—Felix Sabates, Cy Bahakel, and Rick Hendrick—first approached the NBA about an expansion team in 1985 and were initially met with skepticism, and even ridicule, in many quarters.

Shinn and his crew had the last laugh, however, when Charlotte was awarded the franchise in April 1987.

Shinn sold the NBA owners on Charlotte, and fans showed his faith was well-deserved, as more than 14,000 season tickets were sold before the opening tip-off.

Often outgunned by the established NBA teams (though they still won 20 games), the Hornets nevertheless have stood out. The players hit the court in teal and purple uniforms created by noted designer Alexander Julian. An alumnus of UNC-Chapel Hill, Julian was paid for his work with monthly deliveries of authentic North Carolina barbecue to his New York digs. The team's mascot, Hugo—a mean, lean fighting bee—was designed by Cheryl Henson, daughter of Muppets creator Jim Henson.

Currently with the largest arena in the NBA, the Hornets led the league in attendance its first season—the first time an expansion team had done so in any major pro sport. Players rated Charlotte fans as the noisiest in the NBA, and the fans purchased team souvenirs and memorabilia well above the league average.

Although the NBA newcomers have quickly won over the hearts of Charlotteans, fans remain faithful to their longtime favorites. UNC-Charlotte plays its home basketball games in the Coliseum, and Davidson College and Johnson C. Smith University (JCSU) also have their share of local hoop fans. In the fall, ACC football is popular, as is that played by Davidson and JCSU, which plays in the city's Memorial Stadium. Soccer fans cheer on UNCC.

Sporting events are an important and healthy part of the Charlotte life-style. From youth leagues to the games of the NBA Hornets, there is something for everyone to enjoy. Here, the Sting soccer team (orange) battles against a rival team. Photo by Paul Epley

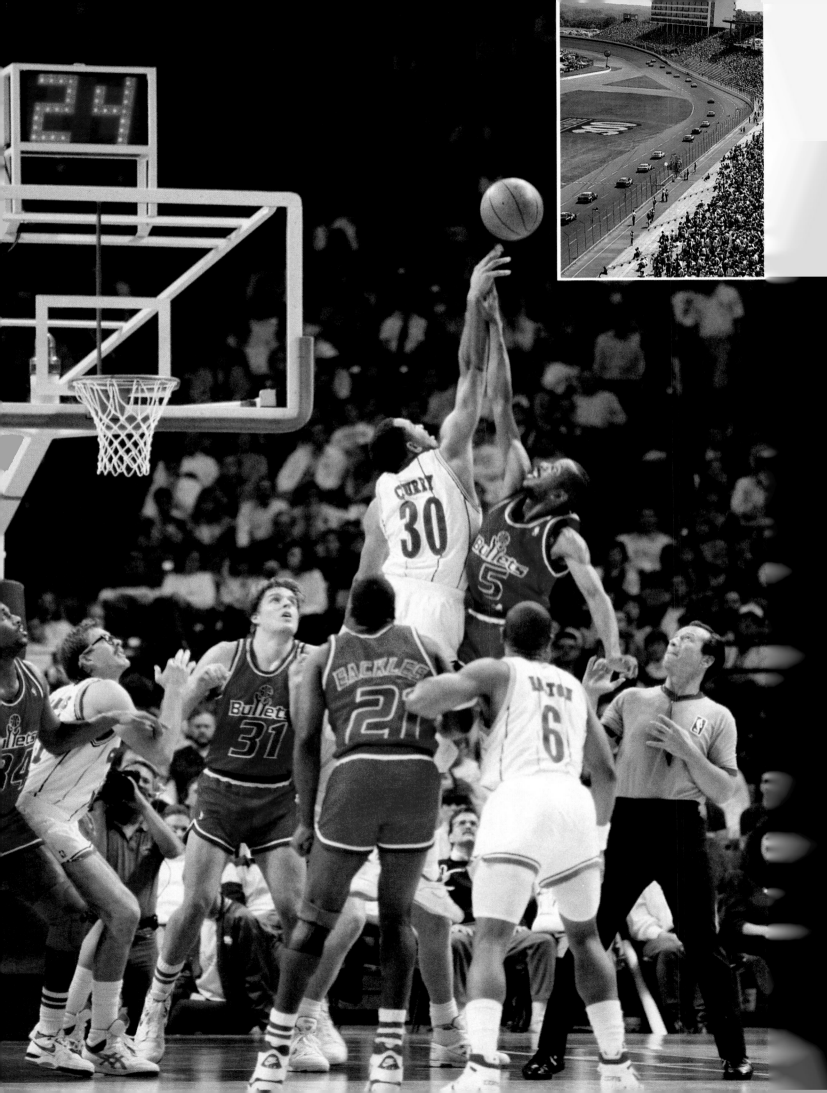

It's not just the traditional college and pro teams that turn on Charlotte sports fans. In August 1988 some 60,000 of them turned out for the Carolinas Invitational Tournament, which featured U.S. and foreign Olympic teams in basketball, gymnastics, wrestling, cycling, and baseball. It was the first time such a variety of U.S. Olympic teams had come together for a single event, and its success ensured that more Olympic-caliber competitions will come to Charlotte.

Even as new sports traditions are being introduced in Charlotte, old ones are not only staying strong, but are changing with the times to retain their old fans and attract new ones. For example, minor-league baseball is a longtime tradition throughout North Carolina, and Charlotte has hosted a minor-league team (with the exception of 1973-75) since the 1920s. Today's AA team, the Charlotte Knights, is affiliated with the Chicago Cubs and is owned by George Shinn of NBA Hornets fame. The team traces its history back to 1976, when it was a Baltimore Orioles farm team (taking on the name of the Charlotte O's in 1979) owned by the Crockett Family, best known for its wrestling promotions.

The team played at Griffith Park (built in 1939 and renamed Crockett Park in 1976) until 1985, when it was almost completely destroyed by fire. Its general manager, Frances Crockett, was known for her often outlandish—but highly successful—promotions, and she was named AA General Manager of the Year by the *Sporting News* in 1981, when she was one of only five women GMs in all of baseball. She hung on with the team—which played in makeshift facilities at what was left of the old park—until 1987, when her family sold the team to Shinn, who promptly renamed the team the

Knights. The 1989 season was its first as part of the Cubs farm system, and also its first in its new home in York County, South Carolina.

Other sports also have a long tradition in the area. For example, although not technically part of Charlotte or Mecklenburg County, the Charlotte Motor Speedway has been an important part of the local sports scene since it opened in 1960. Originally located in the northern part of Mecklenburg just beyond the city limits, it was annexed into Cabarrus County in 1987.

The speedway makes Charlotte a NASCAR center by hosting some 20 events each year that attract about 700,000 people. The largest of these is the Coca-Cola 600, the longest race on the Winston Cup Circuit and the second most-attended sports event in the U.S. (The top event, the Indianapolis 500, is held on the same weekend, over the Memorial Day holiday.) Other major events include the Winn-Dixie 300 and the Winston, also held in May, and the Oakwood Homes 500, held in October. The speedway also boasts of trackside condominiums and a clubhouse, the Speedway Club, which offers meeting and banquet facilities.

Racing in Mecklenburg County dates back to the 1920s when the Charlotte Speedway operated in Pineville. It opened in 1924, when carpenters completed the 1.25-mile wooden track in 40 days, using four million board-feet of lumber. Specta-

ABOVE: *The Carolinas Invitational Tournament displayed the athletic talents of both U.S. and foreign Olympic teams. Photo by Mark Fortenberry*

FACING PAGE: *The Charlotte Hornets clash against the Washington Bullets at the 25,000-seat Charlotte Coliseum. Photo by Mark Fortenberry*

FACING PAGE (inset): *Auto racing has been a popular sport in the Charlotte area since the 1920s when the first Speedway was constructed in Pineville. The current Charlotte Motor Speedway facility, located just north of Mecklenburg County, is host to more than 20 events throughout the year. Photo by Mark Fortenberry*

The Carolina Invitational Tournament in Charlotte provided a showcase of skill and stamina for Olympic-caliber cyclists. Photo by Jane Faircloth/Transparencies

tors recall that the place reeked because the drivers used castor oil for lubrication. The wooden track had a lot of problems, and the facility was closed in the late 1920s for safety reasons. In 1942 all the remaining salvageable lumber went to the war effort.

After World War II two dirt tracks were established in Charlotte: one where Tryon Mall is now located, and one off Wilkinson Boulevard near Little Rock Road. That second track was the site of the first Grand National stock-car race in June 1949. The purse was $5,000.

Many drivers got their training for the sport in less-than-legitimate ways. Junior Johnson is among those who learned to drive fast with consummate skill by running moonshine and outspeeding the authorities.

For those whose idea of racing turns more to fast feet than fast cars, there's the annual Charlotte Observer Marathon, held the first Saturday in January. When first run in 1977, the marathon attracted some 1,700 runners, who ran for the glory but no prize money. In the 1989 event, 5,385 runners participated in the marathon, 10K, and fun run, for a purse totaling $36,600.

Charlotte is also home for the Heat, which won its team tennis league championship its first two years in existence, as well as for the PaineWebber Seniors Invitational, which attracts top-name senior players from across the country.

For pro sports fans in Charlotte, the future looks bright. Shinn has said that one of his goals is to bring a major league baseball team to Charlotte, and efforts are already under way to bring the NFL to the area. Businesses from both North and South Carolina, joined by their two governors, have formed a committee to convince NFL owners to choose the region as a site for an expansion team. The demographics of the area—which boosters refer to simply as Carolina—make it a prime location. With a population of about 10 million, it is the fourth largest TV market in the U.S.

Charlotte is a city that loves its sports, but it is also a city that appreciates the arts and is committed to making them an integral part of everyday life for all its citizens—rich and poor, black and white, young and old. It is not mere boosterism to say that there is a strong consensus in the community which believes that the arts make life better and are something children should be exposed to and encouraged to embrace. That commitment is followed up financially from the public and corporate sectors, as well as individuals, amply demonstrated in the support received by the Arts and Science Council.

The council, one of the oldest in the country, was chartered in 1958, and today it serves nearly 50 members and affiliate organizations throughout Mecklenburg County with financial support, technical assistance, and centralized services. It provides annual funding for groups such as the Mint Museum, the Charlotte Symphony, the Afro-American Cultural Center, and Discovery Place, as well as grants to members for specific projects, including the North Carolina Print and Drawing Society, the Charlotte Shakespeare Company, and the Singing Christmas Tree Concert. In addition, the council provides funds to nonmember groups for arts-related projects and activities,

such as the Nevins Center for a theatrical troupe of retarded people, to International House for an international arts exchange, and to the Charlotte-Mecklenburg Senior Games for an art exhibit by seniors.

This money is raised by an annual fund drive held each February. It is highly successful, and from 1981 to 1988 the council distributed more than $12 million for arts activities. Support for the council has grown dramatically over the years, increasing from $333,000 raised in 1977 to more than $1.9 million in 1988. Although Charlotte-Mecklenburg is the 48th largest area in the U.S. in terms of population, it ranks 10th in terms of total dollars raised for the arts through its united arts campaign and second in per-capita giving (an average of $4.17 per citizen).

The area also ranks second in the number of companies—approximately 60—that allow their employees to make contributions in support of the arts through payroll deductions. About 51 percent of the funds raised by the council comes from individuals, compared to the national average of 37 percent, according to the American Council for the Arts.

In 1986 the council took on a new activity to showcase the arts in Charlotte-Mecklenburg and to provide area residents with a different way of celebrating New Year's Eve. First Night Charlotte is a family-oriented outdoor celebration held uptown featuring performances by council members, including barbershop quartets, puppeteers, theater troupes, steel-drum bands, and the opera. As midnight approaches, a giant crown ascends to count down the final seconds of the old year, bursting into green and white lights as the new year begins. As many as 75,000 people have attended the fete in one night.

The council also held its first annual Vanguard Awards presentation in November 1987 to honor local arts leaders and supporters. Lynn Redgrave and Walter Cronkite were the MCs for the inaugural event; in 1988 Tony Randall and Kathleen Sullivan did the honors.

Charlotteans' commitment and generosity to the arts don't stop with the Arts and Science Council. The city's residents are known for being big dreamers and visionaries, and in recent years they have put their pocketbooks, muscle and know-how together to bring to reality their dream of a performing arts center located uptown. The center, part of the NCNB Tower complex at the Square in the heart of uptown, is scheduled to open in 1992. Designed by internationally acclaimed architect Cesar Pelli of New Haven,

Connecticut, the center will have two performance halls, one with 2,100 seats and one with 450, plus rehearsal and support space.

Not only will the facility be a showcase for the performing arts and generate further uptown development, but it also will be an important educational tool for the county's children. The Charlotte-Mecklenburg school system made a commitment early on to have all its students visit the center.

The process of achieving that dream will be well over a decade long by the time the $38-million facility opens its doors. The origins go back to the mid-1970s, when a cultural action plan called for a performing arts center to be located uptown. Task forces appointed by the mayor, and later by the Charlotte Uptown Development Corporation (a city agency that pro-

From a planned performing arts center and theatrical productions to a variety of art galleries and a symphony, Charlotte is truly commited to the arts. The production of The Crucible *by Theatre Charlotte is shown here. Courtesy, Theatre Charlotte*

motes development in the area), continued to explore ways in which one could be built. Then, in early 1987, an 11-member task force considered proposals from developers for a joint public-private venture. Input from users and citizens was also considered.

The accepted package came from NCNB Corporation (the holding company of NCNB National Bank), Texas-based Lincoln Properties, and Charlotte-based Charter Properties, which were already working together on the bank's 60-story office complex at the Square. A key part of that package was the donation of $3 million worth of land by the Belk Foundation, the charitable arm of the Belk family, owner of Belk Stores.

The next step was approval, by a two-to-one margin of city voters, of a $15-million bond referendum in November 1987. This money is being used for the center's construction, adding to the $15 million pledged by the state. The city of Charlotte will own the land and the facility and will lease it to the North Carolina Performing Arts Center at Charlotte Foundation, which will manage and operate the center.

The foundation was formally organized in January 1988. Its board plans to raise another $22 million for construction and operating costs and for a general arts endowment of $10 million. That fund drive officially began in the fall of 1989, and supporters expect to meet their goal by the summer of 1990.

The scope of the performing arts center is unprecedented for a city of Charlotte's size. Charlotteans, however, are used to supporting the arts through a combination of bond money and corporate and private contributions. One such example is the Mint Museum of Art, which opened in 1936 as the first art muse-

um in North Carolina

In 1985 the Mint tripled its size to more than 50,000 square feet, financed by $3 million in bonds and $4.5 million raised from the business community and private contributors (exceeding the original goal of $2 million). The expansion was the result of a donation by Charlotteans Harry and Mary Dalton. They gave their collection of American and European paintings—considered the best private collection in the state—to the Mint, provided that the museum had the space to display it.

But the expansion enabled the Mint to do much more than that. Exhibition space was improved and expanded for its Delholm Gallery, one of the best collections of pottery and porcelain in the U.S. An entrance was built on Randolph Road, making the museum more accessible to the entire community, both physically and mentally. As a continuation of those efforts, new programs were added, such as monthly social mixers, an outdoor jazz concert/movie series, and family celebrations. In September 1987 the Robicsek Gallery opened, featuring pre-Columbian art.

The number and quality of traveling exhibits also were expanded, and in September 1988 the 73-piece exhibit "Ramesses the Great" opened amid much fanfare and hoopla. Sponsored by the Egyptian government, the Ramesses show visited only nine North American cities during its tour, and the Mint gained prestige and added to its

Financial assistance from Charlotte's public, private, and corporate communities has enabled the Mint Museum of Art to increase its resources, providing the city with a strong cultural awareness. Photo by Matt Bradley

BELOW: *Eager young artists create colorful chalk drawings during the annual Kids' Art event at Spirit Square. Photo by Diane Davis/Transparencies*

BOTTOM: *This printmaking studio is one of the numerous facilities Spirit Square offers for classes in the fine and performing arts. Photo by Diane Davis/ Transparencies*

reputation by landing it. More than 600,000 people visited the exhibit during its four-month run. Of those, 87 percent had never visited the current Mint facility, and 90 percent of them said they were likely to visit the museum again.

Financial support from the public, private and corporate sectors made the Ramesses exhibit possible, but so did support of another kind. Some 3,000 community volunteers gave their skills and time to staff the exhibit and provide administrative backup and technical assistance. This made it the largest volunteer effort in the country at the time.

The Mint has always enjoyed generous support. Its original building was built in 1837 as a home for the U.S. Mint (which explains the museum's unusual name) and was located on West Trade Street uptown between Mint and Graham streets. Designed by noted architect William A. Strickland in the Federal style, the Mint officially closed at the outbreak of the Civil War, during which it served as a Confederate headquarters and hospital. Later it was used as a meeting hall for community groups.

In 1933 it looked as if the building would be torn down to make room for expansion of the adjacent post office, but a group of preservationists, led by Mrs. Harold C. Dwelle, led a campaign to save the structure and purchased it for $950. Then, under the direction of of Charlotte architect Martin C. Boyer, the building was demolished and reconstructed at its present site by the Federal Emergency Relief Administration on land donated by E.C. Griffin, Sr. The museum's first expansion occurred in 1967.

Although not as old as the Mint, the Spirit Square Center for the Arts is another popular Charlotte arts attraction that enjoys wide-ranging public support. Its activities cover the visual and performing arts as well as education. When the center opened in 1976 at Tryon and Seventh streets, it was the first step in the creation of an arts and cultural center in uptown, a process culminating in the construction of the performing art center at the Square. The process also has included a new science museum, a black cultural center, numerous galleries, and even the start of an artists' district in First Ward, which some call Charlotte's "future Greenwich Village." All this has contributed to the revival of uptown Charlotte.

This was no more than a pipe dream when Spirit Square opened, but Charlotteans bought into the vision. The renovation of the First Baptist Church facility, where the center is housed, was funded by $2.5 million in city bonds as well as by individual and corporate monies. Today the county government provides operating funds, and the city provides money for capital projects as needed. The 750-seat performance hall, called NCNB Performance Place, is located in the church's sanctuary, which was originally built in 1909. With its beautiful stained-glass windows and near-perfect acoustics, it has gained an outstanding reputation among the regional, national, and international artists who have performed there.

As Charlotte's awareness and sophistication has grown, so has Spirit Square's. In 1983 Knight Gallery was added with $1.4 million from the city and county, with the goal of highlighting pivotal developments in visual arts since 1960. The gallery has matured into a major center for contemporary art in the Southeast, with a national reputation for the range and depth of its exhibits, its cutting-edge approach, and its scholarly work, with several catalogs to its credit.

Spirit Square continues to grow in other ways as well. Its newest expansion and renovation opened in late 1989, featuring increased and improved gallery areas that give more space to local artists, a 250-seat theater, and four times as much space for classes in clay, fibers, acting, dance, and print making. The project, costing $5.6 million, was financed with $2.8 million from the city, as well as with money from businesses, individuals, and grants.

After Spirit Square initially opened, the next big boost for uptown culture was the construction of Discovery Place in 1981. This hands-on science museum, ranked as one of the top 10 science museums in the country based on size, budget, and attendance, received the Travel Attraction of the Year Award in 1986 from the Southeast Tourism Society. More than 400,000 people visit the museum each year, and they enjoy such activities as picking up a starfish in the Aquarium Tidal Touch Pool, playing laser pinball, cooking crystals at the Piedmont Natural Gas Hearth, trying out some 60 experiments in the Science Circus, watching exotic birds in the three-story Knight Rain Forest, and swapping shells or minerals at the Trading Post.

The 82,000-square-foot facility was funded by $7.1 million in bond money and more than $3 million in private and corporate contributions. It too is

BELOW: *Established in 1986 in the renovated Little Rock AME Zion Church, the Afro-American Cultural Center promotes and preserves black cultural history. Photo by Mark Fortenberry*

BOTTOM: *A member of the Johnson C. Smith University Brass Ensemble performs at one of the school's many concerts. Photo by Paul Epley*

expanding, with plans for a 45,000-square-foot expansion that will include an OmniMax Theatre, one of only about a dozen in the U.S. The expansion will open in 1991. Half of the $18 million for the expansion came from a bond referendum approved by voters in November 1988.

Down the street from Spirit Square and Discovery Place is the Afro-American Cultural Center, housed in the renovated Little Rock AME Zion Church. The facility opened in 1986, funded by $1.2 million from the city and a capital fund drive. Through its art gallery, theater, concerts, and classes, the center promotes, presents, and

The Charlotte City Ballet performs a stunning production of the popular fairy tale Beauty and the Beast. *Courtesy, Charlotte City Ballet Company*

preserves black cultural history. The center also opens its doors to community groups for meetings.

These three facilities—Spirit Square, Discovery Place, and the Afro-American Cultural Center—form the nucleus for the growing cultural district uptown. Several galleries have opened in the area, and from September to June on the first Friday of each month, they coordinate their openings in a cultural and social happening known as the "Gallery Crawl." In conjunction with the crawl, the Metrolina Theatre Association sponsors productions through its Experimental Theatre Project.

Music also flourishes in Charlotte, whether your taste runs to the symphony, opera, jazz, country, folk, reggae, or pop. The grande dame of music in the Queen City is clearly the Charlotte Symphony Orchestra. Born in 1932 when it gave its first concert—free—on March 20 at the Carolina Theatre on North Tryon Street, the orchestra's first season began in September of that year..

Today, considered one the nation's

finest regional orchestras, the Charlotte Symphony also has achieved an international reputation. In 1987 it was the only regional orchestra asked to participate in the Summer European Music Festival and played to rave reviews in West Germany, Poland, and Holland during its first international tour.

The Symphony brings delight to Charlotteans in many ways—offering subscription seasons at Ovens Auditorum and Queens College, a series of cabaret concerts, special performances with Opera Carolina or Charlotte's Oratorio Singers, gala concerts with top performers from around the world, free Summer Pops concerts, and free "sidewalk" concerts all over the city. It also brings delight to children through its Lollipop Concerts and two performances of *The Nutcracker* each Christmas season.

Another venerable institution on the Charlotte music scene is Opera Carolina, the largest and oldest opera company in North Carolina. The company made its debut as the Charlotte Opera on May 14, 1949, with the production of *Rosalinda*, and in 1982, performed the world premiere of Robert Ward's *Abelard and Heloise*. Performances have been held in Ovens Auditorium since 1955, and they will move to the new performing arts center when it opens in 1992.

Today the company brings in international talent for its annual season of four productions, which in 1988-89 included *Aida*, *Elixir of Love*, *Die Fledermaus*, and a performance by the Peking Opera. The company is also the largest touring company in the Southeast, and its education and outreach program introduces opera to schoolchildren throughout the area.

Charlotte is also home for one of the few independent oratorio choruses in the country, the Oratorio Singers of Charlotte, begun in 1931. A variety of other groups abound in the city, to either listen to or participate in, such as the Charlotte Jazz Society, the Charlotte Folk Music Society, Chamber Music of Charlotte, the Charlotte Community Concert Association, and the Charlotte Choral Society, which holds its "Singing Christmas Tree" concert each Christmas. A growing number of nightclubs and bars offer jazz, blues, reggae, and rock, while local colleges are another good source of musical entertainment of all kinds.

For dance lovers, there are performances by Dance Central, Catchin' On (a jazz company), the Charlotte City Ballet, and the Charlotte Youth Ballet, as well as by college troupes and visiting artists. For those who prefer dance of another sort, square dancing and clogging are very popular in the area, with several clubs to join and a diversity of places where you can watch or jump into the swing of things.

For those who love the theater, Charlotte's offerings are rich and varied. New, small companies with a flair for the experimental and offbeat take on productions away from the mainstream, and the local colleges serve up an eclectic schedule. Even the most traditional of Charlotte theaters, Theatre Charlotte, offers a depth of productions that challenge and provoke.

Theatre Charlotte was born in 1927 when a group of university women formed a study group. Its first production was held the next year, and

Theatre Charlotte is North Carolina's oldest community theater, dating back to 1927. A scene from The House of Blue Leaves, *just one of the more than 330 productions staged at Theatre Charlotte, is pictured here. Courtesy, Theatre Charlotte*

in 1931 the group became the Little Theatre, a name it kept until 1987. Today it is the oldest community theater in North Carolina, and as of late 1989 the group had performed some 340 main stage productions in front of about a half-million people. With its own facility on Queens Road and a base of about 500 volunteers, it is an integral part of the arts scene in Charlotte.

Theatre Charlotte has grown with the city. In the mid-1980s productions included *Sweeney Todd, Sunday in the Park With George, As Is*, and the first nonprofessional production in the U.S. of *La Cage Aux Folles*. In addition, it also offers the Reading Stage, a program that features readings, study sessions, and analyses of several plays each year. In 1987 Theatre Charlotte was named best community theater by the North Carolina Theatre Conference.

Charlotte also boasts of its own Equity theater company, Charlotte Repertory Theatre. Founded in 1977 as the Actors Contemporary Ensemble (ACE), the company's productions were one of the highlights of Char-

lotte's summers for a decade. In 1989, as the audience for theater in Charlotte grew, Charlotte Rep expanded into a full-time company. It also holds a new play festival every spring.

Summer theater remains vibrant however, with the Central Piedmont Community College Summer Theatre, which attracts about 26,000 people each year to its five productions at Pease Auditorium on campus. Traditionally, three of the productions are longtime popular Broadway musicals. Also during the summer you can enjoy both theater and the outdoors with the traveling productions of the Charlotte Shakespeare Company, founded in 1974. In recent years the company has added indoor productions of Shakespeare and other revivals at UNCC to its free outdoor plays held at city and county parks.

Children's theater is strong in Charlotte, with two companies—Children's Theatre of Charlotte and the Taradiddle Players—performing exclusively for the younger generation. The Children's Theatre, founded in 1948 by the Junior League, is now an

independent group and has its own facility, with a theater seating 300, on East Morehead Street. It offers productions, as well as acting classes and opportunities to perform for aspiring young actors and actresses.

The Taradiddle Players have been performing since 1971 at Spirit Square and at locations throughout the city. Constance Welsh began the troupe in Davidson as a semiprofessional company, which then moved to Charlotte and became fully professional in 1982. In 1988 the North Carolina Theatre Conference awarded Taradiddle Players its top youth division award.

There are also plenty of things to see and do in Charlotte that don't quite fall under the headings of the outdoors, sports, or the arts. For example, there's Carowinds, a 325-acre amusement park that straddles the South Carolina border. Carowinds has been a favorite place for families—especially their teenagers—since 1972. For museum lovers, there's Duke Power Company's Energy Explorium at Lake Norman, where you can learn about electricity through hands-on exhibits; the Nature Museum, a teaching center for young children; and the Hezekiah Alexander Homesite and History Museum, which features the city's oldest remaining structure, built in 1774. Exhibits here focus on local, regional, and state history.

History lovers also will enjoy Latta Place, which is on the National Register of Historic Places; Reed Gold Mine, in nearby Stanfield, where you can tour the underground mines or pan for gold; and the James K. Polk Memorial, where his 1795 birthplace has been reconstructed.

Charlotteans also love celebrations of all kinds, and attending these on an annual basis may very well be one of the most fun things about living here. The New Year is kicked off with First Night Charlotte, sponsored by the Arts and Science Council in uptown. Uptown also is the site of the annual St. Patrick's Day Parade in March.

In April the grandmother of Charlotte's uptown festivals, SpringFest, has become the city's way of celebrating the rites of spring. It was begun in 1982 by Koni Kirschman Findlay and Cyndee Patterson (who also brought the idea of First Night to Charlotte) as a way to foster a positive awareness uptown and to celebrate the visual arts. Now, the three-day festival attracts about 300,000 people with artists' exhibits, some of the best food in Charlotte, and music of all kinds. In addition, organizers of the event award about $30,000 in purchase prices and $5,000 in merit prizes to participating artists. During the event 3,000 community volunteers help make it Charlotte's favorite outdoor festival.

Spring and summer also mean neighorhood celebrations of all kinds, both large and small. The most well-known and well-attended are the

Elizabeth Association Festival in Independence Park in April and the Dilworth Jubilee in Latta Park in August. On July 4 Charlotteans traditionally celebrate with a Pops concert and fireworks display in Memorial Stadium. In August Charlotte is the home for one of the largest Women's Equality Day celebrations in the country.

Celebrating doesn't stop, however, when fall arrives. Come September, Festival in the Park runs for six days in Freedom Park with music, food, and fun. UNCC holds its annual international festival that month, and Charlotte's largest ethnic community, the Greeks, celebrates and shares its heritage with the rest of the city in the Greek Yaisou Festival.

At the end of October, right before election time, the Mallard Creek Presbyterian Church holds the Mallard Creek Barbecue. The event, held since 1929, attracts hundreds who love barbecue, as well as political candidates and their followers, who see it as one last time to shake hands and politick. The Christmas season is ushered into Charlotte with the Carolinas Carousel Festival and Parade. And in early December the Shrine Bowl is held in Memorial Stadium. Since 1937 the Shrine Bowl has pitted high school all-star teams from North and South Carolina in a clash that benefits the Shriners' children's hospital in Greenville, South Carolina.

Simply put, Charlotteans are as serious about playing as they are about most everything else they choose to undertake.

Each April the three-day SpringFest celebration draws about 300,000 revelers with its art exhibits, delicious food, and musical concerts. Photo by Mark Fortenberry

CHARLOTTE'S ENTERPRISES

Charlotte is alive with many economic and cultural opportunities. Photo by Mark Fortenberry

Networks

Charlotte's energy, communication, and transportation providers keep products, information and power circulating inside and outside the area.

Westinghouse Electric Corporation, 160

WSOC-TV, 161

WSOC FM-103, 162

Epley Associates, Inc., 163

Duke Power Company, 164-165

USAir, 166-169

Cogentrix, Inc., 170-171

WMIX Radio, 172

WPCQ Channel 36, 173

Southern Bell: A BellSouth Company, 174-175

Photo by Kelly Culpepper/Transparencies

WESTINGHOUSE ELECTRIC CORPORATION

If you've flipped a switch, listened to the radio, watched TV, flown in a plane, or ridden an elevator, you've been touched by George Westinghouse and the company he founded a century ago—Westinghouse Electric Corporation.

Few inventors have matched George Westinghouse in turning today's creative tinkerings into tomorrow's products and services. In his lifetime he was awarded patents on 361 inventions. Before turning his attention to electricity and the first alternating-current (AC) system in America, he invented the air brake and a system of railway signals and switches. He also developed a system for delivering natural gas.

Only five other *Fortune* 500 companies claim charter dates earlier than January 8, 1886, the date Westinghouse was incorporated. Westinghouse of Charlotte is a good indicator of the adaptability that has made that longevity possible.

In 1968 the company broke

Dwarfing the employee at the left, this steam turbine rotor will soon change steam energy into mechanical energy that will then rotate a generator, creating electrical energy. Photo by Bruce C. Ainslie

ground and hired employees for a Charlotte plant to build low-pressure steam turbines for electric utility customers. A year later construction gave way to production.

In the early 1970s the Arab oil embargo and the incident at Three Mile Island were the harbingers of change. The Charlotte plant began to manufacture all types of steam turbine designs in an effort to improve employment stability. However, by the early 1980s the impact of electricity conservation brought on by the embargo reduced employment and forced employee layoffs.

The people at Westinghouse refused to give up. When utilities continued to stress conservation, employees worked to load the plant with service work, repair business, and new designs that would extend the life of existing power plants. Many employees assumed additional responsibility and undertook additional training in company-sponsored and independent courses. Because of their commitment and performance, the plant was selected for more work. When the corporation was forced to close a turbine manufacturing plant in Philadelphia in 1985, it moved the work to the Charlotte

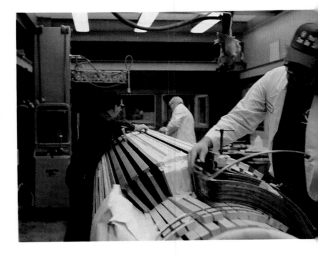

Employees install a copper coil in this generator rotor that will soon be used by a utility to electrify communities around the world. Photo by Bruce C. Ainslie

facility. Three years later, with business still on the decline, another Westinghouse plant closed in East Pittsburgh. Again Charlotte got the call, and its employees showed their commitment and flexibility and met the challenge of adding generators to its product line.

Today at the Charlotte facility 800 employees work in a climate-controlled environment where cranes lift loads of up to 185 tons in 80-foot-high bays. They use state-of-the-art techniques for such processes as welding and advanced tools that will cut products with an accuracy of 1,000th of an inch. Their work includes rough and finished machining of huge rotor forgings, cylinders, and covers, and assembly and winding for turbines, generators, and a variety of associated controls.

After assembly, customer-oriented employees perform dynamic testing on turbine and generator rotors at speeds higher than their normal 1,800 to 3,600 revolutions per minute before shipping by truck, rail, and air to customers worldwide—from South America to Europe, Egypt, and China. At Westinghouse Electric Corporation in Charlotte, the work of dedicated employees is continuing to bring power to people everywhere.

WSOC-TV

The Charlotte television station that today, as an affiliate of the ABC network, operates one of the nation's largest television newsrooms, began in 1957 as an affiliate of NBC-TV.

Now the ABC station represents the 31st-largest market in the United States: 22 counties in North and South Carolina with a population of more than 1.85 million people.

The Channel 9 newsroom includes a set that overlooks a large working space, where the station's staff of more than 100 reporters, producers, and editors puts together newscasts that run from 6 a.m. through noon, and at 6 p.m. and 11 p.m., with newsbriefs in between. They use such state-of-the-art processes and equipment as a full-time Bell Jet Ranger helicopter, named Chopper 9; Radio News Network; the Carolina News Network, the first direct microwave link of its kind in the United States; full-time news bureaus in Gastonia, North Carolina, and Washington, D.C.; and satellite reports from around the country and the world.

The on-camera journalists include managing editor Bill Walker and co-anchor Meg MacDonald of the Eyewitness News 6 p.m. and 11 p.m. weekday reports, news anchors

WSOC-TV Eyewitness News anchors (from left) Harold Johnson, Meg MacDonald, Bill Walker, and Ray Boylan present the area's most complete newscast each weeknight at 6 p.m. and 11 p.m. Courtesy, Richard Ivey, Ivey Custom Color

Cullen Ferguson and Janet England, AMS meteorologists Ray Boylan and Tad Maguire, and sports director Harold Johnson.

This combination of people, facilities, and technology has won a long list of prestigious awards. In 1983 Eyewitness News was honored by United Press International for the Best Newscast in America. In 1984 it received the coveted Edward R. Murrow Award for the Southeast from the Radio and Television News Directors Association. It has been cited by Associated Press and United Press International for a variety of news spots and documentary productions, and won the award for Best Newscast in North Carolina from AP in 1988.

Throughout its history,

A WSOC-TV technical director adjusts the complicated video switching equipment to get ready for telecasts from the station. Courtesy, Richard Ivey, Ivey Custom Color

WSOC-TV has remained committed to a tradition of leadership and innovation in reporting. For example, it was the first western news organization to use a Soviet communications satellite to relay live coverage to North Carolina. Later it was among the nation's first stations to offer all-night news, using a special feed of CNN Headline News from 2 a.m. to 6 a.m.

As an active participant in community affairs, Eyewitness News includes such regular features as "Action 9," with consumer help information; "Healthbeat," to provide information on recent medical advances; "Breakthrough," with facts on new technology; and "Janet England's Family Focus," to help parents and children cope with the pressures of daily life.

At the annual Nine Who Care event, WSOC-TV honors volunteers from 17 counties who have served their communities. It sponsors an extensive entertainment schedule at Springfest as well as an annual Senior Citizens' Christmas Party.

With such a commitment to both the community and television leadership, WSOC-TV every day fulfills its slogan: We Send Our Best to You.

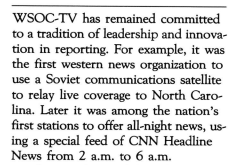

161

WSOC FM-103

Since 1971 WSOC FM-103 has consistently gone to the hearts of its listeners with the country music that reflects the tastes of Carolinians. And, since 1981, this 100,000-watt station has been ranked number one in the market. In short, its success has been unrivaled.

To maintain that position, WSOC FM-103 constantly holds its thumb on the pulse of listener preferences. The station conducts extensive research, asking listeners what songs and features they want to hear year round.

Nine years with WSOC FM-103 have given morning man Bill Dollar a household name in the Carolinas. He wakes listeners with great country songs and everything they need to begin the day—award-winning news with Ed Spencer, Storm Track Radar weather reports from AMS meteorologist Ray Boylan, WSOC FM-103 Sports with Harold Johnson, and Charlotte Police Officer traffic reports.

Then, throughout the day and night, the station's other polished personalities keep the music humming, with solid blocks of 12 country favorites played back to back, every hour. Together with this more-music format is the station's recognized commitment to outstanding news and sports programming.

The station has been recognized by the Associated Press in North Carolina for Best Sport News and Best General News. Its professional news staff has demonstrated an ability to be first on the scene when news breaks in the area.

WSOC FM-103's news team is able to present severe weather coverage in an instant, coordinating life-saving information via Storm Track Radar, WSOC FM-103 meteorologists Ray Boylan and Tad Maguire, and satellite links to the National Weather Service. In addition, WSOC FM-103 maintains a flow of information from area authorities and the Carolinas Skywarn ham radio operators network.

Its sports department actively covers the Southeast's dominant sporting activity, NASCAR racing, which attracts up to a quarter-million spectators to the Charlotte Motor Speedway on race weekends. WSOC FM-103 carries the entire Winston Cup Series as well as broadcasting live from CMS during pole and prerace activities. In addition, it offers listeners extra race-day information, with traffic reports, fan and driver interviews, and insights from nationally known motorsports experts.

Sports fans also tune in to sister-station WSOC AM-93 for coverage of major-league baseball and Charlotte's own minor-league team, The Knights. Starting with spring training, WSOC AM-93 broadcasts more than 300 major- and minor-league games per season, not concluding until the last pitch of the World Series. College and pro-football games are featured on WSOC AM-93 throughout the fall until college basketball begins to dominate the Carolinas sports scene in the winter months. Led by its coverage of the N.C. State Wolfpack, along with other Atlantic Coast Conference teams, no Charlotte area station carries more ACC basketball games than WSOC AM-93.

But simply covering news and events is not WSOC's only task. It also works to be part of the communities it serves. To cover the community events Carolinians care about, the station features hundreds of appearances, remote broadcasts, country concerts, festivals, and parades every year. It annually gives time and contributions to more than 20 charitable organizations, including well-known causes such as the Easter Seal Society, Muscular Dystrophy Association, the World 600 Children's Charities, United Way, the Charlotte Humane Society, and United Cerebral Palsy.

For the more than 245,000 people who listen each day, WSOC FM-103/AM-93 is the place for the best and most country music, and a lot more.

Bill Dollar has become a household name in the Carolinas, handling WSOC FM-103's morning shift from 5:30 a.m. to 9 a.m.

Kitty Ledbetter works the 7 p.m. to 12 midnight shift at WSOC FM-103.

EPLEY ASSOCIATES, INC.

The age of instant communication has revolutionized the way business deals with people. Operating successfully in a fragmented society that is dominated by a demand for immediate information requires that business strategically plan with a keen eye to public issues and people concerns.

Counseling businesses on building understanding of their activities and objectives is the primary purpose of Epley Associates, Inc., a Charlotte based public relations firm that reaches beyond the Carolina borders. Its mission is to develop effective communication strategies and techniques to favorably influence public opinion for the benefit of its clients.

When Joe S. Epley established the firm in Charlotte in 1968, few recognized how the rapid changes in society and technology would affect business in its relationships with employees, the community, consumers, the government, and the media. Epley has built a team of talented public relations practitioners who are dedicated to bridging gaps of understanding and building support for its clients' positions, products, and services through effective communication.

With full-service offices in Charlotte and Raleigh, Epley Associates became the largest public relations firm in the Carolinas and one of the largest in the South. The firm's goal of being on the leading edge of the pro-

Headquartered at 4819 Park Road in Charlotte, Epley Associates utilizes state-of-the-art technology in planning and implementing public relations research and programs.

fession and its record of providing clients with sound public relations advice and service have earned it a national reputation for excellence.

The firm takes pride in its ability to counsel management on preparing for and handling major crisis situations. Its expertise in assisting clients to influence public issues that impact on their operations is a major thrust of the firm's work. Epley Associates also provides a host of other services, including community relations, special events management, research, government relations, internal communications, media relations, graphics, audiovisual presentations, and publicity.

Scores of successful major programs have been developed to help organizations—from *Fortune* 500 corporations to local governments—anticipate and manage situations that affect the organizations internally and externally. Examples include helping major firms such as Philip Morris, U.S.A., Freightliner, International Bio-Synthetics, and Ajinomoto establish

The senior management team at Epley Associates provides a broad background in public relations and other issues that impact corporate success. Seated in a planning session are (from left) Martha Walters, APR, vice-president/Raleigh; Joe Epley, APR, president and chief executive officer; and Gail Rosenberg, APR, director of client services. Standing is Lamar Gunter, APR, vice-president/Charlotte.

operations in the Carolinas. Gala openings and impressive special events were orchestrated for clients such as Burroughs Wellcome, Bahlsen, Charlotte Memorial Hospital and Medical Center, and Marriott hotels. When mergers caused businesses to reorganize and adopt new names, Epley Associates was there to help Grace Equipment Company and Sandoz Chemicals Corporation.

One of the original tasks of the firm was to develop the concept for Carowinds, a major theme park that is still an active client.

In addition to being involved in community and state affairs, Epley's practitioners are recognized for leadership in their profession. All senior practitioners must pass an intensive examination to earn national accreditation in the practice of public relations.

It is the passion for excellence and the demand for effective results in client service that sets Epley Associates, Inc., apart in the public relations profession.

DUKE POWER COMPANY

The twentieth century was in its very first year when Dr. Gil Wylie, a prominent New York surgeon and Chester, South Carolina, native, formed the Catawba River Power Company to harness the power of the Catawba River to run the area's textile and tobacco mills. There were still plenty of skeptics about the value of electricity. But Wylie got a charter to build and operate a hydro-electric plant at India Hook Shoals on the Catawba River and hired a young construction engineer, William States Lee, to do the job.

Three years later, in spite of a great flood on the river in 1901, the two men had the Catawba plant running. It was the beginning of an investor-owned company that, from its Charlotte headquarters, now provides power to more than 4 million people over 20,000 square miles of North and South Carolina.

Its chairman of the board and chief executive officer is William S. Lee, the grandson of its founding engineer.

In 1901 Wylie and Lee dreamed of creating a network of power plants with interconnecting high-voltage transmission lines that would carry power throughout the region. Many people thought the scheme impossible. But their dream moved closer to reality when they got the help of James Buchanan Duke, presi-

Duke's first power plant at India Hook Shoals used rope-driven generators to produce electricity from the flow of the Catawba River.

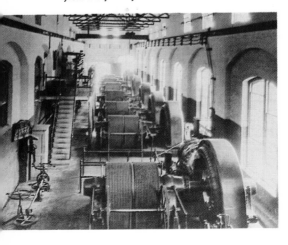

dent of American Tobacco Company and one of the wealthiest men in the country. When Wylie treated Duke for an infected foot in 1904, he convinced Duke to invest $50,000—the beginning of what would become millions—for the formation of Southern Power Company in 1905.

Over the next six decades the sources of power evolved into a diversified mixture of hydroelectric, coal-powered steam, and nuclear energy. Today this diversity ensures that the company can produce a reliable supply of electricity without relying on any foreign source for fuels.

When a severe drought in 1925 demonstrated that the Catawba River alone couldn't meet the region's growing demand for electricity, Duke, just weeks before his death, authorized the construction of a coal-fired steam plant. His contributions to the beginning and success of the company were recognized 10 years later when Southern Power Company was renamed Duke Power Company.

In 1956 the firm's leaders saw that nuclear power might better provide the vast quantities of electricity the growing region needed. Duke Power teamed with two other power companies to design and construct the Southeast's first nuclear power plant at Parr, South Carolina. For the next 10 years it was operated as an experimental program. As a result, Duke Power gained invaluable experience, which it has been able to use in the successful construction and operation of three nuclear

The McGuire Nuclear Station is one of three Duke power-generating plants on Lake Norman, built by the company in the 1960s.

power plants to generate power for its customers.

The success began with the announcement of the Oconee Nuclear Station in 1966. At this station, which began operation in 1973, Duke Power has generated more electricity than any other nuclear plant in the United States. That record of success has continued at the company's McGuire and Catawba nuclear plants.

To retain total control of the quality of each of these plants, Duke determined to use its own employees for design, construction, and operation. The objective was to produce plants that would operate safely and efficiently for decades. While each plant required millions of dollars to construct, the cost of the electricity produced has proved to be far less than that produced by coal, oil, or gas.

When, in 1984, Duke was awarded the Edison Award, the electric utility industry's highest honor, the company was cited for "superior performance in the design, construction, and operation of economical, efficient nuclear power plants."

In addition, the nuclear plants offer environmental rewards in keeping with Duke's commitment to protect the natural resources around its plants. Nuclear plants offer the cleanest available method of generating electricity on a large scale.

The company's environmental

Lake Norman, built by Duke Power in the 1960s to power the Cowans Ford Hydroelectric Power Plant, is the largest body of freshwater in the two Carolinas. Its 520-mile shoreline is home to more than 25,000 year-round residents, and its 32,500-acre surface area is a mecca for boating, fishing, and other water sports.

25,000 residents. Its 32,500 acres of water attract thousands of sailors, boaters, and bass fishermen.

Today Duke Power continues to protect the environment and keep the cost of power consistently below the national average by making the most of existing plants. The company's network of eight coal-fired plants has led the nation in fuel efficiency for 14 consecutive years. And its three nuclear plants typically are ranked among the top 10 in the nation in efficiency.

In addition, Duke sponsors more than 40 energy-management programs that help its 1.5 million residential, commercial, and industrial customers use electricity more efficiently and decrease demand during peak periods. Today Duke Power Company is the seventh-largest investor-owned electric utility in the nation and offers the expanding Piedmont region a reliable, reasonably priced supply of electricity to undergird economic development for the future.

program, which began in the 1920s, has earned Duke Power the National Wildlife Federation's coveted Conservation Award for assembling "the largest and best in-house environmental staff among the nation's electric utilities." This staff monitors the air, water, and environment around each of the firm's 37 generating plants and studies the environmental impact of future facilities. It works with the support of the finest available chemical, biological, and physical and health science laboratories at Duke's Applied Science Center on Lake Norman just north of Charlotte.

The company is particularly proud of its efforts to preserve the natural environment in the Keowee-Toxaway complex in northwestern South Carolina. There the Oconee Nuclear Station and the Jocassee and Keowee hydroelectric stations operate efficiently in an area that includes a scenic 43-mile segment of the Foothills Trail and prized fishing waters

on Lake Jocassee. In the woodlands, Duke protected the habitat of the rare Oconee Bell wildflower. In the lake, it has prevented temperature fluctuations that would harm the lake's trout and black bass—just two of the 75 species of fish thriving in Duke's 24 lakes.

On the 520 miles of shoreline of Lake Norman, built by Duke Power in the 1960s to power the Cowans Ford Hydroelectric Station, there is a growing community of more than

Catawba Nuclear Station, south of Charlotte, was completed by Duke Power in 1987 at the lowest cost of any nuclear plant of its vintage in the nation. The two-unit plant can generate more than 2 million kilowatts of electricity—enough to meet the electricity needs of more than 500,000 homes.

USAIR

USAir has become one of the nation's leading airlines. Long a leader in the Northeast, USAir's recent mergers with California-based Pacific Southwest Airlines (PSA) and North Carolina-based Piedmont Airlines have made it one of America's most popular and prominent airlines.

USAir and PSA operations were integrated in the spring of 1988, while the Piedmont operations were merged into USAir in 1989. As a result, USAir now ranks as one of the nation's largest passenger-carrying airlines.

USAir now carries passengers from coast to coast, as well as supporting heavy traffic along both coasts. Moreover, USAir has committed it-

ABOVE: *Edwin I. Colodny, USAir chairman and president.*

self to international service by continuing to operate a well-established route from Charlotte to London, flying Boeing 767s. It is also pursuing development of a route from Pittsburgh to Frankfurt.

The two recent mergers expanded USAir's primary hubs from Pittsburgh and Philadelphia to also include Baltimore, Charlotte, Dayton, and Syracuse. The Charlotte hub is USAir's largest in terms of daily departures.

Following the Piedmont merger, USAir relocated its main computer center to Winston-Salem, while maintaining its corporate headquarters in northern Virginia. Nearby Washington, D.C., was among the first cities served by USAir when it began carrying passengers in 1949.

USAir first took to the skies in 1939 carrying mail to small towns in the Allegheny Mountains region of western Pennsylvania, making use of a technological breakthrough created by Dr. Lytle S. Adams, a Chicago dentist. Adams developed a device that would enable an airplane to pick up and deliver mail sacks without having to land. He demonstrated his ingenious system at the Chicago World's

Fair, where he met champion glider pilot and businessman Richard C. du Pont.

Du Pont was fascinated. He decided to start a company that would provide airmail pickup and delivery service to isolated locations, using Adams' device. He chartered All American Aviation, Inc., as a Delaware corporation. Then he won bids on two experimental airmail pickup routes for the United States Post Office, connecting cities in Pennsylvania, West Virginia, Delaware, and Ohio. Starting on May 12, 1939, at Latrobe, Pennsylvania, All American Aviation flew for 10 years over the Allegheny Mountains, successfully overcoming some of the nation's worst terrain and weather conditions.

In 1942, after the U.S. entered World War II, du Pont left All American Aviation to help the U.S. Army Air Corps redesign pickup devices for gliders used to transport troops. Major Halsey R. Bazley succeeded du Pont as president.

With the end of the war, All American determined its future lay in carrying passengers as well as mail. In 1949, under the leadership of Robert M. Love, it moved its headquarters to Washington, D.C., changed its name to All American Airways, and began passenger transportation between Washington, D.C.,

Baltimore, Philadelphia, New York, Pittsburgh, Buffalo, and Cincinnati—as well as smaller cities in between.

By 1953, when the airline changed its name to Allegheny Airlines, Inc., it had expanded its routes to Erie, Pennsylvania; Cleveland, Ohio; and Parkersburg and Huntington, West Virginia. Based in the populous East with its many important short-haul markets, Allegheny grew rapidly, developing new ticketing, reservations, and baggage-handling systems to meet the increasing demands of short-haul air transport.

In 1953 Leslie O. Barnes was named president and Henry A. Satterwhite joined the board of directors. Satterwhite served as chairman of the board from 1956 to 1978. He and Barnes piloted Allegheny through the "feeder-line" era, through mergers with Mohawk and Lake Central airlines, and into the jet age.

In 1959 Allegheny expanded to several New England cities and became the first airline to put the Convair 540 turboprops into service. By 1963 the firm that had started with 11 DC-3s had a fleet of 38 aircraft—23 Convair 440 jetprops and 15 Martin Executives. The growing fleet required increasingly specialized facilities, so Allegheny moved

its maintenance, engineering, flight operations, and flight-control personnel from Washington to a new multimillion-dollar facility at Greater Pittsburgh International Airport.

In 1966 Allegheny introduced its first pure jet, the DC-9. The company's last piston-engine aircraft, a Convair, was phased out of service in September 1977.

During the late 1960s, when the regulated environment afforded carriers little flexibility to enter and exit markets, Allegheny developed a program to replace service at smaller cities on its route system that were not generating sufficient traffic to sustain economic air service with jet aircraft. USAir entered into agreements whereby certain carriers operating smaller, propeller-driven aircraft provided service at such cities under the name Allegheny Commuter.

The first Allegheny Commuter flight took off on November 15, 1967. A full network of regional airlines contract with USAir to carry several million passengers per year between local and connecting hub airports under the general name of USAir Express.

Allegheny was ready for more, but in the era of federal regulation of air transportation, an airline could only grow through acquisition. By merging with Indianapolis-based Lake Central Airlines (effective June 1, 1968), the Allegheny system expanded to 77 airports serving an area in which more than 50 percent of the nation's population lived.

Allegheny stretched its regulated wings even farther in 1972, when it merged with Mohawk Airlines based in Utica, New York. That merger made Allegheny the nation's sixth-

largest passenger-carrying airline.

With its expanded route system, its strong Allegheny Commuter network, and a fleet of 37 DC-9s, 31 BAC 1-11s, and 40 Convair 580s, Allegheny was positioned for continued growth. In 1974 it became the first local-service airline to make itself totally self-sufficient, allowing it to be removed from the federal subsidy program.

Barnes retired as president in 1975, and the board of directors elected Edwin I. Colodny to succeed him. Colodny had joined Allegheny in 1957 as assistant to the president; he held several other executive positions before being named chief executive officer. Colodny is now chairman of the board and chief executive officer of the airline and its parent firm, USAir Group.

Passage of the Airline Deregulation Act in 1978 led to radical changes in the U.S. airline industry. The new law brought with it a rapid growth in passenger volume on all scheduled airlines in the United States. Allegheny was no exception. With both the business and vacation travel markets expanding rapidly, each month brought new records for numbers of passengers carried.

To meet new public demands, the airline modernized its equipment,

phased out the last of the Convair 580s, and became an all-jet fleet. With both public interest and value growing, the company's stock was listed on the New York Stock Exchange.

Responding to the new competitive atmosphere, Allegheny adopted innovative pricing practices offering travelers a variety of discount fare plans. It also started service to Houston—followed by new service to Orlando, Tampa, and West Beach. The following year Allegheny added flights to Birmingham, Phoenix, Tucson, New Orleans, and Raleigh-Durham.

Allegheny had become a major airline and was planning to expand its route network nationwide. But market research revealed that much of the public still, incorrectly, perceived the company as a small, local-service carrier. Consultants suggested that Allegheny would not shake the "small and local" image without changing its name. Corporate executives sought a name that would reflect the airline's new size and scope. On October 28, 1979, Allegheny Airlines became USAir.

In December 1986 USAir Group (the holding company for USAir) announced that it had agreed to purchase PSA. With the ap-

proval of the Department of Transportation, that purchase became final in late May 1987, and the operations were merged in the spring of 1988. With the acquisition, USAir became a major carrier in the California market, one of the nation's busiest air travel corridors.

On March 6, 1987, USAir Group announced that it had agreed to purchase Piedmont Aviation, a North Carolina-based airline with a history and tradition remarkably similar to that of USAir. Department of Transportation approval was received on October 30, 1987. The acquisitions of Piedmont and PSA gave USAir a comprehensive network of service throughout both the East and West coasts, convenient connections to USAir cities nationwide, and international service to Canada, the Bahamas, and Great Britain.

With its modern fleet of comfortable, quiet, and efficient aircraft; its flexible operations hubs; and its strong balance sheet, USAir is one of the nation's most successful airlines. The company has flown through the storms of deregulation, emerging stronger than ever with both continuous profits and outstanding customer loyalty.

According to Colodny, "The company has reported a profit in every year since 1976." He says, "Our number-one objective is to remain financially strong. Over the years we have followed a policy of controlled growth. We will stay strong by continuing prudent financial planning and by continuing to serve our markets well. Our scheduling philosophy has been geared to serving the business traveler, and we will continue this emphasis."

In 1984 USAir introduced America to the latest aviation technology with a new aircraft type—the Boeing 737-300. This 138-seat twin-engine jet, which USAir helped design, is one of the most advanced, fuel-efficient, and quiet jets of its size and range. Its large on-board storage compartments brought new convenience to business travel. In

mid-1988, with the operational merger with Piedmont in sight, of USAir's 95 firm orders for additional aircraft to be delivered by 1991, most were for Boeing 737-300s and the larger Boeing 737-400s. Indeed, Piedmont was the launch customer for the 400 series and USAir now operates approximately 20 of these aircraft.

Although it operates one of the youngest fleets in the industry, USAir has continued to modernize. Also, by replacing older aircraft with quiet, new 105-passenger Fokker 100s, it has moved its fleet closer to the Stage Three quiet noise standard established by the United States Department of Transportation.

With these new aircraft and the increased strength created by the mergers have come new service and routes for USAir passengers.

To support the greater level of service, USAir is building a major maintenance facility at Charlotte

and has already opened a training center and parts distribution center there. These facilities, worth more than $100 million, will bring several hundred additional jobs to the Charlotte area by the end

of 1991.

As it moves into the 1990s, USAir is making its Charlotte hub an important part of its continued expansion across more of the United States and the world.

COGENTRIX, INC.

Cogentrix began in 1983 as a one-man operation, the creation of George T. Lewis, Jr., an engineer who has been in the power-generation industry all his life. The idea that ultimately produced Cogentrix, a privately held corporation that develops, owns, and operates standardized cogeneration power plants, was a simple one. First, Lewis wanted to take advantage of the Public Utility Regulatory Policies Act (PURPA) passed by Congress as part of the National Energy Project, which followed close on the heels of the Arab oil embargo in the late 1970s. PURPA requires utilities to buy power from qualified cogeneration plants, that is, nonutility power plants selling steam to industrial users and electricity to utilities. Second, Lewis proposed to build standardized, modular plants that would result in considerable cost savings.

Lewis took the idea to his then-employer, the Charles T. Main Company in Boston, where he was a senior vice-president responsible for utility design and development. Unable to convince other Main officials that cogeneration presented a golden opportunity, Lewis resigned and came to Charlotte, determined to put his idea into action. Lewis knew Charlotte and the area well, having lived and worked there during the years he managed a district office for the Charles T. Main Company. He moved quickly once he arrived, hiring Duke Power Company to design small, coal-fired cogeneration plants. Then, designs in hand, he went about the business of "matchmaking" with electric utilities and industrial steam users.

In late 1984 Cogentrix began construction on its first three plants, all in North Carolina. By early 1986 two 35-megawatt plants were supplying steam to West Point Pepperell

Corp. textile plants in Lumberton and Elizabethtown, and another 35-megawatt plant was sending steam to a Guilford Mills textile plant in Kenansville. Carolina Power & Light, now Cogentrix' largest utility customer, buys all the electricity the three plants generate—an arrangement that suits the utility very well. CP&L was more than pleased to achieve its goal of adding load capacity without taking any of the risks

George T. Lewis, Jr., president and chief executive officer of Cogentrix, Inc.

of building or operating a plant and without investing any of its own money to do so.

From day one the Cogentrix formula has been to simplify, standardize, and economize. Currently Cogentrix' standard modules are the 35-megawatt plant, which produces between 20,000 and 60,000 pounds per hour of steam, and the 55-megawatt plant, which produces between 60,000 and 120,000 pounds per hour for an industrial host.

Those first three Cogentrix projects were quickly followed by other successful start-ups: Roxboro, North Carolina, in August 1987; South-

port, North Carolina, in September 1987; Hopewell, Virginia, in October 1987; and Portsmouth, Virginia, in April 1988, with an additional 20-plus projects now on the drawing board.

Lewis, who is president, chief executive officer, and sole owner of Cogentrix, is quick to point out that a major reason for his company's success is the first-rate team he has assembled, a staff that includes Lewis' three sons and whose four senior members, exclusive of Lewis, have a collective total of 75 years of engineering, consulting, and electric utilities management experience. Add Lewis' lifetime of industry experience, and that total is considerably more than 100 years.

In a seven-year time span, Cogentrix has rapidly expanded from a one-man operation to its present staff of 400. Outside the home office in Charlotte, construction-crew size at the job sites varies, depending on current project needs. The firm moved into a new 30,000-square-foot corporate headquarters in the Arrowpoint Business Park in late 1988.

Another important factor in the Cogentrix success story is its ability to oversee all phases of a project. Although Lewis originally retained Duke Power for design services, the company now has complete capability to manage construction from design to operation. Following start-up of a new plant, an operations and maintenance group keeps the plant operating at peak efficiency and in compliance with utility standards and procedures. Lewis' efforts have been recognized by his peers. The Cogeneration Institute of the Association of Energy Engineers named Lewis the Cogeneration Professional of the Year in 1987. Virtually everyone connected with Cogentrix' projects points out that Lewis' familiarity and contacts within the electric utility industry and his choice of quality suppliers are also among the contributing factors in the company's success.

As for the industrial steam users, they, too, are pleased with their purchasing arrangement from several standpoints. Reliability is an issue for them, as it is for utilities. Stable energy prices are important as well, and because coal prices are more predictable than are oil prices, these companies can plan their energy costs more accurately. Finally, the firms are saving the capital investment that would have been required had they built the steam-generating facilities themselves.

When Lewis was looking for a home for his new company, he was attracted by Charlotte's transportation capabilities and the city's legal, engineering, and investment banking services. Lewis and Cogentrix are returning the favor to the area. Cogentrix plants in North Carolina are, for

ABOVE: George T. Lewis, Jr. (left), with his son, Robert "Bob" W. Lewis, president of Cogentrix Development, Inc.

BELOW: Robert W. Lewis (top right), David J. Lewis, and James E. Lewis (bottom right).

the most part, constructed in locales blessed with a plentiful but untrained work force. Cogentrix hires locally as much as possible, training staff from the ground up. The firm provides courses for control operators at entry and advanced levels, a system maintenance and troubleshooting course, and a basic academic course for power plant operators.

When Cogentrix builds a plant, it represents a long-term commitment to the community; a Cogentrix plant has a 30-year life expectancy. Cogentrix works hard to be a good neighbor and is committed to protecting the environment, beginning in the planning and design stages and continuing through construction and plant operation.

At a time when energy production and conservation are critical, and in the wake of slower growth rates and other impediments to the construction of large, capital-intensive power plants, Cogentrix is effectively filling a special niche in the nation's power-generation industry. As for the future, George Lewis believes prospects are bright, saying now that Cogentrix is established in the marketplace, the only limitation on the future is imagination.

In view of what his company has accomplished thus far, the Cogentrix, Inc., future looks bright indeed.

WMIX RADIO

Turn the radio dial to 104.7 FM seven days per week, 24 hours per day, and hear current and past hit music that appeals to adults, ages 25 to 54. It is the sound today's adults enjoyed when they first developed their musical tastes.

That sound is one of the secrets of success for MIX 104.7, says general manager Jake Gurley. It is carried by 100,000 watts of power from an antenna 1,230 feet above the average height of Charlotte to 55 counties in the two Carolinas—from Asheville to Fayetteville, from Winston-Salem to Camden. It is heard by more adults than any other contemporary station in the Charlotte area, in spite of increasing competition from new stations.

Combine that musical sound with the station's wild and informative morning team, a creative advertising campaign, and a unique promotions program, and the result is a winning mix of news, information, and entertainment. Those are the elements it takes to keep the station's target market listening, Gurley says.

On the air, Chuck Boozer, MIX 104.7 morning man, maintains top ratings with a combination of wild antics, zany characters, and unexpected guests. Off the air, he participates in

The WMIX "music monster." Courtesy, Tony McGee Photography

a wide variety of charitable events. He has pushed himself in a wheelchair for 140 miles to raise money for muscular dystrophy. He sat in every seat in the new Charlotte coliseum to raise $15,000 for I Wish I Could, a charity for terminally ill children.

With Boozer from 5:30 a.m. to 10 a.m. are a group of the city's most widely known radio personalities. News director Karen Barnes brings the latest news and insight into the area's events. Weatherman Alan Archer has received the Award for Excellence in Broadcast Meteorology from the American Meteorological Society. Traffic reporter Trooper Dan has guided morning commuters for 10 years. And former NFL star

The WMIX 104.7 studio and offices are located at 137 South Kings Drive in Charlotte. Courtesy, Tony McGee Photography

quarterback Roman Gabriel gives his perspective on sports of all kinds.

The station's other wide-ranging talents include production director Fred Story, who adds to the station's programming with his Sunday night jazz show. Off the air, he also leads the nationally known jazz band, Flight 108.

WMIX' broadcasting strength and programming are a long way from where the station began in 1971, when it was a 3,000-watt classical music station. It gained more listeners in its target market by changing to a beautiful music format in 1972. Then, in 1982, when more people between the ages of 25 and 50 had grown up during the age of rock music, WMIX changed to its current format of more contemporary sounds.

Today it is one of 15 stations owned by EZ Communications of Fairfax, Virginia. Jake Gurley, who has been with the station for more than 10 years, says he expects that format to keep bringing in adult listeners. But, he says, as more teenagers who have grown up with today's pop sounds become part of WMIX' target market, MIX 104.7 will probably start appealing to them, with more of their kind of music.

WPCQ CHANNEL 36

For WCNC-TV, Charlotte's NBC affiliate station, which reaches more than 600,000 households from Spartanburg, South Carolina, to Boone, North Carolina, being part of the community is an important job.

In September 1988 the station, which is owned by the Providence Journal Company, began broadcasting from a new 1,936-foot transmission tower in Gaston County. Since then its strong, clear signal has brought viewers such popular network programs as "The Cosby Show," "Cheers," "Matlock," and "L.A. Law."

Charlotteans depend on WCNC-TV for the area's first newscast, "News 36" at 5:30 p.m., also the only hour of local and national news with "News 36" at 6 p.m. and "NBC Nightly News with Tom Brokaw" at 6:30 p.m. The station's staff of young, aggressive broadcasting professionals takes an investigative look at the news to uncover the story be-

hind the headlines. Their efforts are supported by the news-gathering capabilities of a satellite truck, which allows reports to be made live from any location.

Even the station's weather reports have an unusual twist. The station offers the area's only outdoor weather broadcast—which has even been done from the top of the WCNC-TV tower—so viewers actually see what is happening.

The station's coverage of sporting events has included reporting and commentary by such noted professionals as veteran NASCAR driver Benny Parsons and football star Roman Gabriel. In addition, WCNC-TV is the only Charlotte affiliate to cover every Hornets game, including interviews of players, even when the team is on the road.

As part of its commitment to

The News 36 Team are (from left) Jim Celania, Tom Miller, Jesse Johnson, and Steve Raleigh.

the community, WCNC-TV has taken an increasingly active role in supporting the area's charitable and civic needs. The station is proud to be the title sponsor of WCNC-TV JazzCharlotte. This two-day event, held every September, features a wide variety of music, food, and entertainment for the whole family. More than 100,000 people flock to uptown Charlotte to experience the fun of WCNC-TV JazzCharlotte. At the 1989 Springfest in uptown Charlotte, WCNC-TV sponsored an entertainment stage for the first time. And its staff members are actively involved in such organizations as the Charlotte Division of Make A Wish.

As WCNC-TV moves into the 1990s, it expects to attract even more viewers with its aggressive approach to involvement in the lives of the people in its 21-county broadcast area. WCNC-TV is Charlotte's up-and-coming source for news and entertainment.

SOUTHERN BELL: A BELLSOUTH COMPANY

With the introduction of Computer Access Terminals (CATs), services technician Robert Kingry is able to contain assignments quicker and more accurately. Here, using a CAT, Kingry makes his own investigative tests from a telephone pedestal to help pinpoint a customer's line trouble. Photo by Nancy Pierce

At the North Carolina state headquarters of Southern Bell in Charlotte, the watchword is "technology." But it's not technology only for its own sake. Instead, the goal is to help customers communicate better, faster, and more easily through state-of-the-art equipment.

That equipment is the latest in a line that extends back to the 1870s, when Alexander Graham Bell and Thomas Watson struggled to find a way to transmit the sound of the human voice through electrical impulses along a wire. Their historic moment of success came on March 10, 1876, when Bell said, "Mr. Wat-son, come here. I want you." It began a revolution in the way we communicate.

The revolution reached Charlotte on January 18, 1880, when Western Union Telegraph Company installed the city's first telephone in the drugstore of Dr. T.C. Smith and connected it to another one in the residence of Colonel Frank Coxe. By 1904 there were hundreds of phones in Charlotte, and the system that operated them was managed by Southern Bell.

During the ensuing decades Southern Bell has established a reputation for reliability while continuously en-hancing Charlotte's communications with new services. When the nation's telephone system changed in the 1980s, Southern Bell became the company that provided Charlotte's residences and businesses with their dial tone as well as long-distance services to cities within its calling zone. It also provides the facilities linking local customers with long-distance service outside the calling zones. Its equipment also transports computer and video signals.

The telephone system, which at first was run entirely by manual labor, became entirely automated and then computerized. Now all of Southern Bell's 1.5 million North Carolina customers are served by computerized switching systems.

The advanced technology makes possible a variety of special features, such as Touch-Tone and the Custom Calling Services—call waiting, call forwarding, speed calling, and three-way calling—that many people enjoy. In 1988 Southern Bell began offering TouchStar^{SM}, the next generation of advanced services.

"For all our customers, both business and residential, living in the Information Age will be something like being in a giant telecommunications shopping mall," says Joseph P. Lacher, vice-president for North Carolina. "You will be able to pick and choose those services you want just as you choose products and services when you go to a mall or grocery store."

Southern Bell also offers an array of service options for businesses. Its ESSX™ service gives a business the capability of a PBX system with up to 10,000 lines without the business having to purchase and maintain expensive equipment that will become obsolete. Southern Bell's

LEFT: *Service representative Brenda Hill spends a great deal of her day taking requests to establish, move, or change customers' telephone numbers. Hill is one of approximately 130 service representatives located in Charlotte. Photo by Nancy Pierce*

BELOW: *Southern Bell designed a network that has connected more than 5,000 state employees. The network is maintained 24 hours per day by employees such as electronic technician Joe Hankins. The network helps the state government service North Carolinians more quickly, efficiently, and cost effectively. Photo by Nancy Pierce*

MegaLink^{SM} service transmits wideband data at 1.5 megabits per second—fast enough to send the 1,315 pages of *War and Peace* in seven seconds.

Early in 1989 Southern Bell capitalized on a ruling by the Federal Communications Commission to offer one-stop shopping to multiline business customers. The ruling allows the company to sell and maintain both customer equipment and network services through one organization. After installing new accounting procedures required by the ruling, the firm recombined its network sales and service organizations with those of the nonregulated Southern Bell Advanced Systems entity, satisfying requests from customers who yearned for one point of contact.

One aspect of the Information Age not readily apparent is transmission technology. But the company is moving swiftly to install one of the newest innovations: fiber-optic cable. This cable is made of hair-thin glass threads through which laser flashes travel at the speed of light to provide the highest-quality voice, data, and video transmission available. A

Computer attendant Eddie Hicks may not move with the speed of an IBM computer, but he enjoys the race. He loads data file cartridges into C-tape drive units at the Charlotte Data Processing Center. Employees like Hicks manage complex equipment so that even a child can dial grandma for a chat. Photo by Nancy Pierce

single strand can carry up to 16,000 conversations simultaneously. By the end of 1989 Southern Bell will have installed 26,000 miles of fiber-optic cable in North Carolina in only two years.

"North Carolina has a modern telephone network that is second to none," says Lacher. "It is critical for the economic health and growth of our state that the network remain strong. Telecommunications is part of the infrastructure businesses and industries examine when deciding whether to locate in North Carolina, and those decisions mean jobs for our citizens."

New technology, however, isn't the only way in which Southern Bell's 7,200 employees in North Carolina contribute to the state. Many employees, one-third of whom work in the Charlotte area, are active in their community's cultural and charitable projects. Vice-president Lacher quickly became involved in the community after assuming his post in January 1988. He has been active with the Charlotte Homeless Shelter, the chamber of commerce, and Spirit Square. In the fall of 1988 he chaired a citizens' committee that led a successful drive for $182.8 million in local improvement bonds.

Chapter 35 of the North Carolina Telephone Pioneers, a civic group of long-term and retired employees, gained national recognition for its work when President Ronald Reagan awarded a Presidential Citation to the Fire Safety House. Built on a trailer, the small house is used in a hands-on exercise that teaches children what to do in a fire. Since being dedicated in May 1987, the house has been used to teach some 100,000 children, including a nine-

year-old girl in Mt. Olive who relied on the lessons to escape a fire that destroyed her family's home.

What's more, as a company Southern Bell supports many of the state's educational institutions and activities. That support includes scholarships for students at community colleges, UNC-Chapel Hill, UNC-Charlotte, N.C. State University, N.C. A&T University, Appalachian State University, Davidson College, and Queens College.

In the Information Age, Southern Bell continues its tradition of providing service to the community while it advances the technology of its services.

8

Manufacturing

Producing goods for individuals and industry, manufacturing firms provide employment for many Charlotte area residents.

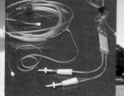

Charlotte Pipe and Foundry Company, 178-179

Pepsi-Cola Bottling Company of Charlotte, 180-181

Hoechst Celanese Corporation, 182-185

ICI Americas Inc., 186-187

E.I. du Pont de Nemours and Company, 188-189

The Pneumafil Group, 190-191

Dexter Plastics, 192-193

Okuma of America, 194-195

Sandoz Chemicals Corporation, 196-197

Homelite/Textron, 198

Verbatim Corporation, 199

Frito-Lay, Inc., 200-201

Barnhardt Manufacturing Company, 202-203

Philip Morris U.S.A., Cabarrus Manufacturing Center, 204

Photo by Paul Epley

CHARLOTTE PIPE AND FOUNDRY COMPANY

What uniqueness of thought had prompted him to establish a foundry in an area that had never known one? Alabama was the recognized center of the pipe manufacturing industry. Charlotte had concentrated its energies upon production of textiles and ancillary machinery and equipment. It doubtless required uncommon originality and daring to pursue the untried direction of pipe manufacturing.

A Foundry, Volume I

These words were written about the founder of Charlotte Pipe and Foundry Company, Willis Frank Dowd. He began the business in 1901 in Dilworth, when Charlotte was a town of some 22,000 people. As daring as his new venture was, its potential expressed itself tenaciously through early fires, economic downturns, illness, and death. The small pipe company of 25 employees in 1901 became today's manufacturing giant at five locations with 1,100 employees. The sales territory that was originally Mecklenburg County is today 46 states and several foreign countries. And the original product line of cast-iron drain, waste, and vent pipe and fittings has flourished into a myriad of products in both cast iron and plastic.

But some things have remained the same. Today the Dowd family re-

An aerial view of Charlotte Pipe's foundry in 1988—still situated on South Clarkson Street where it was built in 1909 following a fire that destroyed the Dilworth plant. The foundry has enjoyed numerous expansions.

mains personally involved in the management of the company—this leadership now extending to great-grandsons of the founder. The philosophy that originated with him—that a company has to be bigger than any one man—is reflected today in the accumulated integrity and aspirations of the many men and women who work at Charlotte Pipe.

The founder of Charlotte Pipe and Foundry Company was distinguished by more than his vision. Until his death in 1926, Willis Frank Dowd was active in Charlotte's religious and civic life. He was a charter member of Pritchard Memorial Baptist Church, serving it as both a deacon and a member of the board of trustees from its origin. For his city, he served as a member of the board of aldermen and as a director in two

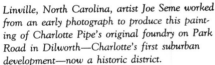

Linville, North Carolina, artist Joe Seme worked from an early photograph to produce this painting of Charlotte Pipe's original foundry on Park Road in Dilworth—Charlotte's first suburban development—now a historic district.

of its leading banks.

Willis Frank Dowd II was only 30 when he inherited the presidency, but he had been well tutored for his role. Since age 11 Frank had carried the title of "office boy," and when not in school was busy with foundry duties. After education at Woodberry Forest School and North Carolina State College, he returned to work at the foundry.

The rare talent that Frank brought to the business was personal charm, which translated into selling ability. To his personal warmth, he added persistence and untiring stamina to become a one-man dynamo sales department. When he retired from the presidency in 1963, the company's sales territory stretched from Pennsylvania through Georgia.

Technological advances during the 1950s were so sweeping that they virtually amounted to a revolution in foundry methods. Charlotte Pipe recognized the necessity for change and instructed two of its engineers to design and implement the "new" foundry. Wesley Thompson, vice-president/production, and

Some key members of Charlotte Pipe management team (from left): Roddey Dowd, Jr., vice-president; Edward H. "Ned" Hardison, president; Frank Dowd, Jr., chairman, executive committee; Roddey Dowd, Sr., chairman of the board; and Frank Dowd IV, vice-president.

Frank Dowd III spent most of the 1950s visualizing and actualizing a state-of-the-art facility. Frank described it later as "like going from a horse and buggy to the automobile." By 1957 the new foundry was in production.

It was a proud and progressive attainment, but it was only the beginning of a climate of change and modernization that continues today.

For the plumbing pipe industry, however, the greatest change was yet to be. It was reflected in the caption of an ad appearing in national industrial magazines in April 1969: "This fitting cost us several million dollars. You can get it for $3.50." And it bore the logo of Charlotte Plastics. The ad produced a near-shock wave in the plumbing industry, for Charlotte Pipe had historically been an advocate of cast-iron piping materials. But the research of Frank Dowd III and his brother, Roddey, had convinced the organization that plastic would have a star role in the future of the industry.

In April 1965 the company bought 182 acres of land in Union County for a possible future plant site. Frank spent time in Europe studying the latest technology of the French, Austrians, and Germans. He describes the results of his explorations: "Having obtained the latest ideas and thoughts, we came back and designed the plant ourselves. We didn't know a thing about plastic pipe, but a plant's a plant. If you want to make a product, there's a certain way you go back upstream to do it, and we designed the plant that way and, amazingly, we made very few mistakes—and none of them fatal."

From 1967 to 1988 Bart Hodges was general manager of the plastics operation. He has presided over tremendous growth of the division for the past 20 years, until today Charlotte's Plastics Division is the largest producer of plastic drain, waste, and vent pipe and fittings in the United States. The plant in Bakers, Union County, has been expanded five times until today it comprises 600,000 square feet of manufacturing space and employs more than 600 people.

In 1982 a second plastics-manufacturing plant was built and put into production in Cameron, Texas, and in 1988 still another was activated in Muncy, Pennsylvania. Investment in new technology and new products continues in both the foundry and in the Plastics Division.

Frank Dowd III served as president from 1963 until 1973, when he was succeeded by Roddey Dowd. Frank's talents and training are in engineering and production. Roddey's major contribution has been in marketing and in the establishment of corporate identity.

On July 12, 1984, Edward H. "Ned" Hardison moved from executive vice-president to president, the first person from outside the family to pilot the company. Today Roddey Dowd, Jr., and Frank Dowd IV, great-grandsons of the founder, are vice-presidents. Each has been trained in the ranks as their fathers were before them, having spent time in every job in both divisions. The "uncommon originality and daring" of Willis Frank Dowd is being carried forward by a fourth generation.

A 1988 aerial view of Charlotte Pipe's Plastics Division plant in Bakers, North Carolina. In 1967 a single building housed the operation that today is one of the largest producers of plastic pipe and fittings in the United States.

PEPSI-COLA BOTTLING COMPANY OF CHARLOTTE

When Charlotte's Pepsi-Cola Bottling Company was ranked in the top 100 privately held North Carolina companies in 1988, it was also one of the 10 largest bottling companies in the Carolinas. With gross sales of more than $50 million, its 275 employees sold and distributed Pepsi-Cola in seven North Carolina counties: Mecklenburg, Union, Stanley, Cabarrus, Gaston, Cleveland, and Lincoln.

Those figures were the result of eight years of rapid growth, a rate of almost 10 percent per year. They are the latest success story in the history of an organization that began in the barn of a man who had been the bookkeeper of a grain company. And they were achieved under the leadership of that man's granddaughter.

In 1905 Henry Barksdale Fowler was persuaded by New Bern pharmacist Caleb Bradham to market his new soda fountain drink, Pepsi-Cola. He formed the company's first franchised bottling plant. His family helped him bottle the drinks at night so he could sell them by day.

Within three years Fowler owned the first motorized delivery truck in Charlotte, even though the city of 17,000 had no paved streets. It was the first motorized beverage truck in the United States.

Fowler explained the purchase by saying it was the best advertisement he could have. In the coming years it became the first of a fleet; but Henry Fowler never learned to drive.

One night when a driver lost his truck and the product in a dice game on the edge of town, Fowler had another driver take him to win the truck back. He also took his wife, Sadie, to drive it home to Charlotte.

As the company grew, Fowler became known for his hard work and fair dealings with employees. In fact, he continued to work 10 to 12 hours a day, six days a week, until he was in his eighties. The morning after PepsiCo honored him at age 86 with a banquet attended by actress Joan Crawford and PepsiCo president Alfred Steele, Fowler was at work at 7:30.

Although Pepsi-Cola suffered two bankruptcies in its first 40 years, Fowler managed to keep the Charlotte bottling company running.

ABOVE: *Henry Barksdale Fowler marketed his new soda fountain drink, Pepsi-Cola, in 1905. That same year he formed the company's first franchised bottling plant. Today Pepsi-Cola Bottling Company of Charlotte is one of the 10 largest bottling companies in the Carolinas.*

BELOW: *In 1908 this truck delivered Pepsi-Cola to Charlotte-area residents. It was the first motorized delivery truck in Charlotte and the first motorized beverage truck in the United States. The driver, pictured here, is Will Hayes.*

An artist's rendering of Pepsi's new modern 48,500-square-foot headquarters building.

Later his continuous use of the Pepsi-Cola name helped Pepsi defend its "cola" trade name against a suit by Coca-Cola, which wanted to claim proprietary rights.

Today the bottling company is led by the third generation of Fowler's family: granddaughter Dale Halton, who is president and chairman of the board. And she is acutely aware of her responsibility to the family tradition of hard work and success in a company with a strong family orientation. In fact, the company's employees praise the way it makes employees feel that they are a needed part of the Pepsi "family."

While PepsiCo has stimulated sales with new soft drinks, the bottling company has increased the number of local promotions and improved the service of its distribution system. By giving every employee incentives for attendance and performance, Charlotte's Pepsi-Cola Bottling Company has stimulated all employees to work harder for their customers. "We try to show employees that we care about them and about the community," Halton says.

As a result, the firm experiences less than 5-percent turnover in employees each year. Employees like to talk about the profit-sharing and benefits plans that reinforce their loyalty. And several women have shortened their maternity leaves by bringing their new babies to the office for several months.

A number of its top managers have been with the company since the days of Henry Fowler. They believe in its active management style—an atmosphere in which so few memos are written that there are no secretaries and no dictating equipment.

In addition, the firm continues Henry Fowler's tradition of involvement in the local community. Fowler, who was chairman of the Mecklenburg County Commission in 1932, made it a practice to supply every church picnic with Pepsi.

Today the company's Pepsi-Cola

of Charlotte Foundation, created by a contribution of 10 percent of pretax profits, supports a wide variety of charities, the arts, and educational institutions. Dale Halton, who was nominated as Charlotte Businesswoman of the Year in 1987, has served on the board of directors for the Charlotte chamber and the UNCC Athletic Foundation, on the advisory board of public radio stations WFAE and WDAV, and on the boards of the First Citizens Bank, UNCC Foundation, and the Charlotte Symphony Board. And the company is known for its gifts of Pepsi to community events.

In 1985 a modern 48,500-square-foot building replaced the bottling company's old buildings on South Boulevard. The firm's Midland warehouse was recently expanded to accommodate demand in Cabarrus, Union, and Stanley counties. In addition, plans are under way to expand the Gastonia plant by 1991.

Dale Halton and her Pepsi-Cola Bottling Company family clearly intend to be part of the picture as Charlotte grows.

HOECHST CELANESE CORPORATION

The 1987 merger of American Hoechst Corporation and Celanese Corporation created Hoechst Celanese, a *Fortune* 100 industrial with a diversified product line, an international customer base, and substantial financial and research and development resources.

The new Hoechst Celanese Corporation also has roots deep in the history, the growth, and the fast-paced forward thrust of the City of Charlotte, Mecklenburg County, and the Carolinas.

Beyond the Carolinas and the United States, Hoechst Celanese is part of the Hoechst Group, a worldwide organization developing, producing, and marketing a broad spectrum of chemicals, pharmaceuticals, advanced materials, and other high-technology products. The Hoechst Group's world headquarters is at the offices of Hoechst AG in Frankfurt, West Germany.

Worldwide, Hoechst employs approximately 200,000 people in 230 companies. Those thousands of people are involved in all segments of the worldwide chemical industry.

The approximately 24,000 Hoechst Celanese employees in the United States develop, manufacture, and market chemicals, fibers and films, engineering plastics and ad-

Textile and Technical Fibers groups personnel at the Dreyfus Research Park have made significant contributions to the world of manufactured fibers. Among them are fibers that resist soil, silk-like polyester filament yarns, stretch polyester yarns, and the first polyester tire yarn specifically designed for radial tires.

vanced materials, printing plates, dyes and pigments, pharmaceuticals, and agricultural and animal-health products.

Worldwide, Hoechst Group research and development expenditures of approximately $4 million every business day—more than one billion dollars annually—support the innovative activities of 14,000 researchers in 14 countries.

Hoechst and Hoechst Celanese are known globally for their technological and scientific sophistication, their dedication to producing quality products, and their commitment to developing and manufacturing products that are helpful to people.

The Charlotte Connection
Charlotte has been part of the Hoechst Celanese story since the spring of 1925, when the nearly brand-new, fibers-producing Celanese Corporation opened a three-person sales office on Tyron Street in the central city. The steady growth of Celanese's fibers business and the start up in 1948 of the South's first manufactured-fibers plant at nearby Rock Hill, South Carolina, led to the construction and occupancy in 1954 of the company's Charlotte office building at 6000 Carnegie Boulevard. Development of the Dreyfus Research Park on Archdale Drive soon followed.

Over the years, as Celanese grew and merged its fibers, chemicals, and merchandising strengths with the worldwide strength and expertise of Hoechst AG to form Hoechst Celanese, Charlotte became home to sev-

Production-testing operations such as this at the Separations Products Division's modern state-of-the-art-equipped facilities in Charlotte's South Point Business Park ensure that the division's Celgard® microporous flat-sheet and hollow-fiber membranes meet customer requirements.

eral of the corporation's business groups.

Those Hoechst Celanese organizations are the Textile Fibers Group, the Technical Fibers Group, and the Film and Fiber Intermediates Group, all headquartered at the Carnegie Boulevard office building; the Specialty Products Group's Separations Products Division in the South Point Business Park; and the Chesapeake Drive operations of the Specialty Chemical Group's Colorants and Surfactants Division.

Through these business entities, Hoechst Celanese employs approximately 1,500 people in Charlotte and Mecklenburg County. Approximately 10,000 people are employed in the Carolinas, about 600 of them at the Dreyfus Research Park. This Charlotte facility is one of four major research centers operated in the United States by Hoechst Celanese, which invests approximately $200 million each year in research and development.

The Colorants and Surfactants Division's tele-marketing program is on the cutting edge of dyes technology, permitting the matching of custom color shades by telephone and computer.

Hoechst Celanese's southeastern data center is at the Carnegie Boulevard facility, as are the sales and marketing offices; the law, human resources, and supply and distribution functions; the customer service operations; and the administrative staff organizations of the three fibers and film groups.

The Technical and Textile Fibers groups manufacture their products at Shelby and Salisbury, North Carolina; Spartanburg and Rock Hill, South Carolina; Narrows, Virginia; and in Canada, Mexico, and Belgium. Marketing offices are in New York City, Los Angeles, Atlanta, and Akron. Film and Fiber Intermediates Group facilities are at Spartanburg and Greer, South Carolina, and at Wilmington, North Carolina.

The products manufactured by the Hoechst Celanese organizations based in Charlotte/Mecklenburg range from Trevira® polyester and acetate fibers used in clothing, carpeting, and tires to fabric dyes and polyester film for video tapes to specialty membrane separations and filtra-

tion products. Some products are on the cutting edge of innovation. The Separations Products Division's Celgard® microporous flat-sheet and hollow-fiber membranes, for example, are used in blood oxygenation equipment (critical life-sustaining devices used during heart transplants and open-heart surgery), in transdermal drug-delivery systems, in high-performance military and consumer battery systems, and in disposable butane lighters for control of butane delivery for constant flame height.

Textile Fibers Group
This group produces Trevira® and other branded polyester fibers, yarns, and fiberfill and Celebrate!® acetate filament yarns used in apparel and home fashions. Trevira®, the leading polyester in carpeting, also is used in upholstered furniture,

office systems, and nonwoven fabrics. Celebrate!® acetate and Ceylon® polyester fibers are used in curtains, draperies, and bedding products.

With the capacity to produce 1.2 billion pounds of textile fibers annually, the Textile Fibers Group is the nation's largest producer of acetate filament yarns and the second-largest producer of polyester fibers and yarns. In addition, Textile Fibers makes a new Trevira Linenesque™ polyester apparel fiber, and its Comfort Fiber® and ESP® polyester trademarks appear on women's, men's, and children's clothing.

Technical Fibers Group
The Hoechst Celanese Technical Fibers Group is an innovative, worldwide producer of quality polyester filament yarns and staple fibers, filter products, and specialty fibers and materials for numerous industrial applications.

This group is the world's largest producer of high-denier polyester filament yarns for tire cord, rubber-related markets, seat belts, coated and laminated fabrics, vinyl-coated yarns, and webbing.

The group's high-denier polyester filament yarns, which are produced at Salisbury as well as Canada and Mexico, are used in tire cord, seat belts, coated and laminated fabrics, vinyl-coated yarns, and webbing. Low-denier polyester filament yarns, produced at Shelby, are used in core thread and for other industrial applications.

Since the mid-1950s the Technical Fibers Group's Filter Products Division has been a major, international producer of acetate tow for cigarette filters at plants in Virginia, Canada, Mexico, and Belgium. The group's newest tow plant, in Jiangsu Province of the People's Republic of China, is a joint venture with a division of China National Tobacco Co.

The Filter Products Division also makes acetate flake for fibers, photographic film, tape, and molded products in Virginia and at Rock Hill.

Spunbond polyester products manufactured by the Technical Fibers Group at Spartanburg are sold for roofing and geotextiles. Polyester monofilament products from Spartanburg are used in papermaking, conveyor belts, and zippers. Moreover, the group markets high-performance specialty fibers for use in making advanced composite materials and specialty cellulose acetate products used in health care and pharmaceutical applications.

Film and Fiber Intermediates Group

The Charlotte-based Film and Fiber Intermediates Group is composed of Polyester Film and Polyester Resins divisions and Cape Industries, as well as the administrative functions supporting the three fibers and film

At work in this Dreyfus Research Park laboratory are personnel of the Filter Products Division of the Hoechst Celanese Technical Fibers Group. This division has been a major, worldwide producer of acetate tow for cigarette filters since the mid-1950s.

groups.

Cape Industries at Wilmington, a joint venture with American Petrofina, produces the major polyester raw materials dimethyl terephthalate and terephthalic acid.

At Greer, the Polyester Film Division operates research and development, marketing, and manufacturing facilities for Hostaphan® polyester film. This product is processed by Hoechst Celanese customers into audio, video, and computer recording tapes; microfilm and drafting films; food-packaging materials; solar-control window film; adhesive tape; and labels and decals. This division also markets Trespaphan® polypropylene film and acetate films produced by Hoechst AG.

From Spartanburg and Greer, the Polyester Resins Division is a major supplier of resins for soft drink bottles, food packaging, food-storage containers, frozen-food trays, and strapping. Its polyester-fiber-grade resins are used in textile, monofilament, and nonwoven products.

Dreyfus Research Park

Personnel of this 453,000-square-foot, campus-like complex on a 128-acre site serve the Textile and Technical Fibers groups and support activities of the PBI Products Division, which produces its polybenzimidazole fire-retardant fibers at Rock Hill and is part of the corporation's New Jersey-based Advanced Technology Group.

This major research center's mission is to provide customers with new and improved products, to design manufacturing processes that certify that these products will meet specifications, and to make certain that Hoechst Celanese has the best technology in the world.

Dreyfus Research Park scientists have developed a significant variety of new products. Included are fibers that resist soil; polyester fibers that stretch; silk-like polyester yarns; PBI fibers that do not burn and are used to protect astronauts, fire fighters, and race car drivers; and polyester tire yarn specifically designed for radial tires more dimensionally stable than anything else on the market. Currently, the facility's scientists are converting new resins into high-performance fibers for advanced composites markets.

However, they have done more than develop new products. They also have created new, better, and faster ways for their customers to use Hoechst Celanese products in their manufacturing processes. One such innovation is a filament yarn that can be processed 24 percent faster at customers' textile mills, an achievement that received a national New Product of the Year Award from the Society of Professional Engineers. Better filters are possible because of the Celstar® microprocessor control system the Dreyfus staff developed for the tobacco industry.

At the same time, the Dreyfus Research Park staff has an exceptional, award-winning record of personnel and environmental protection because of persistent adherence to a strict set of safeguards and proce-

A PBI Products Division technician performs a vertical burn test on a fabric of PBI (polybenzimidazole) fibers. These fibers do not burn and, in addition to varied other applications, are used in protective garments for fire fighters, astronauts, and race car drivers.

dures. Safety measures cover everything from emerging procedures to periodic audits of all chemicals being used or stored at the Archdale Drive site. Consequently, park personnel repeatedly have won awards from the North Carolina Department of Labor, the National Safety Council, and the Chemical Manufacturers' Association for their success in practicing on-the-job safety and accident prevention.

Separations Products Division

The Separations Products Division is a leader from its quiet, new, modern Mecklenburg County location in the development and production of specialty membrane separations and filtration products. The division is the worldwide strategic center for specialty separations activities of Hoechst AG and is part of the corpo-

ration's New Jersey-based Specialty Products Group.

Celgard® microporous flat-sheet and hollow-fiber membranes are the foundation of the Hoechst Celanese family of membrane products. Celgard membranes combine the selectivity of membrane separations processes with the chemical stability, flexibility, and durability of specially engineered polymeric materials. Because of their unique characteristics and reliable performance, Celgard® membranes are used in high-technology applications across a broad range of industries.

The Separations Products Division also produces and markets membrane-based components and systems for specialty separations applications featuring both Celgard® microporous membranes and Hoechst Nadir® ultrafiltration membranes. These products have applicability in such things as pharmaceutical, biotechnology, food and dairy, beverage, specialty chemicals, and hazardous-waste processing.

Colorants and Surfactants Division

Many of the dyes and organic pigments that color American clothes and home furnishings, the chemicals that make them work, and chemicals used in producing textiles result from the work at the Chesapeake Drive facilities of personnel of the Colorants and Surfactants Division of Hoechst Celanese's Specialty Chemicals Group of New Jersey. Their products are used in virtually every kind of clothing and home-furnishing fabric—from dress to leisurewear, from hosiery to military and career apparel uniforms, from sheets and draperies to carpet and upholstery.

Hoechst Celanese is widely recognized as the industry's most technically innovative and advanced supplier of such products. The corporation is the United States' largest producer of Remazol® fiber reactive dyes for cotton and rayon and of sodium hydrosulphite.

Other Hoechst Celanese dyes for

natural fibers include Hostalan® for wool and Hostavat® and Naphtol® for cotton and rayon. The company makes Samaron® for polyester and Remalan® for nylon fibers. Remazol/Samaron® and Imperon® pigments are produced for printing and padding blends of natural and manufactured fibers.

The Specialty Chemicals Group also develops and manufactures surfactant (surface-active) products and finishing agents broadly used in the textile and fiber industries, as well as for formulating household, industrial, and institutional cleaners and detergents.

The Community

Hoechst Celanese Corporation's contributions and employee volunteers are in the thick of life- and environment-enriching activities in Charlotte/Mecklenburg and the other communities and states in which the firm operates.

The company was a major contributor to the founding of UNC-Charlotte, Charlotte's Spirit Square, Discovery Place, the North Carolina School of Science and Mathematics, and the Charlotte/Mecklenburg Chapter of the National Urban League. Annual United Way contributions from the firm and its employees in the Carolinas and Virginia amount to nearly one million dollars annually.

Charlotte's Johnson C. Smith University, Central Piedmont Community College, Queens College, the YMCA, Alexander Children's Home, and the Charlotte Treatment Center are among the other frequent recipients of a Hoechst Celanese policy calling for "a complete program of community involvement, including contributions and volunteer activities supportive of and responsive to the best interests of employees, their families, and their communities."

The objective is to help make Hoechst Celanese communities more attractive and more rewarding places in which to live, while ensuring that Hoechst Celanese Corporation and its employees are recognized as responsible and desirable citizens.

ICI AMERICAS INC.

The products of ICI Americas Inc., a subsidiary of Imperial Chemical Industries PLC of London, serve virtually every major industry. They include pharmaceuticals, plastics, polyester films, agricultural chemicals, specialty chemicals, paints, polyurethanes, dyes, electronics, advanced composites and ceramics, fibers, security devices, and aerospace components. In all, there are more than 15,000 ICI products sold to 150-plus countries that are made at 220 manufacturing sites in 40 countries. No wonder ICI calls itself a world-class organization.

ICI markets the hypertension drug Tenormin®, which protects the hearts of 3 million people in the United States every day, and the liquid antacid/antiflatulent Mylanta®, which soothes the stomachs of millions of U.S. adults each year. The firm produces the dye that colors one out of every four pairs of blue jeans in the world. It makes the fiber for one-fourth of all the world's computer ribbon. And its agricultural chemicals help grow more food than those of many other companies in the world.

From its Wilmington, Delaware, headquarters ICI Americas directs the activities of about 17,000 people at plant sites, research and development laboratories, agricultural research farms, and sales and technical service offices nationwide. Its products benefit from the extensive research and development capacity of the ICI Group, which uses the knowl-

At the Charlotte plant, ICI manufactures chemicals for the textile industry and conducts research on new dye products and methods.

edge of about 10,000 scientists worldwide and 500 subsidiaries worldwide. In fact, worldwide ICI has filed an average of 16 patents every working day for the past five years.

Charlotte is an active participant in this innovative international business. It is the home of research, manufacturing, and distribution facilities for several ICI products.

The oldest of these facilities is the ICI Charlotte plant. It was constructed in the early 1940s by the Armour Company for processing oils from cotton and rapeseed, and was later purchased by Arnold, Hoffman and Company, Inc., for manufacturing chemicals for the textile and paper industries. Since ICI purchased Arnold, Hoffman in 1950, the firm has expanded the plant's manufacturing capabilities and added a warehouse and research laboratories.

Now the hub of ICI America's activities in the textile market, its 65 employees manufacture specialty chemicals for the textile and the pulp and paper industries, and it makes biocides for the paint industry.

Also housed in the Charlotte plant, the ICI Colors & Fine Chemicals Division operates its Dyes Application Research Laboratory (DARL) for the textile wet-processing industry. There researchers develop new dye products and new methods of application and establish standards of quality for those products. Moreover, the laboratory offers dye and application evaluations for the printing industry, including screen and roller-print applications as well as high-temperature steaming.

The DARL customer service sec-

ICI Americas headquarters in Wilmington, Delaware, is the corporate center of all of its operations in the United States.

tion provides exact laboratory matching of shades and offers customers technical training in all areas of dye application. Its services include telephone support services such as computer shade matching and color analysis for customers and field technical representatives.

Since 1970 ICI Americas has also operated its 100,000-square-foot Charlotte Distribution Center on I-85 North. While it originally distributed only textile chemicals and dyestuffs for the Piedmont textile market, it now provides regional and national services. Among its logistical services are just-in-time inventories, sampling, computerized certificates of analysis, and same-day deliveries.

The distribution center still supplies ICI textile dyes and intermediates, colorants, leather dyes, and dyeing agents to major southeastern textile manufacturing plants. But it also delivers ICI specialty products, including nonchlorine swimming pool chemicals, surfactants, polymer additives, photo chemicals, and silicones; ICI general products such as Saffil®

Aluminum fibers for insulation in industrial furnaces; fluorocarbon solvents for cleaning and degreasing electronic components; and Perspex® plastic for molding bathtubs, whirlpool tubs, and shower stalls.

The Charlotte Distribution Center supplies distributors with ICI agricultural products such as Gramoxone®, Ambush®, Torpedo®, Cymbush®, Karate®, Demon®, Cyclone®, Prelude®, Reflex®, Tornado®, Fusilade®, Weather Blok®, Gro-Safe®, and Talon®. From the center ICI specialty polyester films, Fluon® coating for the wire and cable industry, chemical dispersants for the paper industry, and specialty resin coatings for automotive parts, wood, plastic, and metal are sent to their industrial users.

In 1986 ICI acquired The Glidden Company and assumed ownership of the most recent addition to the ICI Americas family in Charlotte—the 16.5-acre Glidden Industrial Coatings facility, whose 150 employees manufacture, test, and sell powder coatings for factory applications. Unlike liquid solvent paints,

This ICI warehouse stores products manufactured in Charlotte for distribution to U.S. customers.

which were used in the past on products such as appliances, automobiles, and metal machinery, these new-generation ICI acrylic and polyester finishes do not pollute the air during application. The colored powders are electrostatically attracted to the metal and then baked on, to form a hard, durable finish. Acrylic powders are primarily used on appliances, while several different types of polyester powder coatings are used for industrial equipment, automobiles, outdoor furniture, and other products that must withstand the effects of outdoor weather and corrosive chemicals.

For each of these ICI Americas manufacturing, research, and distribution facilities, Charlotte provides an excellent distribution site and a high quality of life for employees. As a result, Charlotte is an important part of ICI Americas as it continues to become an even greater world-class family of companies.

E.I. DU PONT DE NEMOURS AND COMPANY

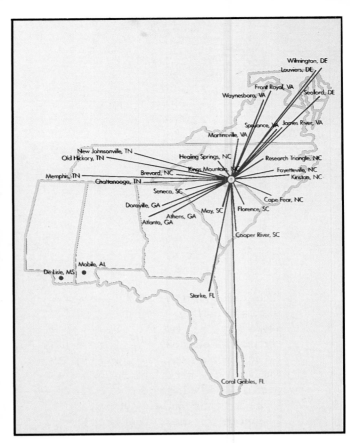

When young Eleuthere Irenee du Pont emigrated from his native France to the United States in 1800, he soon spotted the need for quality black powder in his adopted country. As an apprentice to the distinguished chemist Antoine Lavoisier, du Pont was well tutored in modern scientific method and the craft of making black powder. He believed he could make better powder than was available from domestic mills.

In 1802 E.I. du Pont de Nemours and Company was founded on the banks of the Brandywine River near Wilmington, Delaware. From that simple beginning has evolved one of the largest, most diversified international corporations on the modern industrial scene.

During its first century the Du Pont Company remained essentially a black powder manufacturer. Then, in 1902, its centennial year, Du Pont management made the decision to diversify by developing new products through research. Its laboratory in nearby New Jersey was among the first research facilities operated by any corporation in this country. A year later an experimental station was established on a 152-acre site on a bluff overlooking the Brandywine River just downstream from the original powderworks.

The decision to undertake a formal research program was pivotal in the firm's development, transforming Du Pont into a science-based company and giving birth to a tradition of discovery and diversification that continues to the present. Now nearing its 200th anniversary, Du Pont is the prototype for the global corporation that is expected to be preeminent in the twenty-first century.

Early research concentrated on ways to expand the company's existing explosives business, but the focus soon included a variety of chemical processes unrelated to explosives. For example, to extend the firm's Fabrikoid synthetic leather business, a 1910 acquisition and Du Pont's first important venture outside the explosives business, research into other synthetic fabrics was undertaken.

In 1921 Du Pont began producing a European discovery called Fibersilk, a man-made fiber known today as rayon. The company's commercial introduction of nylon in 1938 marked the beginning of the man-made textile industry worldwide, and Du Pont has since become the world's largest and most diversified supplier of man-made fibers. In the United States and around the world, Lycra spandex, Dacron polyester, Orlon acrylic, and Antron nylon are household names.

ABOVE: Du Pont's Charlotte site provides support services to its customers by serving as an extension of its various locations and by offering responsive, competitive resources and services that add value to its competitive position.

LEFT: More than 800 employees, including 260 Du Ponters, reside in these four buildings that make up Du Pont's Fairview Road site, approximately 200,000 square feet of space. From here seven different departments serve primarily the company's southeastern sites and businesses.

Today, largely withdrawn from explosives, Du Pont has more than 90 other major businesses. The company's products and services number in the thousands and can be found in most major market sectors—from agriculture to coal, construction, electronics, fibers, health care, imaging systems, petroleum, and transportation. Du Pont has manufacturing and processing operations in some 40 countries on six continents. The company continues to develop and produce "better things for better living" in an unending quest to improve the quality of life for people worldwide.

A dynamic synergy was created between the city of Charlotte and the Du Pont Company during the 1940s, when the firm first began operations there. Du Pont's mission in Charlotte then, as today, was to provide support services for its customers by serving as an extension of

their locations and to offer those customers responsive, competitive resources that add value to their competitive positions.

In the early days in Charlotte, the Du Pont Fibers Department conducted a marketing operation in uptown Charlotte, and the Organic Chemicals Department ran a testing laboratory on Old Steele Creek Road. By 1969 the Fibers operation had moved to the current Fairview Road site. In 1982 the Engineering and Fibers departments joined forces to form a regional office on Carmel Road, which three years later was also moved to the Fairview location.

As the needs of its customers have become more complex and diverse, Du Pont has kept pace, aided in significant measure by the growth and development of the city. Du Pont management believes the dynamism of this rapidly growing area contributes to the operation's effectiveness and value to its customers. An international airport and expanded airline service provide easy access to customers across the region, indeed, across the Atlantic. The increase in excellent meeting facilities and cultural and educational opportunities also have contributed to the vitality and creativity of Du Pont's employees.

Today some 300 people are at work in Du Pont's Fibers, Engineering, Materials and Logistics, Finance, Automotive Products, Information Systems, Polymer Products, and Medical Products departments, which primarily serve the company's southeastern sites and businesses. Approximately 500 contract employees provide support in the areas of engineering, finance, computer systems, reprographic, and secretarial and clerical services.

Four buildings on Fairview Road house the 260 Du Ponters and the 500 contract employees in 200,000 square feet of space. Another 20 Du Ponters work at the company's paint warehouse on Interstate Street; 15 employees staff a laboratory on Old Steele Creek Road; and approximately 15 Du Ponters work out of their homes. Conoco Inc., a wholly owned Du Pont subsidiary, manages a 40,000-square-foot warehouse for investment recovery on Old Steele Creek Road and handles product transportation for several of the local Du Pont departments.

Du Pont is dedicated to certain principles that have been hallmarks since its founding and are the cornerstones of its exemplary reputation. The safety of its employees, neighbors, and customers is a matter of the highest priority at Du Pont, and it is the firm's long-standing policy that no product will be offered unless it can be manufactured, distributed, stored, used, and eventually disposed of safely. One outgrowth of this policy is a safety record that is among the best of any manufacturing company. In fact a Du Pont employee is many times safer at work than home.

From the outset Du Pont has also been committed to an unending quest for quality. The reliability of its gunpowder and explosives won the firm wide acceptance among the pioneers who pushed the American frontier beyond the Appalachian Mountains, giving birth to the legend that the West was won with Du Pont powder. That quest continues as the company seeks always to make products and provide services of the highest quality.

For almost two centuries the firm has prospered. One key to its success and longevity has been faithful adherence to these and other principles. At the same time, Du Pont has remained flexible, adapting its philosophies, strategies, and businesses to keep pace with a rapidly changing and increasingly complex world economic, social, political, and industrial environment.

THE PNEUMAFIL GROUP

In 1946 Hans C. Bechtler, the head of a Swiss engineering firm, founded a unique new business for the U.S. textile industry. Headquartered in a former machine shop in Charlotte, Pneumafil Corporation first offered U.S. spinning companies a vacuum system for collecting broken ends and improving productivity. Such a system was widely used in Europe but had yet to be introduced in the United States. Charles R. "Pete" Harris soon joined the company as its first president.

Within a few years of the company's opening, the Pneumafil System was considered standard equipment on spinning frames. The firm's research and development professionals were also developing lint- and dust-control systems for a wide variety of other textile machines, and Pneumafil was expanding its areas of expertise into other industries.

This was the beginning of The Pneumafil Group, which now consists of three very different companies—Pneumafil Corporation, Luwa Corporation, and Southeastern Metal Products Incorporated. Under the leadership of chairman and chief

A Luwa Corporation Process Division evaporation system installation.

executive officer Bob Barbee and vice-chairman Andreas Bechtler, each of the three operates with its own identity and includes several specialized divisions. But all of them support Pneumafil's one central goal: to meet the specific needs of customers with high-quality products and service.

The original company, Pneumafil Corporation, today encompasses four separate divisions. Its Textile Division still offers the industry's premier lint- and dust-control systems as well as total mill air-conditioning systems. Its revolutionary Automatic Panel Filter has quickly gained wide acceptance for its compactness, efficiency, and simplicity. And as the leading total-mill air conditioning source, its systems provide the precise humidity and temperature controls that are required by the modern textile plant.

The company's expertise in filtration led to the formation of its Industrial Air Filters Division, which developed the reverse air bag filter for collecting wood particles from the air in the woodworking and furniture manufacturing industries, a process that allows companies to meet stringent OSHA standards. With that beginning, the division has become involved in coal, chemical, fumes, pharmaceutical, cement, rock products, and general industrial applications.

The Specialty Air Products Division is another outgrowth that manufactures filtration systems on a worldwide basis for gas turbine intakes and steam turbines. It also manufactures special humidifiers for automotive plants.

During the Korean war, in re-

A Pneumafil Corporation Metal Products Division engineered cabinet for meeting exacting government and military specifications.

A Pneumafil Corporation Textile Division Automatic Filter Panel for efficiently controlling dust and lint.

sponse to a need for quality metal fabrication work, Pneumafil created what became the Metal Products Division to manufacture the cabinetry required for military electronic equipment. For more than three decades this division has continued to earn its reputation as a reliable producer of engineered cabinetry for government and military use. Its custom products are widely known to meet the exacting specifications necessary for the protection of electronic equipment located on ships, aircraft, and military bases.

By the 1980s the Pneumafil name no longer covered the diversity of the group's many products. In 1984 Pneumafil purchased Luwa Corporation from its Swiss parent, Luwa AG. Today Luwa's three divisions are an outgrowth of its sale of European high-tech equipment. Luwa's Process Division is widely recognized as a world leader in thin-film evaporation technology for major manufacturers of chemicals, food, specialty polymers, and pharmaceuticals. The Process Division also markets granulation systems to those industries and others. It is the sole North American licensee and distributor for the Buss AG Process Technology division of Basel, Switzerland, and Fuji Paudal, Ltd., of Osaka, Japan.

A Pneumafil Corporation Southeastern Metal Products Division electronic enclosure for a variety of industrial uses.

Luwa's Fluid Systems Division began as an exclusive distributor for high-performance Swiss-built Maag pumps, which provide increased quality and productivity for polymer producers and extruders. As the division's expertise in this field has grown, it has expanded to also offer specialized valves and controls for the extrusion and polymer markets.

When Luwa AG developed a process by which it could draw metal into a very deep bowl shape and began manufacturing Euro-style sinks, Luwa Corporation created a Builder Products Division for their distribution. Today the division offers a variety of Euro-style sinks and faucets, mirrors, and cooktops made by a number of outstanding European manufacturers. Its products are sold to home owners through an extensive national distribution network involving kitchen-bath showrooms, architect specifications, and custom home builders.

At the beginning of 1986 Pneumafil added still another member to its expanding family of companies when it purchased Southeastern Metal Products Inc., a contract manufacturer of precision stampings and custom metal products. Southeastern, unlike Pneumafil's specialized Metal Products Division, produces a standard line of high-quality enclosures for electronic equipment used in a variety of industries. At Southeastern's 90,000-square-foot Charlotte plant, it performs virtually every function in metalworking, from fabrication and welding to finishing and assembly.

As each of these new companies and divisions has become part of The Pneumafil Group, it has joined in supporting the firm's purpose, stated in the company's 1954 slogan: "Pneumafil just doesn't happen to be good. . . it's made so on purpose." In each Pneumafil company, employees pledge to "provide supe-

A Luwa Corporation Builder Products Division high-tech, European-style work center and faucet.

rior customer satisfaction through superior quality products and associated services at competitive prices—best value, and listen to customers to understand their needs and treat them in a professional and responsive manner."

At the same time The Pneumafil Group and its employees are committed to their record as major contributors to Charlotte's arts organizations and the United Way. By supporting a strong community as well as the quality of its products, Pneumafil's employees are continuing to support the growth of its diverse family of companies.

DEXTER PLASTICS

Although Dexter Plastics is a relative youngster on the American corporate scene, it is nonetheless a prosperous, rapidly growing division in a company with a distinguished heritage of more than 200 years devoted to providing the American and international marketplaces with quality products.

The Dexter Corporation of Windsor Locks, Connecticut, has come a long way since Seth Dexter started his sawmill in 1767, branching out a year later into cloth dressing and wool scouring. By the 1830s the business was further diversified, when Charles Haskell Dexter began papermaking experiments that eventually led the company into nonwovens and related specialty fiber materials.

But it was under the leadership of David Linwood Coffin, who traces his lineage to the founder, that sales of the *Fortune* 500 company's specialty materials began to skyrocket, climbing from $9.4 million in 1958, the year Coffin became chief executive officer, to the best-ever year of 1988, when sales hit $827 million. Dexter now operates in 16 countries on 5 continents and has 31 major production facilities, providing specialty materials to a broad range of industrial, commercial, and consumer markets.

With an eye to the future, Dexter management launched, in October 1985, its two-year New Directions program, which led to combining one previously acquired and two newly acquired specialty formulated plastics companies to create Dexter Plastics. Those acquisitions were Alpha Chemicals & Plastics Corp. of Newark, New Jersey, which gave Dexter entry into the thermoplastics business through its polyvinyl chloride compounding facilities; Research Polymers International of Grand Prairie, Texas, which launched the company into the compounding of

Lawrence P. Doyle, president of the Dexter Plastics Division, which is headquartered at Dexter Plastics Pineville location.

thermoplastic polyolefins; and Rutland Plastics Inc. of Pineville, North Carolina, where Dexter Plastics is headquartered.

Samuel F. Rutland founded Rutland Plastics in Charlotte in 1962 to produce vinyl plastisols for industrial applications. The company later expanded its product line to include urethane elastomers, epoxy and adhesive plastisols, compounded PVC, and unique colored plastisols for use in the silk-screen-printing industry. Rutland technical expertise in formulating products for air-filter gaskets, sealants for fuel and oil filters, and coatings for fabrics and metals also added significantly to the company's sales. Says Rutland, "Our staff of chemists and engineers have always taken pride in our reputation for having the best technology, quality, and customer service of anyone in the business."

In 1974 Rutland expanded manufacturing capability by adding a second plant in nearby Pineville to produce rigid and flexible polyvinyl chloride formulations. The original plastisol plant also was relocated to Pineville from Charlotte in May 1986, when a new plant and corporate offices were completed on Rodney Street.

Sam Rutland recalls the time he and his employees were preparing to observe the firm's 25th anniversary. "It's a mark of achievement for a company to have 25 successful years, and we had planned a gala affair to celebrate—but we didn't quite make it. The Dexter Corporation acquired Rutland Plastics on the last day of December in 1986."

The PVC Compounding business management team includes (standing, from left) Joseph Groder, Samuel Harwell, Reese Sumrall, Michael Vaden, and Gil Christopher.

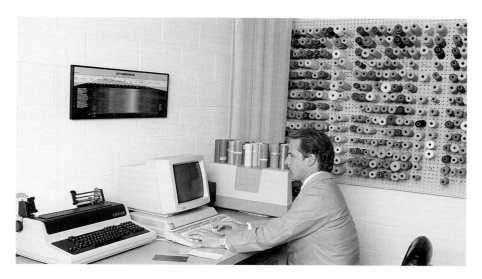

Dexter PVC resins provide both color and light stability as a coating for yarns supplied to weavers of exterior use fabrics.

After the acquisition by Dexter, Rutland notes, "25 years didn't seem like such a long time, at least not in comparison with Dexter's 220-plus years in business. We were suddenly a 'new' company once again." Rutland adds that although The Dexter Corporation is an old company—the oldest listed on the New York Stock Exchange—in many important ways it is new: "It's new in its technology, new in its products, new in its forward thinking, and it's filled with a zest for accomplishment." Sam Rutland continues to be active with the new Dexter Plastics businesses.

Dexter Plastics, one of three operating divisions organized around the parent company's core plastic businesses, is one of the five largest compounders of engineered blends and alloys in the $30-billion plastic materials industry in this country.

The Pineville facility employs approximately 125 people and has 150,000 square feet of manufacturing space, with the capability of producing 100 million pounds of polyvinyl chloride compounds and plastisols annually. Combined capacity for Dexter Plastics' six manufacturing plants, which have a total of 600,000 square feet of space and 550 employees, is 250 to 300 mil-

lion pounds of product annually.

Lawrence P. Doyle, who became president of Dexter Plastics in August 1987, states, "Over the next three to five years, we expect growth of 5 to 10 percent in polyvinyl chloride specialty compounds, 20- to

25-percent growth in elastomeric thermoplastic olefins, as well as significant growth in engineered blends and alloys."

Those chemical terms perhaps have little meaning to the average person, but it is also probable that not a single home in America today is without one or more products manufactured in whole or in part with one of Dexter Plastics' products.

Among the firm's many trademarks is ONTEX™, a diversified fam-

ily of high-performance thermoplastic alloys used in interior and exterior automotive body components—bumpers and trim, for example. There is also SUPER-KLEEN™, a family of flexible and semirigid compounds proven to be absolutely harmless to human cells that are ideally suited for the manufacture of child-related products—teethers and pacifiers, for example—as well as food and beverage applications and medical devices.

Doyle notes that his company's choice of the Charlotte-Pineville area for its headquarters has proven to be a good one. "This location is readily accessible to the growing plastic-processing industry in the Mid-South and to the North American car market centered in Detroit,

Alpha™ flexible PVC materials are nationally recognized in the medical industry.

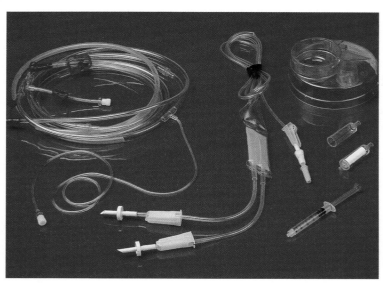

where we now have an Automotive Technical Center. The area's international airport, good business climate, and low energy costs are definite pluses that fit perfectly with our plans for growth over the next several years."

Look for Dexter Plastics' growth to include expanded testing and research laboratories and additional manufacturing facilities—not only in this country, but in Europe and the Far East as well.

OKUMA OF AMERICA

The United States headquarters and manufacturing operations for the Japanese-owned Okuma of America is located on a 30-acre site at 12200 Steele Creek Road in southwest Charlotte.

Celebrating the opening of a new Charlotte plant with glasses of Japanese wine is not all that unusual these days, considering the recent trend toward Asian cuisine. But when guests toasted a new manufacturing plant with sake on November 18, 1987, it reflected much more than gourmet tastes. The occasion was the opening of the first Okuma manufacturing plant not on Japanese soil, and the sake symbolized a new union between East and West.

Okuma Machinery Works Ltd., one of Japan's oldest and most respected firms, has been making metal-cutting machine tools for more than 90 years. Today the company is the world leader in the manufacture of computerized numerically controlled (CNC) machine tools and systems, with worldwide sales of more than $700 million.

In 1984 Okuma of Japan established a sales and marketing operation on Long Island, New York, to sell and service imported CNC lathes, machining centers, and grinders to the North American market.

Following three years of highly successful operations, it was decided to search for an American production site to complement Okuma's

manufacturing facility in the city of Oguchi, Japan, where the firm employs 2,000 workers.

Okuma found what it was looking for in Charlotte. The new

Okuma plant, located on a 30-acre site on Steele Creek Road in southwest Charlotte, contains 175,000 square feet of production, design, and administrative space and features a showroom for displaying and demonstrating its many machine tool products. The complex also houses the sales and service arm of the company, which moved to Charlotte from Long Island, New York, in 1988. U.S. Okuma operations employ about 250 people in Charlotte, of which 40 are Japanese and 210 are American.

Though the company's products may be unfamiliar to the general public, they are used in virtually every industry in the world, from automobile manufacturers to aerospace and defense contractors. Well known for quality and state-of-the-art technology, Okuma produces a wide range of machine tools, from lathes, machining centers, grinders, and CNC systems to machining cells and flexible manufacturing systems.

Okuma is unique from its competitors in that it makes both the ma-

The Japanese and American presidents of Okuma: Mickey Iwata and John D. Hendrick.

chine tool and the technically matched computer control that operates it. The firm can also integrate several machines, work-handling devices, industrial robots, material transporters, and control systems into a single, unified manufacturing system that is completely automated.

In 1988, with its Charlotte plant in full gear, Okuma enjoyed North American sales of $167 million—up from $134 million the previous year. The Charlotte plant ships 60 machines each month and anticipates a rate of 100 to 120 per month by 1991. The company now has about 16 percent of the American lathe market and 5 percent of the machining center market.

A network of 30 distributor organizations provides local sales and service throughout North America, Mexico, and South America.

Okuma's reputation has been built on a constant search for perfection by upgrading the performance, quality, and reliability of its products.

The Japanese members of the

CNC lathes are completed on a 12-station assembly line that balances the workload and disciplines the production schedule in delivering a finished machine every four hours.

Okuma team in this country are proud of their company's distinguished heritage—a pride that is now shared by their American colleagues. This combination of cultures, peoples, and talents is best symbolized by the Okuma logo: two pieces of metal conjoined in a perfect union.

At this Japanese-American company, all employees are members of a team working in harmony to achieve the common shared goal of excellence.

The people of Okuma believe this union is the company's major strength. One example of Okuma's confidence in American management is the appointment of John Hendrick as the new president of Okuma Machinery, Inc. Hendrick is one of only a handful of American executives who run Japanese-owned companies in the United States.

Though Okuma's Charlotte plant is demonstrating Yankee ingenuity it has borrowed some Japanese management practices. The company has instituted several long-term employee benefit programs and plans to implement others, including student exchanges between American and Japanese families.

As Okuma's Charlotte facility moves toward an almost totally American work force, the cooperation of people working together forges a bond that guarantees the firm's American-made products are in the best tradition of Okuma Machinery Works of Oguchi, Japan.

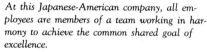

SANDOZ CHEMICALS CORPORATION

In 1886 Edoward Sandoz, a businessman; Dr. Alfred Kern, a dyestuff chemist; and 10 workmen began their labors in a small dye-manufacturing plant in Basel, Switzerland. They were the nucleus of what has become the worldwide group of Sandoz Ltd. companies.

The American chapter of the Sandoz story began during the post-World War I economic and industrial boom. Wool, silk, cotton, and leather processors wanted unusual dyes to enhance and brighten their products.

In 1919 the Sandoz Chemical Works opened for business in a tiny office in Lower Manhattan, marking the beginning of a continuing series of innovations in the science of color application—innovations that have helped make virtually every color in the rainbow available to industry. After maintaining its headquarters in the metropolitan New York area for more than 60 years, Sandoz Color and Chemicals moved its offices and laboratories to the Southeast. At about the same time Sandoz acquired the Sodyeco Division of Martin Marietta, and the two units were merged in July 1984 to create Sandoz Chemicals Corporation.

The merger was a reaffirmation of the commitment of these two industry leaders to provide reliable, top-quality products to their dye- and chemical-consuming markets. Charlotte, formerly a district office, became Sandoz Chemicals' headquarters. Kenneth L. Brewton, Jr., who earlier had spent several years in Charlotte as field sales manager, returned to the city to serve the company as president and chief executive officer.

Says Brewton, "The decision to make Charlotte our headquarters was based in part on the fact that the cost of doing business in the northeastern United States was becoming increasingly prohibitive and on the fact that being in Charlotte put us closer to our customers in the textile industry, which is one of our biggest markets."

An aerial view of Sandoz Chemicals' headquarters facility. The Charlotte skyline is in the background.

The firm's employees work at its Charlotte facilities on Monroe Road, which house the company's central offices and customer service laboratories, as well as other support groups that serve the paper, metals, coatings, plastics, household, and personal products industries, and the long-standing textile industry accounts. Today Sandoz Chemicals offers the widest range of dye classes in the United States and an extensive line of specialty chemicals, pigments, and intermediates.

The Mount Holly, North Carolina, plant near Charlotte is one of the major American Sandoz manufacturing units, with eight separate buildings totaling some 400,000 square feet of production space. Sulphur dyes, vat dyes, and specialty chemicals are the main products of the plant, which contains state-of-the-art equipment. Its industrial waste-treatment programs are among the most sophisticated in the country. Other Sandoz manufacturing plants are located in Martin, South Carolina, and in Fair Lawn, New Jersey. "Unless someone is directly involved in one of the industries we service," notes Brewton, "chances are they'll have little or no knowledge of the products we make." Chances are excellent, however, that most Americans come into daily contact with items that have been manufactured with products supplied by Sandoz. For example: Sandoz products play an important role in every step of the complex textile preparation, dyeing, printing, and finishing processes. The Sandoz textile laboratory evaluates dyes, fluorescent whitening agents, chemical auxiliaries, and preparation and finishing agents for their ability to enhance fabric quality and marketability. Sandoz chemists have developed a broad range of colorants and additives used in the manufacture of plastics and synthetic fibers.

The paper industry also has come to rely on Sandoz for such developments as a dyeing system for the continuous coloring of paper, and the company's fluorescent whitening

An exterior view of Sandoz Chemicals Research and Development Center, which opened in the fourth quarter of 1988. Staffed with senior-grade scientists and equipped with state-of-the-art facilities, the new unit will spearhead dye and specialty chemical product development.

agents are considered the industry standard for producing long-lasting whites on all grades of paper. Sandoz paper specialists are knowledgeable in most facets of the paper-manufacturing process and often work directly in the paper mills to solve production problems.

The ink industry is another important market for Sandoz colorants, which are used in printing inks for lithography, metal deco, aluminum, and polyethylene packaging. Sandoz colorants also are widely used for producing inks to print tissue and paper towel products.

Sandoz pigments and ultraviolet absorbers are used in automotive finishes, and Sandoz dyes and chemicals are used in a host of consumer and military aluminum products. The company also markets a broad range of organic intermediates for use in dye, photographic, pharmaceutical, plastics, and agricultural chemical-processing industries.

Sandoz products also play an important role in the manufacture of plastics, and Sandoz dyes and auxiliary chemicals add color, softness, and washability to leather products. And the company manufactures and markets a broad spectrum of chemi-

cal auxiliaries for such highly specialized applications as corrosion inhibitors for metals; high-purity, state-of-the-art materials for the electronics industry; and colorants and other products for such diverse applications as detergents, personal care products, and household cleaners.

On January 19, 1988, Kenneth Brewton announced the expansion and relocation of the firm's research and development facilities to The Mallard Creek Center in University Research Park. "This project," Brewton says, "demonstrates Sandoz' commit-

ment to both the Charlotte community and to our own further development of quality dyes and specialty chemicals, particularly for the American textile industry."

The center includes state-of-the-art equipment, the latest computer technology, and a staff of highly qualified personnel, including several Ph.D.s, to meet the company's long-term research goals. "The chamber of commerce was a great help in that Charlotte is an excellent city in which to operate a facility of this type. More important, the chamber proved to us that Charlotte is the most cost-effective site," says Brewton. He also notes, "The center is an important demonstration of our ongoing commitment to providing the technical expertise, quality products, and manufacturing know-how our customers throughout the United States have come to expect from Sandoz."

An aerial view of Sandoz Chemicals' Mount Holly plant. Situated on the Charlotte side of the Catawba River, the facility has more than 400,000 square feet of manufacturing space. Dyes and specialty chemicals are the main products produced at this site.

HOMELITE/TEXTRON

Today the Homelite Division of Textron Inc. is a leading force in the field of portable outdoor power equipment. A totally integrated company, it has a heritage and commitment to the consumer, agricultural, and construction equipment markets. The company operates worldwide and is backed up by the most expansive sales and distribution network in the industry.

The name Homelite and its product line are as well known in the Fiji Islands as in Peoria, Illinois. That's because Homelite products are sold throughout continents, not just countries. From North and, South America, Europe and Asia, Australia and Africa, Homelite has an office, plant, warehouse, or distribution outlet somewhere. A large sales organization supported by more than 3,000 office and factory employees backs up Homelite's efforts worldwide.

With the broadest array of portable outdoor power products in the industry, Homelite has a product to fill most any need. Products run the gamut from an innovative lightweight hedge trimmer for home-owner use

to a state-of-the-art chain saw designed for use on the farm or a heavy-duty diesel-powered water pump for light-industrial applications.

The company has 19 categories of products with 155 different models, each designed for specific applications at home, on the farm, or at the industrial work site. Products range from lawn and riding mowers, string trimmers/brushcutters, power blowers, tillers, chain saws, water pumps, generators, pressure washers, and a wide line of construction equip-

ment products.

Homelite has four manufacturing plants in the United States, plus warehouse distribution and parts facilities that cover the globe. And Service Schools provide full factory-trained personnel in more than 12,000 authorized service centers.

The synergy of Homelite/Textron is responsible for its successful presence on the world scene. The company fills an important worldwide need and responsibility in the field of outdoor power equipment.

Homelite's broad array of portable outdoor power products run the gamut from an innovative lightweight hedge trimmer for home-owner use to a state-of-the-art chain saw designed for use on the farm.

198

VERBATIM CORPORATION

Founded in Sunnyvale, California, 20 years ago, Verbatim today is a Charlotte-based international corporation with a reputation for product innovation and uncompromising quality.

From the very beginning Verbatim has been at the forefront of the flexible data-storage media industry. Its first two products—full-size and mini-size data-storage cassettes—market firsts, were followed in the 1970s and 1980s by pioneering developments in 8-inch, 5.25-inch, and 3.5-inch data-storage disks. The Verbatim DataLife™ and DataLifePlus™ brands are valued by users of computer systems using removable media who demand faithful data storage.

Verbatim chose Charlotte in late 1982 as the site for its second U.S. manufacturing facility. The sprawling manufacturing site, located north of the city in University Park, began production of the company's magnetic storage products in 1983.

The Eastman Kodak Company acquired Verbatim in 1985 and with the added resources of Kodak, Verbatim continued and expanded its role as an industry leader. In 1987 Verbatim moved its company headquarters from California to Charlotte, which is now the home to 2,500 employees worldwide, including 400 people who live in the Piedmont. The corporate headquarters serves a global manufacturing and marketing network located in the United States, Ireland, Australia, Brazil, Mexico, Japan, and India. Verbatim sales offices are located in key market areas in the United States, Europe, Latin America, Asia, Australia, and Japan.

Verbatim's engineers and research scientists are developing the next generation of data-storage devices, which will use thermo-magneto-

Since its inception Verbatim has been at the forefront of the flexible data-storage media industry.

optical technology. This technology is the basis for a 3.5-inch erasable optical drive and disk system, which is nearing market introduction.

So important is this technology that Verbatim, Kodak, the state of North Carolina, the University of North Carolina at Charlotte, and Central Piedmont Community College have formed a task force to develop educational curricula and expand the transfer of this exciting, new technology from the research laboratories into the educational systems.

Verbatim has added to the manu-

Charlotte is home to Verbatim's corporate headquarters and U.S. manufacturing.

facturing, scientific, and educational resources of the state and the community. It lends a stimulating international flavor to the city; Verbatim employees and their families from many overseas locations come to Charlotte to work and live. With an eye to the future, Verbatim expects to continue as an industry leader and innovator in the development, manufacture, and service of world-class data-storage products.

FRITO-LAY, INC.

A young ice cream salesman named Elmer Doolin stopped for lunch in a small San Antonio cafe one day in 1932. While he waited for his five-cent sandwich to be prepared, Doolin noticed a plain package of corn chips on the counter. On a whim he spent another nickel for the corn chips, a decision that would change the course of his life.

Inside the package was a tasty corn-dough snack, which Doolin decided he would like to produce and sell. He bought the recipe for the corn chips, the Fritos brand name, 19 retail accounts, and the equipment he needed to make the chips—a converted, hand-operated potato ricer—and began turning out corn chips in his mother's kitchen. Plant capacity in those early days was about 10 pounds an hour, with daily sales running from $8 to $10, for a profit of about $2.

That same year another young entrepreneur, Herman W. Lay, also was starting his own business, selling the potato chips products of an Atlanta company. In 1939 Lay, who had become one of the firm's major

distributors, accepted an offer to buy the organization, which he renamed H.W. Lay & Company.

The two firms joined forces in 1961, becoming Frito-Lay, Inc., an organization with a basic business philosophy: Make the best product possible, sell it at a fair price to make a fair profit, and make service a fundamental part of doing business. Today the company's products, Lay's®, Ruffles®-brand potato chips, Fritos®-brand corn chips, Doritos®-brand tortilla chips, and Chee*tos®-brand cheese-flavored snacks, are among the most widely recognized products on the American scene.

Since 1972, when Frito-Lay began operating in North Carolina, the firm's retail sales have increased from $400 million to $3.5 billion annually. In a company noted for the quality of its management and the efficiency of its operations, Frito-Lay's Charlotte and Salisbury facilities have achieved enviable records.

The Charlotte operation, with approximately 500 employees, is one of the company's most technology

Frito-Lay continues its tradition of leadership in community involvement programs by initiating the Charlotte, North Carolina, area's first Adopt-A-School relationship. The Charlotte plant formally adopted Nations Ford Elementary School and its 550 students during a ceremony on November 17, 1988. Activities include tutoring, lunch pals, art/entertainment, computer literacy, and plant tours. Approximately 40 of Frito-Lay's employees invest their time weekly in these activities, which are designed to enhance the student's social, emotional, and academic development. The relationship is an excellent example of the commitment that Charlotte area businesses have made to support public education.

driven and efficient facilities, producing some 70 million pounds of product annually. In 1986 Charlotte employees won the highest honor the firm bestows on its plants, the Leadership Award. Charlotte was both the first of the company's 37 plants nationwide to work one million hours without a lost-time accident and the first plant to repeat the accomplishment. In total, Charlotte employees worked approximately three years in a manufacturing environment without a single accident requiring an employee to miss work, a record of which the employees are jus-

Teamwork is at the heart of many successful United Way campaign, education, and involvement programs at the work place—everyone working together creates a winning effort. In Charlotte, North Carolina, for example, Frito-Lay, Inc., employees contributed $115,670 to the United Way of Central Carolinas, Inc. The company's motto is "The United Way and Frito-Lay, partners in caring."

tifiably proud.

Frito-Lay's Salisbury plant employs approximately 100 people, and of the plant's 80 hourly technicians, one-quarter have worked there since it opened in 1972. The plant consistently produces 16 million pounds of snacks each year, which averages out to about 300,000 bags every day. Salisbury plant employees, too, are proud of their record of producing and distributing 100 percent of their orders on time for five consecutive years—the only one of the company's United States plants that can make that boast.

In total Frito-Lay employs approximately 1,100 North Carolinians in manufacturing, sales, or distribution, more than any other snack manufacturer in the area. The Charlotte and Salisbury facilities produce a combined total of 85 million pounds of product yearly, and more than 300,000 cases of Frito-Lay snacks leave the two plants weekly for distri-

bution by the company's sales force in retail stores throughout the southeastern United States and along the Atlantic seaboard. In North Carolina, 400 sales personnel stock the snacks directly on the retailer's shelf, and the first non-Frito-Lay person to touch the snack bag is the customer.

To Frito-Lay's management, the company's success can be explained with a single word: people. The firm's achievements are the result of the individual men and women who have worked hard to make a difference, not only on the job but also in their communities.

For example, Joe Collins, manager of the Charlotte plant, is active in Charlotte community affairs, serving on the boards of WTVI Public Television, the Better Business Bureau, the Charlotte Chamber of Commerce, the Manufacturer's Council, Belmont Abbey College, and the Carolinas Minority Suppliers Development Council.

The community involvement of Frito-Lay employees isn't limited to top management, however. Anna Fenno and Jerry Mitchell teach business skills to local Junior Achievement members. Jeanne Oliver was a volunteer for the four-month Ramesses exhibit at the Mint Museum, and Virginia Gregory is on the board of directors of the Caroli-

nas Minority Development Supplier Council.

The company, too, is deeply involved in community affairs. In 1988 Frito-Lay spent more than $950,000 with minority vendors in the Carolinas, but the firm's concern for minority businesses is not limited to contracts. Frito-Lay sponsors marketing seminars for minority business owners and lends its management expertise to the Larry Danner Machine Shop through the Adopt-A-Vendor program. The company also has "adopted" Nations Ford Elementary School, a partnership that has proved rewarding and worthwhile not only to the students and teachers but to the employees of Frito-Lay as well.

Frito-Lay, Inc., employees actively support some 20 organizations and associations with purposes as diverse as athletics, history, medicine, and the performing arts. The University of North Carolina at Charlotte, the Charlotte Symphony, Spirit Square, Discovery Place, WDAV Public Radio, the American Heart Association, United Cerebral Palsy, Carolina Opera, To Life Counseling, and the United Way are among those organizations that have benefited from the financial resources, time, and talent of Frito-Lay's active, committed employees.

BARNHARDT MANUFACTURING COMPANY

In 1989 the automated bleaching facility of Barnhardt Manufacturing Company in Charlotte will prepare 12 million pounds of cotton for use in surgical dressings and cotton-tipped cosmetic applicators.

In the nine decades since this family-owned business was formed by Thomas M. Barnhardt in 1900, it has become one of the nation's largest manufacturers of bleached cotton. It was first established in response to a need: to use the quantities of unbleached cotton fibers that were too short for use in textiles. Barnhardt Manufacturing Company used them to produce layered batting for quilts, buggy seats, and horse collars.

Since inception it has repeatedly developed new products and organized new subsidiaries to meet the needs of a growing industrial country. Now Barnhardt's products include nonwoven cotton filters that remove impurities from liquid acrylics, acetate, and rayon before they are made into synthetic yarns. The firm also processes polyester fibers into batting and cushions, for use in

furniture, at four plants in Charlotte, Hickory, and High Point, North Carolina, and Ocala, Florida.

Barnhardt's subsidiary, Carolina Absorbent Cotton Company, formed in 1930, is a major supplier of cotton products for hospitals, nursing homes, surgical supplies, pharmaceutical houses, and beauty supply houses throughout the United States. Its products range from surgical sponges and fillers for pharmaceutical bottles to cotton coils for use by beauty salons. It also distributes a wide range of hospital textile products, including sheets, towels, draperies, and gowns for patients and operating room personnel.

Another subsidiary, Richmond Dental Cotton Company, which Barnhardt purchased and moved from Niagara Falls, New York, in 1947, manufactures cotton rolls, balls, gauze, and pellets. It distributes them with dental tissues and swabs

---

Barnhardt Manufacturing Company dates back nine decades, and today is one of the nation's largest manufacturers of bleached cotton.

to dental supply companies in the United States and many other parts of the world.

Through a third subsidiary, North Carolina Foam Industries, in Mt. Airy, Barnhardt manufactures foam cushions for furniture in about 30 different densities and 100 different degrees of softness. Each cushion must be formed to exactly fit the furniture manufacturer's specifications for size, shape, and feel. It may be simply buffed or wrapped in synthetic batting and covered with muslin, and it may also be shaped for use in mattresses.

Each of the firms in this modern diverse collection of businesses has grown from the one-room plant and office cottage Tom Barnhardt established on what is now the site of the company's bleaching plant and headquarters. Behind his desk hung a sign that said: "Do not criticize unless you can remedy." He continuously looked for ways in which his products could remedy problems in the nation's growing number of industries.

That goal led him to produce

the first cotton batting to replace "curled hair" automobile upholstery in a 1911 Packard. It also made him the first producer of cotton filters for manufacturing rayon in 1914. Time after time, the company recognized more opportunities and met the challenge.

When World War I increased the demand for orthopedic padding, Barnhardt became a major supplier for the American Red Cross. As the demand for bleached cotton grew, Barnhardt constructed its own bleachery in 1929.

When northern furniture manufacturers moved south to take advantage of North Carolina's plentiful supply of hardwoods, upholstery fabrics, and workers, Barnhardt became a preferred supplier of cotton batting for cushions and upholstered furniture.

When, in the late 1930s, the U.S. Department of Agriculture offered incentives to companies that could help use the nation's 20-million-

With a host of subsidiary companies, Barnhardt Manufacturing Company's products include non-woven cotton filters that remove impurities from liquid acrylics, acetate, and rayon before they are made into synthetic yarns.

bale surplus of cotton, Barnhardt developed a chemical treatment that made it flameproof. As a result, it could be used as an insulating material that was more efficient than other materials available at the time. Moreover, it became known as an effective fire-resistant material for mattresses and upholstered furniture.

During World War II Barnhardt received the Army-Navy "E" Flag, the nation's highest award for civilian production, for its enormous efforts to meet the heavy medical needs of the Army. Since that time Barnhardt has further expanded by adding the dental supply firm and the foam manufacturing company to its list of businesses.

Over the years it has been

guided by each successive generation of the Barnhardt family. After Tom Barnhardt's death in 1946, he was succeeded by his three sons: Thomas, Jr., Jacob, and James. His daughter, Nell, became president of Richmond Dental Cotton Company.

Now Thomas M. Barnhardt III is company president, and Jacob C. Barnhardt, Jr., heads North Carolina Foam Industries. They work with other members of the family, including several fourth-generation Barnhardts, to ensure the continued expansion of Barnhardt Manufacturing Company.

"We can continue to grow through competitive pricing and good service to our customers," says Tom Barnhardt. "We'll be able to achieve that by modernizing our equipment and facilities, increasing efficiency, and reducing our costs."

Like their grandfather, today's Barnhardts are striving to use the company's products to best meet the needs of customers.

PHILIP MORRIS U.S.A.,
CABARRUS MANUFACTURING CENTER

With diversity comes strength. Charlotte's economy draws its strength not only from the diverse base of business and industry within its borders but also from the diversity of the surrounding communities, such as its neighbor to the north, Cabarrus County.

It's in Cabarrus County that Philip Morris U.S.A. operates an international showpiece cigarette manufacturing facility that is a major economic force in Cabarrus and Mecklenburg counties.

The Philip Morris U.S.A. Cabarrus Manufacturing Center began production in 1983 as the world's most technologically advanced cigarette manufacturing plant. The facility is designed to produce a staggering 60 billion cigarettes per year—enough to circle the earth 120 times. The cigarettes are made at lightning speed with highly sophisticated machinery guided by the skilled hands of approximately 1,600 employees. The world's most popular cigarette brand, Marlboro, is made in Cabarrus County along with other leading brands.

Each year the plant processes more than 120 million pounds of to-

Recognized as an international showpiece in cigarette manufacturing technology, Philip Morris' Cabarrus Manufacturing Center spans 250 acres of a 2,100-acre site in Cabarrus County.

bacco leaf, much of which is bought in North Carolina. This places the company in a special niche in North Carolina's tobacco industry, which itself employs about 90,000 people directly and 167,000 others indirectly. That's one of every 10 North Carolina jobs.

The Cabarrus Manufacturing Center stands as an architecturally striking example of the successful blending of a manufacturing facility with its natural surroundings. Located just north of Charlotte along Highway 29, the manufacturing center stretches a half-mile in length and is situated on 250 acres of the company's wooded, 2,100-acre site. Philip Morris is also credited with helping open a corridor for development north of Charlotte that begins at the University of North Carolina at Charlotte.

Each year the manufacturing center attracts thousands of visitors from around the nation and world who are fascinated by its highly auto-

mated production processes and immaculate grounds. During the free tours, visitors are also treated to viewing an extensive collection of North Carolina artisan craftwork, including the world's largest hanging quilted tapestry and an impressive collection of paintings, pottery, earthenware, and basketry.

Through the dedication and quality work of its employees, as well as its strong partnership with the citizens and leaders in the area, Philip Morris will continue to contribute great strength and diversity to the Charlotte region in the years to come.

The Cabarrus Manufacturing Center is part of Philip Morris Incorporated (Philip Morris U.S.A.), the oldest operating unit in Philip Morris Companies Inc. Among the leading cigarette brands produced by Philip Morris U.S.A. are Marlboro, the number-one selling cigarette in the world; Benson & Hedges; Merit; and Virginia Slims.

Philip Morris' success has been created by dedicated people producing the finest quality cigarettes in the nation. Marlboro and Merit are two of the brands made at the Cabarrus Manufacturing Center.

Chapter 9

Business and Professions

Greater Charlotte's business and professional community brings a wealth of services, ability, and insight to the area.

Charlotte Chamber of Commerce, 208   Price Waterhouse, 209   Royal Insurance, 210-211   Broadway & Seymour, 212-213

Johnson & Higgins Carolinas, Inc., 214   Parker, Poe, Thompson, Bernstein, Gage & Preston, 215   KPMG Peat Marwick, 216-217   Deloitte Haskins & Sells, 218

Robison & McAulay, 219   First Union Corporation, 220-221   NCNB Corporation, 222-223   The FWA Group, 224-225

Page 205: photo by Diane Davis; right: photo by Matt Bradley

Interstate/Johnson Lane,
226-229

Aetna Life & Casualty,
230-231

Cansler, Lockhart, Burtis &
Evans, 232-233

Bell, Seltzer, Park and Gibson,
234-235

CHARLOTTE CHAMBER OF COMMERCE

The Charlotte Chamber of Commerce has been working for the economic health of the Charlotte/Mecklenburg area since its beginnings in 1879.

Known in the earliest days as the Greater Charlotte Club, the organization has had a lasting and positive influence on the Charlotte/Mecklenburg of today.

In 1915 the Greater Charlotte Club gave way to the incorporation of the Charlotte Chamber of Commerce. The certificate of incorporation set forth the purpose of the organization: ". . . to encourage, advance, and promote the industrial, commercial, civic, and social interests of the City of Charlotte and its surrounding territory."

The Chamber has been at it ever since.

Over the years the chamber has a notable record of accomplishments. It championed the cause of highways in the Carolinas long be-

fore state and local government became involved. Chamber automobile caravans trekked over rutted dirt roads to neighboring states to spread the message shortly after the turn of the century. The chamber hired the first city planner to recommend a location for the city's first skyscraper, the Independence Building. The paving of Charlotte streets, the construction of a city auditorium (and another along with a Coliseum in the 1950s), and the location of the Norfolk-Southern Railway through Charlotte were all results of chamber efforts.

In recent years the chamber furthered the cause of industrial development and supported measures to build better roads, increase the city's accessibility by attracting interna-

The downtown Charlotte skyline—the Charlotte Chamber of Commerce has, for 108 years, been actively involved in economic development and business advocacy in the area. Photo by M. Fortenberry

tional flights to Charlotte-Douglas International Airport, construct a major coliseum for national sporting events, and create a regional center for the performing arts.

In 1989, under the leadership of First Union Corporation's John Georgius, the chamber's volunteer chairman, the organization worked with business leaders to support improvements in the Charlotte/Mecklenburg school system; worked to solidify the Metrolina region into an economic, cultural, and political unit; and devised a number of programs to give better direct assistance to small and minority businesses.

Altogether those efforts add up to enormous improvements in the lives of the people of Metrolina. Today, after nearly 110 years, the Charlotte Chamber of Commerce, one of the oldest and largest chambers in the country, is doing more than ever to make the region greater than it has ever been before.

PRICE WATERHOUSE

Every year in Hollywood representatives of Price Waterhouse share the spotlight with celebrities at one of the country's most public events, as they guard the contents of the envelopes for the Academy Awards. That outward symbol of general trust is a small reminder of the solid reputation this major international firm has amassed during almost 140 years of business.

The *Wall Street Journal* has called the firm "generally regarded as the blue chip among the nation's largest accounting firms." The U.S. Senate subcommittee on Reports, Accounting, and Management has said, "Price Waterhouse is in a class of its own as the most influential of the Big Eight firms."

That reputation of quality has been upheld by the Charlotte office of Price Waterhouse since 1961, when the firm opened its first Carolinas location. Today the more than 180 professionals in the Charlotte office represent clients in every industry, including banking, soft drink bottling, communications, manufacturing, apparel, and real estate.

The overall performance of these Charlotte professionals constantly sup-

A Price Waterhouse senior accountant working in the funds management department of a large bank.

A regional partner meeting of Price Waterhouse in Charlotte.

ports the firm's widely accepted reputation for excellence in every aspect of accounting, while its professionals have also developed an unusual level of expertise in representing financial institutions and in the field of mergers and acquisitions. Among the firm's clients are some of the area's most prominent companies: NCNB Corporation, BarclaysAmericanCorporation, North Carolina Federal Savings and Loan, Coca-Cola Bottling Company, Siecor Corporation, and Alcatel NA, Inc.

At the same time the Charlotte office also actively contributes to the total firm's commitment to serve small and medium-size companies, as well as the community. Its professionals are proud participants in such non-

profit organizations as the United Way, WTVI Public Television, the Charlotte Repertory Theatre, and the Mint Museum.

The office staff takes pride in being part of a tradition that began when Samuel Lowell Price started performing audits in London in 1850 and continued with his partnership with Edwin Waterhouse in 1865. By 1890 the company's clerks were serving enough clients in the United States to open the first independent U.S. office.

In the ensuing century Price Waterhouse has grown to include more than 100 American offices staffed by almost 950 partners and a total of more than 12,000 men and women. The Charlotte office is part of a worldwide organization of more than 400 offices in 100-plus countries and territories. The total staff of more than 37,000 professionals serves one of the most prestigious client rosters in the country. The accounting organization provides services to more *Fortune* 500 clients than the other Big Eight firms and more *Forbes* 100 multinational corporations than any other firm.

Today the Charlotte office, which has more than doubled in size in the past five years, continues to make the Price Waterhouse name synonymous with excellence and expertise in the field of accounting.

ROYAL INSURANCE

At first glance, the contemporary 340,000-square-foot corporate office complex in southwest Charlotte doesn't look like the U.S. headquarters of a nearly 150-year-old British company. Its three-story barrel-vault atrium, 1.5-acre man-made lake, and 40-acre grounds with a softball field, tennis and basketball courts, and jogging/fitness trails appear to be the work of a very youthful corporate giant.

On the ground floor, in 50,000 square feet of data-processing area, the firm's mainframe computers operate virtually on their own. Even the new unmanned mailmobiles, which traverse the entire complex six times per day and stop for 20 seconds at predesignated unloading points, reveal a company that looks forward instead of back.

Yet these facilities are indeed a fitting environment for a historic insurance corporation. They symbolize the spirit that has driven the corporation to take advantage of new opportunities for growth since it began as a fire insurance company for local merchants in Liverpool, England, in 1845. Just six years later it recognized the potential for business in the United States and established a New York office on Wall Street.

From this willingness to identify opportunity and seize it has grown one of the largest property-casualty insurers in the United States, with a network of nearly 100 offices and

6,000 employees nationwide. This openness led Royal to move its U.S. headquarters to Charlotte from New York in 1986, when its management recognized the advantages of Charlotte's prosperity and attractive lifestyle.

Moreover, in each Royal office, employees act on the company's clear sense of mission. In fact, in the 1980s the firm's employees summarized their understanding of the Royal tradition in a statement called "The Royal Vision." It declares their commitment to quality, innovation, teamwork, and opportunities for recognition, and it ends by asserting, "We will be the 'best of the best' . . . in every job, in every office, every day."

That commitment has made Royal part of U.S. history. When much of Chicago burned in 1871, Royal paid $3.3 million in fire insurance losses. It was the second-largest disbursement made by the many insurers in the city. In 1906, after the great San Francisco earthquake and fire, only five of the 243 insurers involved paid their claims in full. Three of those who honored all claims—a total of $13.9 million in settlements—were member companies of what is today Royal Insurance.

In addition, Royal's commitment to innovation and creativity has contributed much to its growth and success. Since the beginning Royal has

openly sought new ideas and areas for expansion. It has, for example, taken advantage of opportunities to merge with other thriving insurers. Chief among these was its 1919 merger with The Liverpool & London & Globe, a company that, like Royal, had begun in Liverpool in

Royal provided the builder's risk insurance during construction of the 25,000-seat Charlotte Coliseum, home of the NBA Charlotte Hornets.

the mid-1800s and, soon afterward, opened a U.S. office to meet the protection demands of America's surging economy.

In 1979 the worldwide operation was reorganized into profit centers, and Royal Group, Inc., was formed as the holding company for Royal's U.S. subsidiaries. Royal Group, Inc., is a sister company to other holding companies in the United Kingdom, Canada, and elsewhere, and these in turn are subsidiaries of Royal Insurance Holdings plc, the worldwide parent. In 1989 Royal once again expanded its capabilities by acquiring Maccabees Life Insurance Co. of Michigan. The addition quintupled Royal's life insurance business, from about $50 million in premiums to more than $250 million.

That number, however, is still only a small part of Royal's overall U.S. business, which totals more than $2 billion in annual premiums. For the most part, the company derives its revenue from a wide variety of property and casualty offerings.

Through its General Insurance Division, Royal protects the property of individuals, small to medium-size businesses, and some large commercial lines. Its personal insurance lines include policies for homes, condomin-

Prompt, efficient claim service is an important part of the insurance coverages offered by Royal.

iums and apartments, automobiles, boats, and personal articles.

With its Challenger series of policies, Royal provides an automated insurance protection program for small and medium-size businesses, while its Business Protection Portfolio (BPP) is designed for larger companies.

All of these are offered and serviced by independent agents through offices in territories across the United States. Royal believes it can operate most effectively by placing authority and responsibility as close to the customer as possible.

Commercial accounts requiring specialized underwriting techniques are served by Royal's Special Insurance Division. The professionals in its Special Risks area can meet the needs of corporate risk managers and write domestic as well as international property and casualty coverage. In addition, the Royal All-Marine Specialty area provides coverages for ocean and inland marine, aviation, and boiler and machinery risks.

In all these areas, Royal's Charlotte headquarters plays an important role. There product managers

and other insurance professionals constantly develop improved methods of coverage. Moreover, they use the company's enormous data-processing capabilities to increase efficiency through automation.

At the same time Royal and its employees, under the leadership of chairman and chief executive officer William E. Buckley, have quickly established themselves as important members of the Charlotte community. The company has become a supporter of charitable and community service groups, and its employees serve on the boards of numerous organizations.

While the history of Royal Insurance extends 150 years into the past and thousands of miles across the Atlantic, here, in Charlotte, the company continues to uphold its tradition of moving forward into the future.

Designing customized, property-casualty coverages for businesses of all sizes is a Royal Insurance specialty.

BROADWAY & SEYMOUR

In less than 10 years Broadway & Seymour has emerged as a national leader in helping businesses, industry, and government agencies take advantage of computer technology. In late 1980 the firm was founded in Charlotte by Olin Broadway and Bill Seymour, two men with management experience in the computing and banking industries. Their goal was to provide high-quality computer consulting and services to financial service organizations and others.

The Charlotte area proved to be a great place to begin. It offered the new company the resources and expertise of corporations such as IBM. At the same time the city's position as a strong financial center offered the new company an immediate source of customers. From this local base, Broadway & Seymour quickly expanded beyond its original market.

By 1988 the firm was achieving the two partners' goal with a wide variety of financial institutions; federal, state, and local governments; health care organizations; retailers; manufacturers; construction companies; vendors of computer hardware and software; and others. Broadway & Seymour was providing clients with its services through the expertise of almost 400 employees. It had established seven offices nationwide: Charlotte, Winston-Salem, and Raleigh, North Carolina; St. Paul, Minnesota; Atlanta, Georgia; Dallas, Texas; and Norfolk, Virginia. It had also been listed twice by *Inc.* magazine as one of the nation's 500 fastest-growing companies.

Much of Broadway & Seymour's success results from the ability of its staff to provide total expertise in the integration of a new computer system or software into a client's current operating system. It specializes in developing such expertise within a specific industry and applying computerized solutions to the needs of that industry. Many of its customers are in financial service and government, with a growing number in health care and other industries with sophisticated data-processing needs.

Says Broadway, "We are committed to being the leader in offering high-quality computer systems and services that effectively meet the needs of our clients. We back this commitment with our pledge to be ethical, credible, and professional in all that we do."

More than half the company's sales come from its Professional Services Group, through which it provides both technical and applications experience. A client might hire a Broadway & Seymour team to assess the need for a new computer system or software, to manage the installation of a new system or software, or to train its in-house personnel after installation. It might ask Broadway & Seymour to find appropriate software or to custom design such software when standard packages are not available.

Broadway & Seymour's wide variety of experts in the Professional Services Group aid clients by applying their skills in project management, systems consulting, applications programming, operating systems support, documentation, technical training, and personal computer training.

In addition to the Professional Services Group, the firm's Financial Products Group develops and markets standardized software for use by financial institutions. Its most widely known packages have achieved national recognition in the field of branch automation and application of customer information files for improved sales.

MAXIM™, developed by Broadway & Seymour, is a comprehensive software solution that operates on IBM 4700 controller-based hardware. It supports complete branch automation and enhances the branch selling environment by providing immediate access to customer and sales information via in-branch terminals. BANCStar® provides similar automation and selling benefits via a network of personal computers.

LIBERTY™ frees community banks from the restraints of outside service organizations by providing a turnkey data-processing system for use on an IBM's System/36 and AS/400 hardware. It can render consolidated statements, analyze account profitability, and predict the effects of proposed new fee structures.

Each of these products, and others for banks, is enhanced by the services of Broadway & Seymour's

Broadway & Seymour provides high-quality computer consulting and services to nationally based commercial and federal clients. Courtesy, Jon F. Silla Photography

extensive staff of experts, many of whom have worked in the financial industry. They help clients maximize the advantages of their computer software and systems.

During the company's first decade it was able to grow through responsiveness to the changing needs of its clients. As banks were deregulated, for example, Broadway & Seymour provided much-needed products and services for rapidly expanding interstate giants and for emerging community banks.

The company is increasingly called upon for its capabilities in systems integration—combining user ideas, advanced technology, and data processing. A team of Broadway & Seymour professionals may completely design and install a new system or integrate new software within an existing system.

Moreover, Broadway & Seymour constantly seeks new geographical and service areas for expansion, both in the United States and abroad. It repeatedly adds services by adding the expertise of more professional people. It also tests applications of new technology for clients, such as its research into computerized image processing and computer-addressable media, especially for use by banks.

In Charlotte, Broadway & Seymour is working with local education institutions to increase the number of people who are skilled professionals in computer science. According to vice-chairman Bill Seymour, "We know our most important corporate assets are our people."

As Broadway & Seymour continues to grow, this leader in computer systems and services will need more computer-educated people to make that growth possible.

Broadway & Seymour's LIBERTY Banking Software provides in-house data processing for community banks. Courtesy, Jon F. Silla Photography

JOHNSON & HIGGINS CAROLINAS, INC.

Johnson & Higgins, the world's largest privately held insurance broker and human resource consultant, began on Wall Street in 1845. During this time of the tall ships, Henry W. Johnson and A. Foster Higgins plied the ancient trade of "average adjusting," the sharing of losses from cargoes sacrificed at sea by ships in distress. Later, as the industrial revolution took hold, the firm followed its clients' needs on shore and helped bring insurance to an industrializing America.

History records that after the 1906 San Francisco earthquake and fire, Johnson & Higgins saw that "every loss was serviced with satisfactory payments to its clients." In 1912 it was Johnson & Higgins and its Lloyd's partners that placed the insurances on the *Titanic*. Amazingly, in view of today's litigious society, "all claims were collected within less than 30 days."

Since the end of World War II, American business has concerned itself more and more with the retirement and health care needs of its employees. In serving those concerns, Johnson & Higgins has become a leader in the human resource consulting field.

Today, with 65 U.S. and Canadian offices and scores of others in 18 countries, Johnson & Higgins is a globally recognized expert in all aspects of insurance brokering and human resource consulting. In 1988, in order to manage and maintain expertise in the increasingly complex area of employee benefits, the company formed a subsidiary, A. Foster Higgins & Co., to specialize in that client service.

The Charlotte office, Johnson & Higgins Carolinas, Inc., was founded

to quick resolution of claims have won widespread recognition. As a result, the Charlotte office has become North Carolina's principal broker for most of the state's cities and towns, in addition to being the recognized leader in the field of medical malpractice risk management. Its services have included work for the new Charlotte Coliseum and for major firms such as Duke Power Com-

LEFT: John A. McLean, senior vice-president and branch manager at Johnson & Higgins Carolinas, Inc., at One First Union Center. Photo by Donna Bise

BELOW: John A. McLean (far right) consults with senior staff members (from left) Bobby S. Hastings, Fred R. Bailey, David L. Terwilleger, Jr., and Donna E. Leaird. Photo by Donna Bise

in 1974 as the company's 23rd branch office in the United States, with six employees. Today more than 70 professionals under branch manager John A. McLean serve clients with employee benefit advisory and insurance brokerage benefits. The staff of expert account managers, brokers, and claims professionals is committed to keeping the firm on the cutting edge of a rapidly changing business.

The corporation's aggressive efforts to help clients avoid and control casualty losses and its attention

pany, Lance, Inc., Lowe's Companies, Inc., and CCAIR, Inc.

The Charlotte staff, including former branch managers Rodney D. Day III and Brooke N. Williams, is known for its involvement and support of the United Way, the Arts and Science Council, and a multitude of other Charlotte civic activities. Such involvement, combined with a pioneering spirit, is characteristic of Johnson & Higgins, a company that is still privately held, service minded, and entrepreneurial after more than 140 years.

PARKER, POE, THOMPSON, BERNSTEIN, GAGE & PRESTON

Charlotte was still a sleepy southern Piedmont town when Heriot Clarkson opened his law office in 1884. Clarkson and Charles Duls, the partner who joined him in 1888, set high standards of integrity and commitment to public service that remain the guiding principles of the firm they founded, known today as Parker, Poe, Thompson, Bernstein, Gage & Preston. One of the oldest in continuous practice in North Carolina, the firm is comprised of more than 60 attorneys.

As Charlotte has become a leading center of commerce in the Southeast, Parker Poe has kept pace. Its roster of local, regional, national, and international clients includes individuals, industrial corporations, financial institutions, public utilities, colleges and universities, textile manufacturers, retail merchandising chains, real estate developers, contractors, architects, and other types of businesses.

The firm's attorneys have become highly specialized, a reflection of the remarkable changes that have taken place both in the needs of their clients and in the law itself. To ensure that client needs are met efficiently and effectively, the firm is divided into departments: corporate, litigation, real estate and lending, tax, probate, and employee benefits, and government regulation and administration. In recent years the continuing growth of international business in Charlotte and the Carolinas has required local legal services, and the firm responded with the addition of an international practice specialty within the corporate department.

From the firm's founder, Heriot Clarkson, who served on the North Carolina Supreme Court, to William Poe, chairman of the Charlotte-Mecklenburg School Board during a critical time of social and political change, the firm is comprised of individuals committed both to excellence in the practice of law and to involvement in public affairs. Its attorneys are active in federal, state, and local bar associations and other professional organizations, as well as politi-

Parker, Poe, Thompson, Bernstein, Gage & Preston—more than 100 years of service to Charlotte. Courtesy, Steve Knight Photography

cal, educational, cultural, and charitable enterprises. Although the firm has grown rapidly in recent years, doubling in size between 1984 and 1988, its tradition of devoting personal attention to individual clients hasn't diminished.

To accommodate its growing practice, the firm moved in early 1984 from its quarters in the Cameron Brown Building near the courthouse, to the 26th floor of Charlotte Plaza, at the center of the city's business and financial district. Since the major move uptown, the firm has expanded further, into offices on the 25th and 27th floors of Charlotte Plaza as well as establishing an office in Charlotte's South Park area. Recog-

nizing overall growth potential in North Carolina, Parker Poe merged with a firm in Research Triangle Park concentrating on high-technology, intellectual property, and immigration/visa matters.

Parker, Poe, Thompson, Bernstein, Gage & Preston continues to keep pace with the changing and increasingly complex needs of its clients and to play a leading role in community and professional endeavors—qualities that promise to serve the firm well as it moves into the twenty-first century.

KPMG PEAT MARWICK

Even Big Eight accounting firms can have critics. When Peat, Marwick, Mitchell & Co. merged with the international firm of Klynveld Main Goerdeler to form the world's largest accounting and consulting firm, there were people who said it was impossible. KPMG Peat Marwick, however, saw the merger as one more innovation in a tradition of creativity.

Today that unthinkable combination, under the name Klynveld Peat Marwick Goerdeler (KPMG), is still growing. It operates offices in 115 countries. The 135 offices of its U.S. member firm, with more than 1,900 partners, serve thousands of public and private, domestic and international companies. Its clients include small and medium-size businesses as well as major corporations.

Its Charlotte office is the hub of KPMG Peat Marwick's Carolinas Business Unit. In 1988 it employed a staff of 160, double the number in 1986.

In the March 1988 issue of *The Big Eight Review*, editor James C. Emerson said, "Peat Marwick has never been a firm to follow the crowd. It has a history of charting new ground, and that philosophy continues today."

That history began with the 1897 partnership of James Marwick and S. Roger Mitchell in New York. Within 10 years they had established offices in Chicago, Minneapolis, Pittsburgh, Philadelphia, and Winnipeg. After World War I they expanded even further by merging with W.B. Peat & Co. of London. In 1925 KPMG Peat Marwick arrived in Charlotte, merging with the firm of George H. Adams, to form the company's 25th office and the first Carolina office of a national accounting firm.

For almost a century KPMG Peat Marwick has repeatedly found new ways to serve customers and increase market share. It was an industry leader in developing the peer-review process. It was the first

KPMG Peat Marwick's Charlotte office is led by (from left) F. Crowder Falls, managing partner; Jerry R. Licari, audit partner in charge; Peter A. Mihaltian, management consulting principal in charge; and Robert G. Dinsmore, Jr., tax partner in charge. Photo by Diane Davis

firm to develop an audit manual for worldwide use. In recent years it has been an industry leader in providing value-added services.

"The 1986 start up of our Charlotte-based Carolinas management consulting practice, under the leadership of principal in charge Peter Mihaltian, gives us full-service capabilities," says Charlotte's managing partner, Crowder Falls. "We work hard to be considered our clients' valued business advisers."

But in two respects, KPMG Peat Marwick has especially distinguished itself: the firm's approach to serving specific industries and its use of information technology.

KPMG Peat Marwick's size supports its commitment to industry specialization. Partners develop an in-depth knowledge of their clients' businesses, sometimes focusing this knowledge on a narrow market

group. For example, when many accounting firms treated high-technology firms as just another kind of service company, KPMG Peat Marwick established a separate practice for the high-technology industry. Such specialization has paid off in market share. In 1988 Emerson's analysis showed KMPG Peat Marwick was the leader in 11 of the 14 major industry groups.

In addition, KMPG Peat Marwick has committed itself to helping clients benefit from the use of rapidly expanding information technology. Its objective is to get critical management information to clients

Extensive use of computers to take over the quantitative work frees KPMG Peat Marwick professionals for qualitative thinking. Photo by Diane Davis

also to aid Charlotte's Sister Cities Program and other international business and civic efforts.

In addition to numerous other activities over the years, Crowder Falls was active in helping Charlotte start its First Night Charlotte event for New Year's Eve. Now more than 50 KPMG Peat Marwick employees volunteer in support of this popular annual celebration.

Most important, however, is KPMG Peat Marwick's determination to continue its growth through effective use of its size and depth. Says Falls, "The international merger has made it possible for us to offer en-

Frequent meetings keep KPMG Peat Marwick in touch with clients' top management. Photo by Diane Davis

more quickly. In this pursuit the firm is working to develop systems that will directly deliver usable data to management.

The firm worked closely with Apple Computer during the development of the Macintosh. KPMG Peat Marwick was the first commercial customer for these computers and is one of the world's largest users of the Macintosh. A 1987 merger with information technology company Nolan, Norton & Co. enhanced the firm's ability to offer planning and strategic information services.

Like the rest of the firm, KPMG Peat Marwick's Charlotte office has been a leader in the industry and in the community. It was, for example, the first Charlotte CPA firm to hire a professionally trained marketing director, whose job is to get KPMG Peat Marwick's partners recognized by business decision makers. These partners epitomize KPMG Peat Marwick's firmwide philosophy of superior client service and significant community involvement.

Tax partner in charge Bob Dinsmore was instrumental in the develop-

ment of Providence Country Club, one of Charlotte's premier, family-oriented leisure facilities. As a member of the Mint Museum board, his involvement helped ensure a success for the museum's Ramesses the Great Exhibit.

Jerry Licari, audit partner in charge who came to Charlotte in 1986, instigated the firm's annual survey of foreign-owned companies with headquarters in North Carolina. He has used his knowledge not only to serve KPMG Peat Marwick but

hanced service to all our clients through better resources and improved operating efficiencies."

Such service has already given KPMG Peat Marwick a dominant share of Charlotte's market for audit and tax services among small businesses as well as very large ones. Now with its emphasis on technology, specific industry expertise, and development of business advisory services, the Charlotte office of KPMG Peat Marwick is out to maximize the power of its resources.

DELOITTE HASKINS & SELLS

Deloitte Haskins & Sells recognized early the potential for growth and development in the Carolinas and in 1925 opened the first national accounting firm practice in Charlotte. Today DH&S is one of the largest public accounting practices in the area with about 430 personnel, 125 in Charlotte, which is area headquarters for a 10-office group throughout both Carolinas and Virginia. This network of offices provides DH&S a unique ability to be near its clients and to quickly respond to the diverse needs of an ever-expanding clientele. Internationally, the firm provides accounting, tax, and management consulting service through a network of 425 offices in 70 countries.

O. Charlie Chewning, Jr., area managing partner in the Charlotte office, says, "The office's clients run the gamut from the individual tax client and the smaller, middle-market firms to the largest organizations in the area. Our clients include every major segment of business and industry. Although we service large multinational clients, we consider our practice to be local."

The Charlotte practice is in the mainstream of firm-wide activities. DH&S's national textile and apparel industry coordinator and the national public utility industry tax coordinator are Charlotte office partners. Chewning notes, "Charlotte is a lead office in developing new services and approaches to client service." Major new or expanded services include:

Emerging Business Services and Middle Market Consulting to companies with $5 million to $75 million in sales. Highly experienced personnel in this group take a business advisory approach in helping businesses grow and increase profits.

Computer Assurance Services include computer security, contingency planning, and extended computer auditing services.

Executive Financial Counseling Services assist individual clients to develop and implement financial strategies in order to minimize the effects

of taxation and to maximize personal assets. This value-added service is provided by only 14 of the firm's more than 100 U.S. offices.

Corporate Acquisition Services include leveraged buyouts and mergers. Experienced personnel take key roles in developing tax and financial structures for both small and large highly publicized acquisitions.

Management Consulting includes large management information, cost, inventory, and other systems.

Chewning says, "We are committed to taking a business advisory approach in our services and to providing the highest quality professional services available to our

ABOVE: Client service teams comprised of professionals with audit, tax, and consulting skills meet to discuss ways to serve clients effectively. They also work together to plan comprehensive service plans for their clients.

LEFT: Computer assurance professionals help clients with computer security, contingency planning, and extended computer auditing needs.

clients, large and small. Our approach is to provide added value, to give something more than expected."

"Charlotte is a great place to live and work; it continues to change, to grow, to demand, to challenge," Chewning concludes. "We at Deloitte Haskins & Sells have committed our resources to meeting the demands and challenges of businesses in Charlotte and in the Carolinas, now and into the dynamic future ahead. To further meet future challenges, DH&S and Touche Ross, in July 1989, agreed in principle to a combination in the United States as Deloitte & Touche. If combined, the new firm will be one of the world's largest accounting and consulting firms."

ROBISON & McAULAY

For many American businesses, 1973 did not appear to be a particularly good year. Interest rates were almost beyond America's ability to keep the economy under control; gas shortages produced long lines at stations stretching from Miami to Seattle, New York to Los Angeles, and everything in between; and Vietnam and Watergate had the nation in their respective negative grips.

But it was that very same year that a new company in an industry in its infancy was formed in Charlotte, a firm known today as Robison & McAulay. It was—and still is—comprised of a team of highly professional individuals with broad and diverse backgrounds in executive management. Their capabilities have earned the firm an enviable position in the field of executive search consulting.

Executive search is an industry that actually began its development after World War II, but continued to struggle with its identity and professional standards for at least 25 years beyond that.

Largely confined to metropolitan areas of the Northeast, Midwest, and West Coast, this service appeared by 1973 to have significant opportunities in other American cities, particularly for firms that could bring highly qualified executives into their ranks, and especially for professionals who could help develop and establish the very highest of ethics and integrity.

So when the original firm of which Robison & McAulay is a successor was formed, it quickly was accepted for membership in the Association of Executive Search Consultants (AESC), the first firm head-

quartered in the South to be admitted into that prestigious organization. Today the AESC has an active membership from 31 nations and is a self-policing body comprised of the leading search firms in the world and dedicated to a stringent Code of Ethics. The company has been an active member of the AESC since joining that group, and one of its associates has served as a director.

In addition to earning a reputation as a firm that sets the highest standards in its industry, Robison & McAulay also has been named (two times running) one of the top 50 search firms in the United States by *Executive Recruiter News*, the leading publisher in the search business.

The publishing firm of Harper & Row also has included John H. Robison, President of Robison & McAulay, in its book *The Career Makers: America's Top 100 Executive Recruiters*.

The firm's clients represent a full

range of commercial and industrial enterprises, in addition to governmental, educational, and institutional entities. While its client base stretches from the East Coast to the West Coast and five European countries, it concentrates its efforts on behalf of clients in the eastern United States.

While Robison & McAulay's activities take on a global nature, the firm prides itself on its commitment to its community. Corporately and individually it takes an active role in the support of community endeavors, including serving on a number of civic, social, and religious boards and on corporate boards where there are no conflicts of interest with Robison & McAulay's client roster.

From offices in downtown Charlotte, Robison & McAulay's professional staff continues to maintain its leadership role and its success via a strong commitment to hard work, long hours, judicious decisions, and the delivery of consistent service.

FIRST UNION CORPORATION

H.M. Victor would have a difficult time recognizing the bank he founded in 1908.

Victor's Union National Bank has grown into First Union Corporation, the nation's 22nd-largest bank holding company, based on assets of $28.9 billion at year-end 1988. After its scheduled merger, in the fourth quarter of 1989, with Florida National Banks of Florida, Inc., it will rank 14th in the nation with assets of about $37 billion.

Even before the merger with Florida National, First Union had nearly 700 banking offices in five southeastern states, making it the nation's third-largest branch banking network in 1988.

At year-end 1988 First Union ranked 12th in the nation in market capitalization—the value of its stock in the marketplace. On December 31, 1988, First Union's primary capital ratio of 8.09 percent, gave it the top spot—in terms of capital strength—among the Southeast's 10 largest banks. It also employed nearly 20,000 people in more than 1,200 offices in 37 states and two foreign countries.

That's a quantum leap from the superregional's modest beginnings in the Buford Hotel on Charlotte's Tryon Street not long after the turn of the twentieth century.

H.M. Victor raised funds to start Union National Bank by selling 1,000 shares of stock at $100 each, then set up his office at a rolltop desk in the hotel's main lobby. He soon earned a reputation as a conservative banker who always confirmed his customers' credit-worthiness before making a loan. For years Victor even refused to make loans on the newly invented automobile. When he finally relented with a loan on a Model T, he held the owner's keys and title until the loan was repaid.

As Union National—and, much later, First Union—grew, it maintained a reputation for high credit quality, strong financial performance, and excellent customer service. It was this viability that kept the bank

opened during the troubled 1930s, when the Depression closed many others.

In the decades that followed the bank pioneered many areas with its innovative approach to growth and diversification.

For example, Union National Bank was the first Charlotte bank to open a branch office, in 1947. It later was the first to offer a flat-fee checking account, the first to offer a charge card—even before the advent of Visa and MasterCard—and, in 1988, the first in the nation to link its branches by satellite for data transmission.

In 1958 Union National's management, led by president Carl

McCraw, Sr., saw that the future of banking lay in a strong branching network. With a young manager named C.C. Hope, McCraw traveled to New York to study mergers. (Hope was later to become vice-chairman of the corporation, president of the American Bankers Association, and is now a director of the Federal Deposit Insurance Corporation.)

McCraw's and Hope's studies paid off later that year, when Union National merged with First National Bank and Trust Company of Ashe-

ville, forming First Union National Bank of North Carolina.

By 1964 First Union further diversified by acquiring Raleigh-based Cameron-Brown Company, a national mortgage banking and insurance firm. It was this acquisition that enabled First Union to become one of only a few banking companies in the nation that are legally empowered to offer a full line of insurance products. Cameron-Brown, which took the name First Union Mortgage Corporation in 1986, is to-

First Union is known throughout the banking industry for its emphasis on quality customer service as this employee demonstrates in helping a customer determine his financial goals.

day among the nation's 12 largest mortgage banking companies based on mortgage servicing volume.

The late 1960s brought more organizational change, as First Union formed a bank holding company in 1968. Cameron-Brown's founder, C.C. Cameron, became chairman of the new First Union Corporation. And, in 1973, Edward E. Crutchfield, Jr., then age 32, became president of the corporation, at that time the nation's youngest president of a major U.S. banking company.

First Union's new 42-story headquarters building in downtown Charlotte is the tallest structure between Philadelphia and Atlanta. At full occupancy, the one-million-square-foot building will be the workday "home" to an estimated 4,000 Charlotte office workers. It ranks as the largest urban development in Charlotte's history.

By 1985 Crutchfield had also succeeded Cameron as chairman and chief executive officer of First Union Corporation. That year he led an expansion program that encompassed Northwestern Financial Corporation of Greensboro. The merger, North Carolina banking's largest, created the state's second-largest bank, in terms of assets, and First Union's flagship banking operation.

Between 1985 and 1989 First Union has used its powerful statewide foundation as a base to quadruple its assets through 21 mergers with banks in North and South Carolina, Georgia, Florida, and Tennessee. By seeking other banking organizations with compatible managements and philosophies, First Union maintained its reputation for strong financial performance and quality products and service.

The strong banking network First Union built helped it to earn $297 million in net income in 1988. And its net income of $283 million in 1987 made it the nation's top earning banking company. In 1988 First Union's national presence was sufficient to warrant listing its stock on the New York Stock Exchange.

During these growth years First Union's transition has been strengthened by such leaders as Frank H. Dunn, president of First Union National Bank of North Carolina. And the mergers also added the talents of B.J. Walker, formerly of Atlantic Bancorporation. Walker is now chairman of First Union National Bank of Florida and vice-chairman of the corporation.

First Union's sales, marketing, and customer service programs have the support of John R. Georgius, chairman of First Union National Bank of North Carolina and vice-chairman of the corporation. Georgius helped develop the Quality Customer Service (QCS) program, which has become an industry-wide model.

Under the QCS program, First Union constantly trains employees on improved techniques for customer service and sales. Employees earn cash incentives for achieving high standards of service. The corporation's incentive program is just one example of its commitment to providing quality service to its 4.1 million customers and to attracting new customers. Says Georgius, "In the 1990s there should be no question that First Union is one of the finest sales-driven, service-oriented organizations in the United States."

In fact, First Union Corporation is profiled as one of the "101 Companies that Profit from Customer Care" in a new book citing "role models for the new American manager." The highly acclaimed book praises First Union for its QCS program, for its aggressive "mystery shopping" program by an independent firm, and for its in-depth market research into customer definitions of service.

NCNB CORPORATION

Probably the single most reliable fact about NCNB Corporation is its reputation as an aggressive, fast-growing financial organization. Since becoming the first southeastern bank to expand across state lines in 1982, it has transformed itself from a strong North Carolina bank into a super-regional giant with managed assets exceeding $50 billion.

The recent interstate expansion, however, is simply a natural outgrowth of the corporation's long history. It is a history that has consistently included a strong commitment to the individuals who work for the corporation, to its banking customers, and to the Charlotte community.

The high-technology environment of the Funds Management trading floor is the scene of constant activity.

A central customer service department in Charlotte helps customers throughout North Carolina via a toll-free telephone number.

NCNB began with the formation of Commercial National Bank in 1874, when Charlotte was a rural town of just 2,500 people. Through a steady series of mergers and acquisitions, the small local bank became a statewide financial institution with headquarters in Charlotte. In 1960, with the creation of NCNB Corporation, it became the third bank in the United States to form a one-bank holding company.

By 1982, when NCNB expanded into Florida three years before its major competitors, the corporation positioned itself for aggressive interstate growth. Through a special provision in Florida state law, NCNB acquired several banks there and organized them into a single statewide bank.

Within the next three years the corporation further solidified its position as the preeminent southeastern bank through mergers with Bankers Trust of South Carolina, Southern Bankshares in Atlanta, Prince William Bank in Virginia, and Centrabank of Baltimore.

It had also established representative offices in New York; Chicago, Illinois; Nashville, Tennessee; Rockville, Maryland; Los Angeles, California; Dallas, Texas; Baltimore, Maryland; and Richmond, Virginia. In addition, it operated branches in London and the Cayman Islands as well as offices in Sydney, Australia, and Frankfurt, Federal Republic of Germany.

But physical expansion was not the only change. At the same time, in 1987, NCNB implemented a sweeping internal reorganization. In a break with the traditional structure of management aligned with geography, NCNB established divisions dedicated to meeting the special needs of specific customer groups.

It continued to offer customers the broadest-possible range of products and services. It introduced a money-back guarantee of $10 for errors on checking and related accounts. And it offered NCNB customers the ability to get "hometown" bank services through NCNB offices outside their home state.

To support the corporation's rapid growth, NCNB actively sought promising new management talent among recent college graduates and maintained an extensive program for continued training of the

The new 60-story office tower under construction in uptown Charlotte will house NCNB's corporate headquarters by 1992.

Trained customer service representatives help customers at each branch office.

approximately 14,000 employees in the Southeast. Moreover, to retain those employees, the company instituted a series of benefits for employees with children.

"We spend a lot of money training and developing these people," says Hugh L. McColl, Jr., chairman of the board and chief executive officer of NCNB Corporation. "We want the people we hire to stay with NCNB and build careers with the company. Any assistance that we can provide to our employees in balancing the dual responsibilities of their jobs and their families helps them and helps us."

The corporation established a child-care reimbursement fund that allows employees to set aside pretax dollars to pay for child-care expenses. It increased maternity leave from four to six months and created a Phase In option that allows a returning employee to work a reduced number of hours for a prorated salary and still receive full benefits.

It contracted with a consulting firm to help employees locate child care through a resource and referral service. In addition, it offers full-time employees the option of temporarily working on a flexible schedule during a time when they need to spend more time with their children of any age, from infants through teenagers, or with elderly family members.

The corporation's commitment to people has extended into its role in the Charlotte community as well as in service to customers and employees.

The construction of the NCNB Tower at Trade and Tryon streets in the early 1970s established NCNB as a leader in uptown development. In the next decade it invested almost $15 million in participation in the development of Third Ward and Fourth Ward. In addition, it committed $115 million in loans for residential properties in Third and Fourth Wards, and for retail and business offices. It devoted more than $164 million to major uptown projects, including construction of the Independence Center.

In support of the arts and cultural facilities in uptown, NCNB contributed more than one million dollars to physical projects, including Spirit Square's Performance Place.

NCNB's community involvement continued when, in late 1987, NCNB announced it would support the creation of an arts complex within the multiuse development of two blocks at the corner of Trade and Tryon. The cooperative venture with Charter Properties was designed to include a 60-story office tower and a retail shopping plaza.

All that activity did nothing to slow NCNB's progress toward its goals for expansion. In the summer

The headquarters of NCNB National Bank of Florida towers above the Tampa skyline.

of 1988 NCNB made history again, with the announcement that it had reached an agreement with the Federal Deposit Insurance Corp. (FDIC) to manage and operate the restructured subsidiary banks of First RepublicBank Corp., the largest financial institution in Texas and the 13th-largest banking company in the nation.

Under the agreement, which gave NCNB a 20-percent equity investment and a five-year option to purchase the remaining 80 percent from the FDIC, NCNB Corporation created NCNB Texas National Bank as a single institution. NCNB now owns 49 percent of NCNB Texas. Buddy Kemp, president of NCNB Corporation, was named chairman of the Texas bank. Tim Hartman, the firm's chief financial officer, became the bank's vice-chairman and chief financial officer.

The corporation that began as a small-town bank on Tryon Street is expanding into an even larger national financial organization.

223

THE FWA GROUP

There is no better illustration of the commitment of the FWA Group to architectural excellence than the design awards its projects have received—30 since 1980 alone. These include local, regional, and national awards for structures as diverse as the post office in Kings Mountain and the BASF Agricultural Research Center in Research Triangle Park.

The awards are tangible evidence that the firm is, indeed, living up to its goal: "To provide a better quality of life for all who come in contact with our work, whether they be clients or users, by creating attractive, functional, and economically sound facilities for their use and enjoyment."

RIGHT: The Kings Mountain Post Office is recipient of a Presidential Federal Design Achievement Award in addition to three local, state, and regional design awards from the American Institute of Architects. All photos by Rick Alexander Photography, Charlotte, North Carolina

BELOW: Sunset reflects in the curved-glass exterior of this 40,000-square-foot ForestPark office-showroom building in Charlotte. Courtesy, Faison Associates

A 46-acre site in Research Triangle Park is home for the BASF Agricultural Research Center. The 105,000-square-foot complex houses laboratories, greenhouses, and offices.

This commitment to architectural excellence is one reason the firm is now one of the oldest and largest in North Carolina. The diversity of FWA's designs—each created to meet the specific needs of its client—is another.

Founded in uptown Charlotte by S. Scott Ferebee, Jr. in 1953, The FWA Group now boasts 15 principals. Its four offices in Charlotte and Research Triangle Park, North Carolina; Hilton Head Island, South Carolina; and Jacksonville, Florida, serve regional clients. In addition to architecture, its services also include planning, interior design, graphic design, and landscape design.

In 1988 the company's headquarters returned to uptown Charlotte after 25 years in the city's southeastern suburbs. The decision to

Called a "most sophisticated and elegant work of architecture" by the South Atlantic Region AIA Awards jury, the 220,000-square-foot Union Carbide Agricultural Products Technical Center (now owned by Rhone-Poulenc) in Research Triangle Park, North Carolina, was completed in 17 months.

move to a 15,000-square-foot space on the third floor of the historic 220 North Tryon Street building resulted from the partners' belief that the location is more suited to FWA's urban identity and more convenient to its largest clients. They see Charlotte's growth and prosperity as an important basis for the firm's success.

Several major uptown projects have resulted from the group's association with other architectural firms. The FWA Group served as associate architect with JPJ of Dallas, Texas, on the 27-story Charlotte Plaza and the 42-story One First Union Cen-

According to North Carolina Magazine, "The handsome $32-million, 360,000-square-foot College of Veterinary Medicine at North Carolina State University is a brilliant blend of form and function."

"East Bay Trading Company is a grand renovation job and a restaurant that offers good seafood, good wines, excellent service, and a feeling of old and new Charleston."—The Washington Post.

ter. It associated with Thompson, Ventulett, Stainback & Associates of Atlanta on Carillon, a mixed-use office/hotel/retail complex developed by Hesta Properties, Inc. on West Trade Street in Charlotte.

Providing architectural services for such high-rise office buildings is the most recent development in FWA's history of increasing diversity. In several areas, it has established a firm reputation as an architectural firm that can create a winning design and bring a project in on time and within budget.

The BASF Agricultural Research Center and the Union Carbide Agricultural Products Technical Center, both in the Research Triangle Park, are typical of the firm's expertise in designing research facilities that are both beautiful and functional. The 105,000-square-foot BASF complex includes laboratories, greenhouses, and offices beside a lake on a 46-acre site. The Union Carbide Cen-

ter, with its unique use of cobalt blue to define exterior structural elements, was called "a sophisticated and elegant work of architecture" by the South Atlantic Region of the American Institute of Architects (AIA).

In retail shopping centers from Florida to Ohio, The FWA Group has demonstrated an obvious ability to create appropriate architectural variety. They range from the contemporary one-million-square-foot Valley View Regional Center in Roanoke to the renovated tobacco warehouses at Brightleaf Square in Durham. At The Waterfront in Manteo, FWA combined condominiums, shops, offices, and a restaurant in a traditional style that suggests the heritage of this historic fishing village. The historic renovation of East Bay Trading Company in Charleston, South Carolina, has won praise and awards for its combination of aesthetics and function for one of the area's most popular restaurants.

On college campuses and in child-care centers, The FWA Group has created buildings that are aesthetic expressions of their educational function. They range from the award-winning 350,000-square-foot College of Veterinary Medicine at North Carolina State University and the new College of Architecture building at UNC-Charlotte to the much-praised Rodriquez Child Development Center at Fort Bragg.

At Villa Capriani, a beachfront condominium community on Topsail Island, and at Melrose, a members-only national country club on Daufuskie Island, South Carolina, The FWA Group has created environments appropriate to their settings. The rich stucco and terra-cotta de-

tails of Villa Capriani produce a Mediterranean flair. The Low Country style of Melrose reflects the life-style that has enriched the coastal area from Charleston to Savannah.

Such diversity forms the past and the future of The FWA Group. But it is diversity rooted in the architects' steadfast commitment to excellence.

Says founder Ferebee, who has served as National president of the American Institute of Architects, "Architecture is an expression of art, and it is involved with the way we live. Most art is something we look at, but buildings are something we look at and occupy—they have to serve mankind and they are an important element in his life."

Throughout the Southeast The FWA Group continues to make its creations a beautiful and functional element in people's lives.

Valley View Mall in Roanoke, Virginia, is the largest shopping center in southwest Virginia, with one million square feet of floor space. .

INTERSTATE/JOHNSON LANE

Success is rare and difficult to achieve, and people will forever be fascinated by the magazine cover story, the television feature, or the newspaper profile on a successful person or company. The questions are always the same: What is the secret? What can I learn to help me be successful, too? When you have achieved success, how do you keep it?

For Interstate/Johnson Lane, one of the most successful regional securities firms in the United States and the largest headquartered in the Southeast, the answers to questions such as these are not difficult to find, because the responses are usually the same whether they are asked of a broker with 52 years of professional experience or someone just beginning a brokerage career.

Says one veteran whose wisdom has been sought by news reporters from major North Carolina magazines and newspapers, "I laid off of speculation and risky options a long time ago. It's best to be honest with people, to sell quality paper, and to go to bed at night and sleep just fine."

A philosophy such as that has led to some close ties between 80-year-old George Griffin, who can talk about relationships with customers that have continued through second and third generations.

That kind of customer relationship has contributed much to George Griffin's personal success, and with that attitude about business he could be successful anywhere. But he says he first felt like he had found a home when he joined

Interstate/Johnson Lane in 1979. "Customers can feel that; they feel the warmth from the company. I've worked for a New York firm, and it was cold. They could feel that, too."

It is difficult to know whether that attitude about customers existed from the beginning. The individual who started Interstate Securities in 1932 did not leave his philosophy about business, or a company mission statement, for archivists to review.

But the company's longest-term employee, Claude Abernethy, remembers very clearly back to 1951, when he became one of the dozen em-

Interstate/Johnson Lane brokers have long-term relationships with clients. They are often natives of the community, and their focus is to stay close to the customer.

The company's mandate is to help customers understand the choices available to them and to help them find the quality investments that fit their needs. Balanced advice and personal service are the keys to success.

ployees of the Charlotte-based firm. Fresh from Harvard Business School and a brief tour of Europe, Abernethy joined the company as a municipal bond salesman, courting dozens of small, independent banks.

In short order he recognized the opportunity to establish the firm's first branch office in Newton, North Carolina. Abernethy, who in 1989 was named one of the country's top 10 brokers by *Registered Representative* magazine, has served the same community ever since. "That's one of the things that's different about our brokers," he says. "They tend to have long-term relationships with clients. They're often natives of the community, and they aren't going any-

where."

Customer service, strong relationships, community ties, quality products—the theme is the same from branch to branch, from broker to broker. Before the books were written about getting close to the customer, providing quality products and good service, these brokers were doing it.

The results speak for themselves. What began as a sole proprietorship in Charlotte grew to a 60-branch securities company called Interstate Securities that in 1988 merged with another southeast leader to become Interstate/Johnson Lane.

The focus remains the same: stay close to the customer. As the leading independent broker-dealer and investment banking firm headquartered in the Southeast, Interstate/Johnson Lane is well positioned to meet the rapidly expanding needs of this grow-

Customers feel an immediate rapport with the company. Before the books were written about customer relations—providing quality products and good service—Interstate/Johnson Lane was doing it.

Interstate/Johnson Lane's leaders work to keep the company focused on the customer. They are Elmon L. Vernier, Jr., (left) and J. Craighill Redwine.

ing region.

A business that was born at a time when an investment decision often boiled down to a choice between a stock and bond has changed dramatically to meet the far more sophisticated needs of today.

Interstate/Johnson Lane brokers now offer clients a wide range of services that allow them to customize an investment portfolio to fit individual needs. These opportunities include securities and futures brokerage for retail and institutional customers, market-making and underwriting of municipal and corporate securities, investment management, financial advisory services and the sale of mutual funds, unit investment trusts, limited partnership interests, insurance, and other financial products.

"We realize that the financial world is more complicated than ever, with a myriad of products and investment choices jumping out at consumers," says J. Craighill Redwine, chairman and chief executive officer of Interstate/Johnson Lane. "Our

mandate is to help our customers understand the choices available to them and to help them find the quality investments that fit their needs. The investment alternatives may have changed over the years, but balanced advice and personal service are still the key to success, for us and for our customers."

The key to offering such a full range of investment opportunities—with an emphasis on customer service—is the company's inherent flexibility and its large base of capital.

As a large regional firm, with memberships in the major securities exchanges and with approximately 1,300 employees prepared to serve a variety of customer needs, Interstate/

Stemming from its expertise in the Southeast, Interstate/Johnson Lane is a strong force in financing emerging southern companies. The firm's investment banking efforts are as highly regarded as its consumer-oriented services.

Johnson Lane employees work to ensure the company's size doesn't carry with it all the negatives associated with a large, slow-moving bureaucracy. At Interstate/Johnson Lane, many of the most important decisions continue to be made at individual brokerage offices. The company gives its brokers the freedom to serve clients according to the individual's needs—not to force clients into "the company's way of doing business."

"We'll maintain the strength of our customer relationship, and our growth, as long as we don't fall victim to the bureaucratic systems that have dragged down many of the large, New York-based firms," says Redwine. As the company focuses on maintaining the level of service expected of smaller firms, it continues to bring services to its customers that are more typical of the very large brokerage firms.

Interstate/Johnson Lane offers its customers more than 300 over-the-counter stocks. Its research staff follows more than 250 companies, studying each one as if under a microscope, working hard to find the golden nuggets of opportunity and steer clear of risky investments. The firm's investment banking and corporate finance efforts are as highly regarded as its consumer-oriented

services, generating the capital to keep some of the South's most successful companies thriving.

"Because of our expertise in this region, Interstate/Johnson Lane is a strong force in financing emerging southern companies," Redwine says. "In addition, we've become a leader in the Southeast municipal bond market, with strong track records in

North Carolina, South Carolina, and Georgia."

The company has been rewarded for its focus on the customer with a level of client loyalty that would be the envy of any company. A survey conducted in 1988 revealed highly successful broker/client relationships, with clients rating their brokers superior in these key areas: "Keeps my best interests in mind," "Listens to my needs," and "Recommends investments with handsome returns."

In an industry where customers often use the resources of several securities firms, 86 percent of the Interstate/Johnson Lane customers surveyed said they consider the company to be their primary broker, reflecting the high value they place on the advice and account management they are receiving.

A symbol of the success that comes to those who focus on the customer's needs is the company's new landmark office building, the Interstate Tower, which was announced in 1988. The 32-story, 400,000-square-foot building in uptown Charlotte will be a prominent reminder on the Charlotte skyline of what attention to the customer can bring.

"These and other rewards will come to those businesspeople who remember where the successes came from," says Redwine. "We must remind ourselves every day where we started, how we got here, and why we must stay the course."

·J. Craighill Redwine, chairman and chief executive officer of Interstate/Johnson Lane, is a native of Lexington, North Carolina, and a graduate of the University of North Carolina at Chapel Hill. He began his career with Harris, Upham and Company in 1969 and became manager of Interstate's Wilmington, North Carolina, sales office two years later. In June 1985 Redwine was elected president, chief operating officer, and director of Interstate Securities Inc. In 1986 he became chief executive officer, adding the title of chairman the following year. He retained that title with the new

Interstate/Johnson Lane.

Though his responsibilities as chief executive do not allow the degree of customer contact he enjoyed as a broker, Redwine works hard to stay close to the community. His civic work has included serving as a former director of the Charlotte Chamber of Commerce, trustee of the Charlotte Country Day Schools, and a member of the board of the Central Charlotte Association. He also serves as a member of the business advisory committee of the University of North Carolina at Charlotte Graduate School of Business and as a member of the board of directors of Spirit Square Center for the Arts.

Joining Redwine at the helm of Interstate/Johnson Lane is Elmon L. Vernier, Jr., president and chief operating officer. Prior to the merger Vernier served as president and chief executive officer of Johnson Lane. A native of Baltimore, Maryland, Vernier is a graduate of the University of Maryland, where he received a bachelor's degree in addition to a master's degree in business administration. After serving four years in the U.S. Marine Corps, Vernier's professional career began in 1969 with the investment firm Laird, Bissell and Meads, Inc., of Wilmington, Delaware. That company was acquired by Dean Witter in 1973, and Ver-

A symbol of Interstate/Johnson Lane's success at focusing on customer needs is the company's new landmark office building, the Interstate Tower.

Interstate/Johnson Lane has been rewarded with a high level of customer loyalty. A survey conducted in 1988 revealed that clients rated their brokers superior in these key areas: "Keeps my best interests in mind," "Listens to my needs," and "Recommends investments with handsome returns."

nier went on to serve in a variety of positions, including branch manager, regional sales manager, and senior vice-president. In 1984 Vernier joined Johnson Lane as national sales manager. He was named president and elected to the executive committee in 1987 and became chief executive officer the following year.

229

AETNA LIFE & CASUALTY

On July 4, 1853, Americans from coast to coast were celebrating the nation's birth with the usual parades, fireworks, and patriotic speeches. On that same day in Hartford, Connecticut, the Aetna Life Insurance Company was born, brought into the world by a group of respected local citizens and headed by Judge Eliphalet Adams Bulkeley.

At the time life insurance, although it couldn't compete with the glamour of the California Gold Rush, was one of the new enterprises very much on men's minds. The approach by which Judge Bulkeley came to active participation in life insurance affairs was a natural one. Beginning in 1846 he had been both a director and the general counsel of the Aetna (Fire) Insurance Company, founded in 1819—an organization of substance and excellent reputation. Although the immediate outlook was none too promising for the new company, what perhaps stands out most in the ensuing years is Judge Bulkeley's steadfast faith in the ultimate success of the company he served as president until his death in 1872.

His faith was well founded. Over the years Aetna has substantially expanded its insurance coverages, becoming one of the largest investor-owned financial institutions in the world, with assets of more than $75 billion. Aetna is a leading provider of insurance and financial services to corporations, public and private institutions, and individuals.

Well into its second century, Aetna is today a worldwide corporation, with more than 300 field offices throughout the United States and in Canada, Australia, New Zealand, Hong Kong, Chile, Malaysia, Indonesia, Taiwan, and Spain.

Aetna's corporate strategy is driven by a simple objective: to be the best in the business. To Aetna's 41,000 employees worldwide, being the best means working harder, going the extra mile, and being uncompromisingly dedicated to a standard of excellence—serving customers, the

The home office of Aetna Life & Casualty is located in Hanford, Connecticut.

public, independent agents, and shareholders to the best of their ability.

As early as 1940 senior management was interested in opening a full-service branch office in Charlotte, but World War II intervened, and all thoughts of expansion were abandoned. It was not until 1954—after several other locations had been considered and rejected—that the Charlotte office finally was opened.

Thomas S. Carpenter, general manager of Aetna's commercial insurance division and a 30-year Charlotte resident, says, "Charlotte was selected because of its central location and growth potential. Without a doubt, the decision to locate here has been the single most important factor in our rapid growth over the past three decades. We couldn't be more pleased with the quality of life, the strong work ethic of the local work force, the sound local government, and the responsive court sys-

Thomas S. Carpenter, CPCU, general manager of the commercial insurance division of Aetna Life & Casualty. Photo by Richard Mather

tem in the area we serve."

Thirty Aetna employees opened that first office in 3,000 square feet of the Addison Building—in fact, a converted parking garage and the only space available in the uptown area at the time. Today Aetna's offices occupy several floors of Charlotte Plaza, still within sight of the original Addison Building location.

The resemblance ends there, however. Charlotte is Aetna's regional headquarters, with more than 1,000 employees in locations throughout the Carolinas generating more than a half-billion dollars annually in revenue from all lines of insurance. Charlotte is a major location for the company's commercial insurance, employee benefits, and personal financial security divisions. More than $250 million in benefits are paid annually to or on behalf of Aetna policyholders, with state and local governments receiving an additional $16 million in premium taxes from the firm, which leases some 300,000 square feet of office space in the Carolinas.

As a responsible member of the community, Aetna management believes it is important for the company and its employees to be active

in industry, civic, government, and cultural affairs. Over the years Aetna's executives have held high-ranking positions in many insurance industry organizations and in various civic and community groups. Aetna people can be found as active volunteers in most of the community's organizations.

The Aetna Life and Casualty Foundation has made important grants to Opera Carolina, United Way, Mission Air, Project Graduation, Wing Haven, the Lupus Foundation, Homeless Shelter of Charlotte, the Charlotte Housing Authority Scholarship Fund, the YMCA, and to many other worthwhile groups and projects. Like Carpenter, James F. Byrd, who is general manager of Aetna's personal financial security division, believes the decision to make Charlotte the regional office for the Carolinas was a good one. "I've lived in the Carolinas for nine years," Byrd says, "and have watched the area develop and prosper. Today the potential for marketing insurance and financial products looks brighter than ever. Not only is Charlotte experiencing phenomenal economic growth, it is centrally located within the Carolinas and is in excellent position to partici-

Pictured here are the Charlotte branch offices of Aetna Life & Casualty in the Charlotte Plaza.

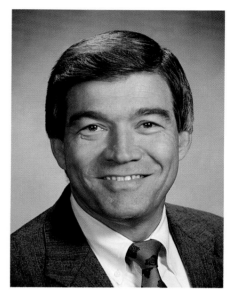

James F. Byrd, CPCU, general manager of the personal financial security division of Aetna Life & Casualty. Photo by Richard Mather

pate in the economic and industrial growth of the whole southeastern region."

As a service-oriented company with a reputation for providing quality products and professional service, Aetna Life & Casualty, too, is in an excellent position to grow along with Charlotte and the region, helping Carolinians fulfill their needs for personal automobile, home-owners, life, and health insurance. Judge Bulkeley and the other Aetna founders would be proud.

CANSLER, LOCKHART, BURTIS & EVANS

Cansler, Lockhart, Burtis & Evans is Charlotte's oldest continuous law practice. Today, well into its second century, the firm engages in a general civil practice, representing a diverse clientele, including a cross section of local individuals, families, and businesses, as well as some of America's largest corporations.

The firm has actively participated in Charlotte's growth and development since 1866, when North Carolina's former governor, Zebulon B. Vance, moved there to practice law. After a brief association with Clement Dowd, then the mayor of Charlotte and later a United States congressman, Vance formed a partnership with Armistead Burwell. In 1874, when the Wilmington, Charlotte, and Rutherfordton Railroad reached the city and made Charlotte a major transportation center, the railroad selected Burwell as its counsel. Its successor companies, Seaboard Air Line and Seaboard Coast Line Railroads, have been important clients to the firm through the years. More than a century later their successor, CSX Transportation, Inc., is still an active and significant client.

After Vance left Charlotte to return to public office as governor and then United States senator, Burwell

Cansler, Lockhart, Burtis & Evans has represented CSX Transportation, Inc., and its predecessors since 1874.

in 1880 merged his practice with that of Platt D. Walker. In 1892 Burwell was appointed to the North Carolina Supreme Court, and Walker associated E.T. Cansler in the firm. After serving as the first president of the North Carolina Bar Association in 1899, Walker was himself elected to the Supreme Court in 1902.

For many years E.T. Cansler practiced law with his two sons, Edwin T. Jr. and John S. Cansler. The Cansler name became synonymous with legal excellence throughout the State of North Carolina. During these years the firm developed an extensive life, accident, and health insurance practice, representing some of the nation's leading insurers, including Metropolitan Life Insurance Company, The Equitable Life Assurance Society of the United States, and New York Life Insurance Company. The Canslers also served as attorneys for both the City of Charlotte and Mecklenburg County.

In 1959, after the death of his father and brother, John Cansler formed a partnership with Thomas Ashe Lockhart, now the senior member of the firm. In addition to

CLOCKWISE FROM TOP LEFT:
Armistead Burwell
Platt D. Walker
E.T. Cansler
John S. Cansler

Tom Lockhart, the firm includes seven other attorneys: John Burtis, George Evans, Bruce Simpson, Tom Garlitz, Mike Allen, Barbara Dean, and Debbie Brewer . Before entering private practice, three of the attorneys served in the military as members of the Judge Advocate General's Corps, one served as a law clerk to a federal circuit judge, and one served as an assistant district attorney.

In addition to its traditional representation of transportation companies and life and health insurers, the firm represents individuals and businesses in a variety of commercial disputes, employers and employees in employment discrimination and other personnel litigation, casualty insurers, self-insured corporations and injured individuals in products liability and other personal injury cases, and both debtors and creditors in bankruptcy and related proceedings.

The firm's attorneys regularly appear in state and federal courts throughout much of North Carolina.

Along with its strong litigation practice, Cansler, Lockhart, Burtis & Evans serves as general counsel to locally headquartered Charlotte Liberty Mutual Insurance Company and as local counsel for a number of national firms, such as The Firestone Tire & Rubber Company and Ford Motor Credit Company. It also represents a diversified and growing list of area businesses in a wide range of commercial activities. The firm's services to its business clients include the formation, merger, acquisition, and liquidation of business organizations as well as advice and assistance in connection with the myriad day-to-day legal problems encountered by such enterprises. A growing area of practice has been the creation and administration of employee benefit plans. The firm also appears frequently before state and local administrative agencies, especially the North Carolina Department of Insurance, on behalf of its business clients.

Cansler, Lockhart, Burtis & Evans has also built a varied real estate practice. In recent years the firm

has been involved in shopping center, apartment complex, and other commercial projects, including three of uptown Charlotte's office towers, the Wachovia Center, the Northwestern Bank/First Federal Building, and the NCNB Plaza complex.

In addition to such commercial projects, the firm regularly represents individual clients in residential real estate transactions and provides them with estate planning, tax advice, and other legal assistance in connection with their financial and personal affairs.

Cansler, Lockhart, Burtis & Evans' lawyers continue to follow the firm's long-standing commitment of service to the public and the bar, recognizing that effective participation in the legal profession also involves a personal commitment to the charitable, educational, and civic life of the community. In recent years the firm's attorneys have served on the board of visitors of the University of North Carolina at Charlotte and the boards of directors or trustees of such charitable enterprises as the Mercy Hospital Foundation and the Episcopal Radio-TV Foundation. Members of the firm have been instrumental in arranging several major gifts to the University of North Carolina at Charlotte and in establishing the John Scott Cansler Lectureship in Trial Advocacy at the University of North Carolina School of Law in

Chapel Hill.

The firm's attorneys also participate regularly in local and state bar association committees and activities, including the Mecklenburg County Bar's various pro bono programs. In addition, Thomas Ashe Lockhart is chair of The General Practice Section of the North Carolina Bar Association.

In 1978, after the death of John Cansler, a resolution was adopted by the Twenty-sixth Judicial District Bar and the Superior Court of Mecklenburg County that stated: "The ideals and standard of excellence which John Scott Cansler exemplified are and will remain an enduring legacy to the legal profession, and to all who were fortunate enough to know this wise and good man." Cansler, Lockhart, Burtis & Evans remains committed to the fundamental concepts of integrity and excellence that John Cansler exemplified and looks forward to serving the Charlotte community for many years to come.

Tom Lockhart (right) is the firm's senior partner.

BELL, SELTZER, PARK AND GIBSON

The law and engineering—seemingly disparate disciplines—have proven to be a most effective combination for this nationally and internationally recognized law firm.

In 1922 Paul B. Eaton, a University of North Carolina graduate from Yadkinville, convinced that southern inventors preferred their legal services closer to home, left his United States Patent Office post in Washington and came home to North Carolina. Eaton chose Charlotte, at the heart of the area's textile industry, as the site for his law office, becoming the first patent law specialist to practice south of the nation's capital.

And although Bell, Seltzer, Park and Gibson is an important resource to local business and industry, it cannot be considered the typical "local" firm. "It's true that we work in a limited, highly specialized area of the law, but we cover a wide geographic area of the country," Bell explains, "and we do a great deal of international work."

In earlier years the textile industry in and around Charlotte accounted for a large percentage of Bell, Seltzer, Park and Gibson's work. The educational background of the firm's name partners eloquently testifies to that industry's im-

Paul B. Bell, president, and Charles B. Park III, chairman of the board and executive committee and head of the firm's litigation department, in the atrium of the office building.

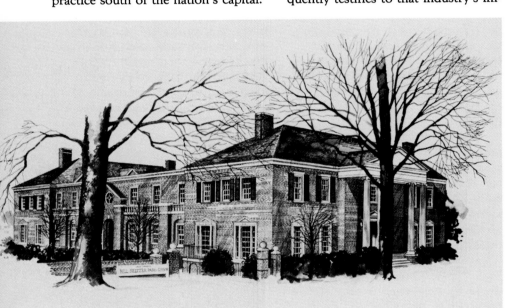

Eaton was joined in 1948 by Paul B. Bell, home after a three-year stint in the Army Air Force and fresh out of Wake Forest Law School. Together the two attorneys began to engineer the growth and development of what has become the largest firm of intellectual property law attorneys in the southeastern United States.

From its East Morehead Street office and a Research Triangle branch office opened in 1981, Bell, Seltzer, Park and Gibson provides a full range of patent, trademark, copyright, trade secret, unfair competition, and related legal services to a long list of distinguished clients.

The law firm's architecturally acclaimed office building, adjacent to the uptown area, houses its Charlotte-based attorneys and support staff, its main library, and its modern computer and communications systems.

portance. With the exception of Bell, each has, in addition to a law degree, a technical degree directly related to the textile industry: Donald M. Seltzer, a degree in textile manufacturing from North Carolina State University; Charles B. Park III, a degree in textile chemistry from North Carolina State University; and Floyd A. Gibson, a degree in textile engineering from Clemson University.

Bell, Seltzer, Park and Gibson has kept pace with the increasingly

complex legal requirements of widely diverse clients, as well as with the explosion of technological development and innovation that has taken place in Charlotte, indeed around the world, since the end of World War II. Today the firm's expertise, in addition to textiles, encompasses virtually every field of technology, including chemicals, plastics, electronics, computer software and hardware, pharmacology, and biochemistry.

The complexities of U.S. and international law, coupled with increasingly sophisticated technologies, have conspired to make the road to becoming an intellectual property attorney long and arduous. Says Bell, "A young lawyer can't just come out of law school and practice patent law."

A science or engineering degree is almost a prerequisite, and in addition to the state bar exam, a patent attorney must pass a separate bar exam to become registered to practice before the United States Patent and Trademark Office. "To become fully proficient in the profession,"

234

Senior partners Donald M. Seltzer and Floyd A. Gibson conferring on a patent matter.

Bell adds, "requires at least a five-year period of internship with a law firm."

Helping clients obtain patents and trademarks by helping guide them through the intricacies of United States and foreign law currently constitutes about half of the firm's practice. Bell, Seltzer, Park and Gibson is, however, actively engaged in the many other important aspects of intellectual property law as well, including licensing technology and franchise services.

Charles Park, chairman of the board of directors and head of the firm's litigation department, observes that, in recent years, "We have a very substantial litigation practice. In addition to frequently complex patent and trademark and copyright infringements suits, a good deal of the litigation involves counterfeiting, which has become a major problem for some of our clients."

Bell, Seltzer, Park and Gibson rep-resents a number of foreign companies, most of which have facilities in the United States or contacts with local firms, in addition to the work it does abroad for North American clients. To support this international aspect of its practice, the firm has more than 100 handpicked representatives in law firms all over the world, as well as in-house translation capabilities in German, French, and Spanish.

Bell, Seltzer, Park and Gibson currently comprises more than 30 attorneys—and still counting—plus a greater number of support staff. As its size increased, the firm began to outgrow its 16,000-square-foot Georgian-style Charlotte office. Ron Morgan, a Charlotte architect, was called in to rehabilitate the existing building, design a new 16,000-square-foot addition, and install new parking and landscaped areas. The project was completed in 1987, and the work was so successfully and beautifully accomplished that it was featured in *Update* and *North Carolina Architecture* magazines.

Bell, Seltzer, Park and Gibson attorneys have a distinguished record of service to the law profession and to the Charlotte community. Charles Park is the only southeastern patent attorney to be named a Fellow of the prestigious American College of Trial Lawyers; Samuel G. Layton, Jr., has served as president of the Licensing Executives Society, U.S.A. and Canada; Paul B. Bell is president of the International Federation of Industrial Property Attorneys, U.S., and has served as president of the Charlotte City Club and the Charlotte Textile Club; and Michael D. McCoy has served as secretary of the Mecklenburg County Bar Association.

In the years since Paul Eaton came home to practice law, Bell, Seltzer, Park and Gibson has been there, working with area inventors and innovators in their own factories, textile mills, and university research laboratories—providing one of the vital services that help make Charlotte the service center of the Southeast.

John L. Sullivan, Jr., head of the trademark department, and associate attorney Martha G. Barber in the firm library.

235

10

Building Greater Charlotte

From concept to completion, Charlotte's building industry and real estate professionals shape tomorrow's skyline.

Waters Incorporated, 238-239

Little & Co., 240

Merrill Lynch Realty, Inc., 241

James M. Alexander Realty, Inc., 242-243

Crosland Erwin Associates, 244-245

Jones Group, Inc., 246-247

Marsh Associates, Inc., 248-249

Childress Klein Properties, 250-251

Rowe Corporation, 252-253

W.R. Bonsal Company, 254-255

John Crosland Company/ Centex Homes, 256-259

D.L. Phillips Investment Builders, Inc., 260

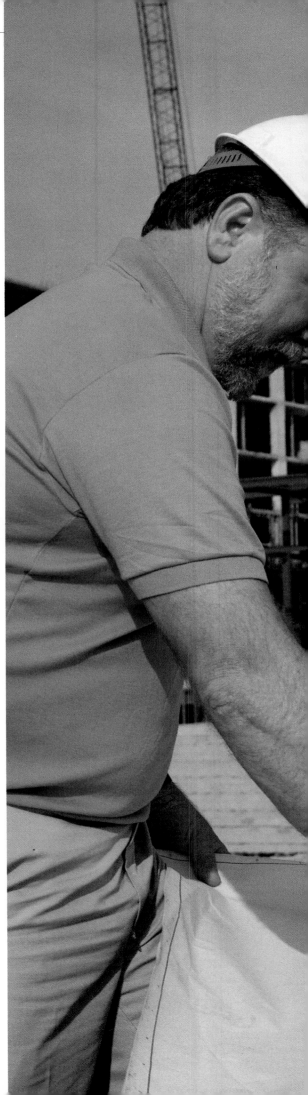

Photo by Paul Epley

WATERS INCORPORATED

This three-story traditional office building of elliptical shape is known as CentrePort One and is located at the Triad Airport in Greensboro, North Carolina. It was the first building in what became a 26-acre office park.

In 1930 Karl M. Waters, Sr., founded the company to sell insurance and manage properties in Charlotte. Today the company he founded is still in the business of real estate and insurance, but its scope has expanded to the development, brokerage, and management of major commercial properties as well as the sale of personal and commercial insurance. Its market area extends throughout the Carolinas.

K. Martin Waters, Jr., joined the firm in 1948 and has successfully guided the company as president since 1953. K. Martin Waters III has, as executive vice-president, forwarded the image, activity, and profitability of the company his grandfather founded. And Robin Waters Griffith, another third-generation Waters, is vice-president/retail development.

They all believe that future growth is possible only by giving active leadership roles to other knowledgeable managers in the firm. "We've been helped by an infusion of young people in responsible positions," says Martin Waters, Jr. "This is not just a family business."

They agree that the success of Waters Incorporated has been the result of the company's creativity and flexibility in responding to changes in the marketplace. At the same time, Waters has earned a reputation for reliability.

Waters' Real Estate Division actively works in all phases of commercial real estate—as a developer, broker of income-producing properties (including residential rental properties), and manager of commercial and residential properties. In addition, Waters often acts as a private placement syndicator of joint ventures for corporate and individual investors.

The company's real estate developments have consistently produced profitable returns and attracted private investors. It still manages many of the properties it originally built. Moreover, the firm's executives are proud to say that Waters has maintained relationships with some clients for more than 40 years.

The growth of Charlotte has played an important role in the growth of the company's real estate. As the city's population rapidly expanded in the 1940s, Waters recognized the need for low-income rental housing. The firm responded by building affordable brick single-family homes for which there is still a high demand. Waters continues to own and manage many of those homes.

When Charlotte's active business environment began to attract more people from outside the area, Waters was one of the first companies to develop mini-warehouses. Today the firm is the biggest manager of those storage facilities in the city.

Today, with a strong business development climate in both North and South Carolina, Waters Incorporated has established itself as an experi-

This one-story structure is a part of Parklane Centre, an office-showroom complex in Columbia, South Carolina.

enced developer of business/office centers and of retail strip shopping centers in areas of suburban growth.

"We want to respond to the many entrepreneurial and high-tech businesses in the area," says Martin Waters III, who has specialized in the company's development of large commercial projects. "Our planned and landscaped office parks provide office, showroom, and storage space to such companies."

Beginning with the 52-acre Park Cedar Commerce Center in Charlotte, Waters has developed business parks in several major cities.

In the North Carolina Triad, it has created CenterPort, a master-planned, 26-acre, multiuse office park. Located just off I-40 in Greensboro, the center includes an Embassy Suites Hotel.

In the nearby North Carolina Research Triangle, Waters has created Greenpoint Business Center and in Columbia, South Carolina, Waters has built Parklane Centre, a 15-acre office-showroom-service park.

Currently it is developing a major Class A office park, which will feature a seven-story Compri Hotel, in Charlotte's rapidly expanding UNCC area.

The company has also recognized a surge in the retail market and an increased consumer demand for inviting shopping areas, especially outside

R. Steven De Conti (left), director of design and construction; J. Arthur Whedon (center), vice-president/property management; and Robert P. Jones (right), vice-president/office business park development.

the Carolinas' urban centers. Robin Waters Griffith is helping Waters Incorporated meet that demand through retail strip centers. The firm has developed a number of 50,000- to 60,000-square-foot shopping centers.

In the Charlotte area, Harrisburg Market includes a Food Lion and a Family Dollar Store, with space for a drugstore, Hardee's Restaurant, and other small shops. In the fast-growing northeastern edge of the city, Newell Hickory Square and Lawyers Square shopping centers offer similar amenities.

In Gastonia, Waters has built New Hope Square, near I-85. In the Triad area, it has developed Eastchester Market shopping center.

While the real estate division is the company's most visible area of activity, Waters' Insurance Division also is a thriving business entity. It provides personal and commercial services from a variety of major insurance companies to individual and corporate clients throughout the Carolinas. Its goal is to offer clients guidance and advice within an atmosphere of trust.

To assure the future growth of Waters Incorporated, the company encourages the professional development of its managers and executives. Both Martin Waters III and Robin Griffith have met the demanding requirements for the designation of Certified Commercial Investment Member (CCIM) of the National Association of Realtors. Robin was the youngest woman in North Carolina to achieve the designation. Martin Wa-

Pictured here are the Waters family members involved in the business. From left is K. Martin Waters III, executive vice-president; K. Martin Waters, Jr., president; and Robin W. Griffith, vice-president/retail.

ters III is now a certified teacher in the program.

All three family members are active in Charlotte's business and civic affairs. Martin Waters, Jr., serves on the board of a savings and loan and a bank, and is a past president of the Charlotte Rotary Club. Martin Waters III serves on the national board of Learning HOW, Inc., an organization for handicapped men and women. Robin Griffith is an active member of Charlotte's Junior League.

In both real estate and insurance, Waters Incorporated looks forward to continuing a strong and gradual expansion in the Carolinas. It will do so by continuing to utilize talented young people to find creative new ways in which to grow with the expanding city and region where it began.

LITTLE & CO.

Little & Co. began as Little Construction Co., Inc., in 1949. William E. Little drew on a construction background when he founded the company; his father and grandfather had owned John P. Little & Son, which erected the Builders Building (1923) and First Methodist Church (1927), among other Charlotte landmarks.

For the first two decades of its existence, Little Construction Co., Inc., operated as a general contractor, specializing in concrete-framed commercial and institutional buildings. Among its more prominent construction projects were two major additions to Charlotte Memorial Hospital (1960 and 1962), Craige and Eringhaus dormitories at the University of North Carolina (1963), the Northwestern Bank Building in Asheville (1967), Holshouser and Scott dormitories at UNC-Charlotte (1968), and the Park Abbey, Park Seneca, and Park View office buildings in Charlotte (1969-1972).

Little Construction Co.'s expansion into real estate development and property management began with the Park Abbey Building. It was Southern National Center, however, that marked a major change in the company's direction.

Southern National Center, a 22-story office/retail/parking complex in uptown Charlotte, was developed by Little Construction Co., Inc., in 1974. The firm, now known as Little & Co., continues to manage the project and retains an ownership interest in it. Southern National Center, in addition to providing more than 500,000 square feet of office space, includes the central business district's largest parking facility—more than 1,500 spaces in an 11-level deck.

Southern National Center also played a critical role in the development of Overstreet Mall. The building's third floor, which is devoted to retail shops and restaurants, is the converging point of four of Overstreet Mall's pedestrian bridges.

In 1981 Little & Co. played an-

Southern National Center, developed and managed by Little & Co., includes a 1,500-space parking facility.

other important role in Charlotte's central business district with its complete renovation of the historic Johnston Building (which was later renamed the UCB Building). The company was also a joint-venture developer of the 22-story First Citizens Bank Plaza, which opened in 1987.

Little & Co. has further diversified its business by moving into residential land development in the Charlotte and Raleigh suburbs. The firm buys land, plans and implements the construction of utilities and roads, and sells improved lots to major home builders.

Little & Co. has remained a family-owned business. William E. Little, founder and president, has been joined by his sons, William E. Little, Jr., and Rodney J. Little. Together, they see their organization continuing to grow with the city. "Charlotte's role as the financial center of the Southeast, its open-shop construction industry, and its pro-growth orientation," says the company's president, "combine to form an economic climate that holds great promise for the future."

A crane that moved on railroad tracks was a key innovation in the Little & Co. construction of a major addition to Charlotte Memorial Hospital in 1960.

MERRILL LYNCH REALTY, INC.

The Merrill Lynch Realty building in Charlotte.

In 1980 there was no Merrill Lynch Realty office in Charlotte. Yet in less than a decade it has become the largest real estate firm in the Metrolina area. With special divisions for relocation services and corporate home sales as well as residential sales, it serves home buyers and sellers from Gastonia and Lake Norman to Monroe.

This rapid growth has been the result of a planned series of acquisitions and an aggressive marketing support program for the company's sales associates. Merrill Lynch Realty, for example, provides associates with continuous training and support materials, while it has created innovative ways to market homes.

According to the office of Charlotte's president, Muriel Helms, Merrill Lynch Realty recognizes that "associates are what makes our company. How good we are depends on how well we recruit them and train them."

Merrill Lynch Realty is the nation's only publicly traded, independent, real estate services firm. It was formed in the 1970s as a subsidiary of the brokerage firm of Merrill Lynch & Co. when that organization began to diversify.

Once the firm identified the growing Charlotte area as the right location for a district office, it purchased the Townsend Company to establish itself in the city. A series of later acquisitions accomplished specific goals for growth.

Moffatt Sherard and Associates provided an entry into the upscale market in 1983. Wightman/Helms offered entry into the builder market and the geographic locations of Monroe and Lake Norman. Finally, in 1987, the acquisition of Alyce Walker Realtors increased the company's customer base and strength.

Today Merrill Lynch Realty offers a wide variety of innovative services that help home buyers and sellers. As a member of Network 50, it helps people who are relocating in all 50 states with professional services. Through association with GMAC Mortgage, it offers buyers many options for financing. Because the exclusive Merrill Lynch Certified Appraisal Program (CAP) assures proper pricing of a home for sale, sellers can sell faster and buyers get loans faster.

Moreover, Muriel Helms says the firm recognizes that part of its job is to keep Charlotte attractive to people and companies who may move here. A past president of the Charlotte Board of Realtors, she has actively participated in committees to review and revise Charlotte's zoning and sign ordinances. "We are very lucky to have a unique combination of strong voices for both development and neighborhood preservation in Charlotte," she says. "That balance

Muriel W. Helms, president of Merrill Lynch Realty/Metrolina.

keeps making the city an unusual and appealing place to live."

In addition, the firm's associates actively work to improve the quality of life in the Metrolina area. Associates have formed a committee for community involvement. One of their first projects was to volunteer and convince the company to become a major contributor to the first two years of Project Graduation, a safe celebration for graduating high school seniors.

For Merrill Lynch Realty that kind of involvement is an important part of making the success of Charlotte part of the company's growth.

JAMES M. ALEXANDER REALTY, INC.

In 1988 a premier Charlotte business publication ranked James M. Alexander Realty, Inc., as the fifth-largest developer in Mecklenburg County. That listing recognized the company's involvement in developing more than 900,000 square feet of commercial real estate from 1981 to 1986. By 1988 the firm's total had risen to more than 1.25 million square feet, worth in excess of $50 million.

The work was accomplished by an organization with just six employees. It is a company founded and led by a man who was born in Fourth Ward's Charlotte Sanatorium Hospital and who has spent most of his working life contributing to the city's development.

Working in partnership with other area developers, Jim Alexander identifies convenient locations within the city and county and develops them for use by businesses. He keeps his own businesses small and contracts with supporting contractors and suppliers to accomplish his goal of creating successful business, office, and industrial facilities.

In addition, James M. Alexander Realty, Inc., manages, leases, and sells properties owned by the Alexander affiliates and a few selected

owners.

"I consider myself fortunate to be in Charlotte when the city is experiencing its most significant growth and to have the experience to contribute to that growth," Alexander says.

He has structured his firm so that it does not have to be continuously in the process of developing new projects. Instead, Alexander and his partners select projects that seem most advantageous and in which he can personally be active. The firm often creates medium-size projects on sites that are sometimes considered too small for investment by huge development companies. Thus, Alexander Realty has been able to take advantage of undeveloped properties in high-growth areas within the city.

The company was a pioneer developer of the highly successful I-77 South corridor in its creation of 77 Corporate Park. About two-thirds of the park's original 330,000 square feet was leased by IBM when the cor-

James M. Alexander at the new Carolina Commerce Center. This 75-acre commercial and industrial park is located on I-77 at Highway 160 just over the South Carolina border. Says Alexander, "Carolina Commerce Center offers tenants the combination of Charlotte's vibrant economy and urban culture, as well as the many advantages of the two Carolinas."

poration first arrived in Charlotte.

James M. Alexander Realty assisted D.L. Phillips Investment Builders with the development and marketing of the 450-acre Phillips Business Park. Beginning in 1978 Phillips developed the land and infrastructure for what is now more than 2.2 million square feet of corporate headquarters, manufacturing, storage, and distribution facilities. These buildings are now owner occupied or investor owned and leased to such companies as Ridgeway Chemicals, Inc., Brad Ragan, Inc., Powertron, Mill Power Supply, White Business Machines, Data South, and Suzy Curtains.

Phillips and Alexander are now using the balance of the acreage in the park as developers for projects such as CenterSouth, an unusually attractive office/showroom/dock high-storage facility and garden office space. The company has also used five acres of the park to develop two high-quality corporate headquarters/office/distribution buildings. Other acreage is still available and will be developed in the near future.

In 1986 Alexander Realty continued its I-77 tradition with the ground breaking of Carolina Commerce Center, a 75-acre mixed-use

CenterSouth, located on I-77 in Phillips Business Park, is a three-building complex that features 125,000 square feet of office and showroom space.

business and industrial park on I-77, five miles south of the Charlotte city limits, at the intersection of SC 160. The park, still under development, includes a bank, an office building, a corporate headquarters and distribution building, and a medical clinic. The park will contain $35 million worth of new construction when completed and employ 1,500 people.

Such enormous accomplishments come as no surprise to those who knew Jim Alexander before the 1950s. He arrived at his career as a major developer after first majoring in chemistry at the University of North Carolina at Chapel Hill and serving as a naval officer in command of an antisubmarine escort ship in the Pacific during World War II.

In 1955 he and a partner established Tar Heel Sash and Door Company, a successful wholesale millwork jobbing company that provided materials for more than two-thirds of the residential starts in Charlotte for many years. There he became a licensed real estate broker, and he learned how multifamily developments could become successful investment projects.

In 1960 he developed a 32-unit complex called 400 Queens Road to show his builder customers that apartments were a profitable investment. One of the first apartment com-

plexes built in Charlotte after World War II, it was the first—and smallest—of Alexander's many developments.

In addition to his involvement in the commercial development along I-77, Alexander and his partners have also successfully created other Charlotte investment ventures.

The 52,000-square-foot Monroe Road Business Park offers tenants easily accessible, visible retail/office/showroom space near the city's center on one of its most heavily traveled central arteries.

Farther east, at 9500 Monroe Road, Sardis Executive Park includes office and office-showroom facilities in a 14-acre landscaped setting.

In South Boulevard Business Park, three buildings provide 34,000 square feet of warehouse space.

James M. Alexander Realty, Inc., also developed Hedgemore Plaza Office Building, with partners Paul Gibson and Penn Mutual Life Insurance Company, in 1981. This nine-story, 150,000-square-foot office building is located just off Park Road in midtown Charlotte.

The company continues to pursue James Alexander's goal: to create successful investments by identifying and developing commercial projects in Charlotte's best locations.

Sardis Executive Park is a 14-acre retail and office/office showroom business park in southeast Charlotte. This vibrant area features tremendous new growth. Five buildings are in place, and eight acres remain for further development.

CROSLAND ERWIN ASSOCIATES

For one of Charlotte's most visible developers of investment properties, success lies in finding prime locations and developing the quality that will produce a long-term return. Crosland Erwin Associates achieves those goals by establishing partnerships with key people in each development, thus sharing the success of the project with those responsible for it.

Company president Mark Erwin says, "We are niche developers, operating outside the mainstream. We find a place in the market where there is less competition and meet a demand."

The firm began in 1982 as a partnership of John Crosland, Jr., and Mark Erwin, an outgrowth of John Crosland & Associates. Among the new partners' first projects was the development of Quail Corners Shopping Center and a historic renovation of uptown Charlotte's Latta Arcade. Three years later, with a variety of major projects under way, the company became Crosland Erwin Associates.

According to John Crosland, Jr., who became chairman of the board, "Mark Erwin brought a driving force and a newly aggressive attitude to the way my family has been developing commercial real estate since 1954."

In the relatively few years since its beginning, the company has created more than a dozen shopping centers, as well as other commercial developments, in virtually all parts of Charlotte. Such rapid growth has been aided by the company's innovations.

With the opening of Outlet Marketplace in 1986, for example, Crosland Erwin created the country's first outlet festival center. The enclosed outlet mall of 220,000 square feet combines shopping with special events, music, and entertainment. At

TOP: *Quail Corners Shopping Center lends a congenial ambience to professional southeast Charlotte.*

LEFT: *Town Center Plaza serves the shopping needs of the rapidly developing University area.*

Charlotte Apparel Center and Days Inn at Fifth and College streets in uptown Charlotte.

A view over the east side of the tree-lined boulevard gateway into the 22-acre CrownPoint development.

its 10,000-square-foot center, a wide variety of community events, including the annual Jerry Lewis Telethon, are held each year.

Waterford Center, just off I-77, was the area's first business center to combine wholesale and retail outlets in a highly visible location. By the summer of 1988 demand for space prompted an expansion of 15,000 square feet in Phase II.

At CrownPoint, Crosland Erwin created the area's first mixed-use park for shopping, hotels, and business use. It includes CrownPoint Plaza Shopping Center, CrownPoint Business Center, and CrownCentre Executive Park.

There the company entered into a public/private venture with the North Carolina Department of Transportation to extend Sardis Road North through the park, providing access to Monroe Road and Independence Boulevard. It is also donating property within the park to the coun-

ty's McAlpine Greenway system. Moreover, land was reserved within the CrownPoint master plan for the future development of a light-rail system into the uptown area.

At River Pointe on Lake Wylie, Crosland Erwin created a prestigious single-family residential development, including a beach, cabana, and pool, and a 60-slip marina. There houses will be built and sold by the area's premier builders.

In uptown Charlotte, Crosland Erwin joined with the city for a unique public/private venture, the 650,000-square-foot Charlotte Apparel Center, completed early in 1989. It includes a 300-room Days Inn hotel and a 900-space parking garage. The center was designed and built to meet the needs of the Carolina Virginia Fashion Exhibitors (CVFE), the country's third-largest apparel show.

As Charlotte has expanded Crosland Erwin has developed shopping centers that meet the needs of new neighborhoods. Centers such as Town Center Plaza near UNCC, The Colonnade on Albemarle Road, Nor-

man Crossing at Lake Norman, Old Hickory at the city's southern edge, and Lake Wylie Plaza bring important services such as grocery and drugstores, dry cleaners, and banks near the city's areas of rapid growth.

In each case Crosland Erwin has used a team of professionals to select and acquire the site, develop the project, and provide leasing and management services. While this team approach applies the expertise of individuals to specific tasks, a systematic review program also ensures that all projects are repeatedly reviewed by top management.

Crosland Erwin's partners assert that Charlotte's pattern of growth, strong leadership in the world of banking, and location as an airline hub assure its future as a center for regional and commercial development. In addition, they say the city's physical beauty and nearby lakes add to its residential appeal.

As a result, they expect to continue to concentrate their efforts in the metropolitan Charlotte area. At the same time they expect Crosland Erwin Associates' managers and partners to maintain their commitment to community service.

"We are a hometown developer, here for the long term, in an exciting, dynamic community," says Mark Erwin. "That means we know we must continue to be involved in its leadership and to participate in the public/private ventures with which we have helped the city grow."

JONES GROUP, INC.

"For the Jones Group companies, commitment to quality is not just policy—it's been the foundation of our business for nearly 100 years."
—Johnie H. Jones, chairman and president

Jones Group, Inc., headquartered in Charlotte, is the largest general contracting company in North Carolina and one of the largest general building contractor in the United States. The Jones Group companies provide diversified construction services to both domestic and international markets, and are part of Philipp Holzmann AG, a West German firm that is ranked as the fourth-largest construction company in the world. The Jones Group companies have grown to enjoy a national, as well as local, reputation for quality-focused, on-time construction and cost-cutting, innovative building techniques.

When James Addison Jones founded the J.A. Jones Construction Company in Charlotte in 1890, he recognized the Queen City as the rising star of the Carolinas. From its inception, J.A. Jones Construction Com-

Jones built Charlotte's tallest skyscraper, One First Union Center, an example of fine craftsmanship and commitment to quality. © Tim Buckman, Rick Alexander Studio

pany has built Charlotte's landmarks. In 1908, upon completion of the first and only skyscraper in the Carolinas, the 12-story Independence Building, James A. Jones moved the firm's offices into its top floor. The view from his windows reflected the changing nature of the city as Charlotte became a major urban center.

Soon the buildings that Jones constructed dominated Charlotte's uptown. As taller buildings became necessary to fill the expanding needs of Charlotte's strong financial community, Jones was there to build them. Today J.A. Jones has once again built Charlotte's tallest skyscraper, indeed, the tallest building between Philadelphia and Atlanta. The pink granite One First Union Center exemplifies the company's fine craftsmanship and commitment to quality.

The Jones Group companies continue the tradition of quality construction. The 12 operating subsidiaries of Jones Group, Inc., with offices nationwide, have unlimited bonding capacity and carry the highest credit and financial ratings.

Metric Constructors, Inc., a merit shop subsidiary headquartered in Charlotte, has built many other Charlotte landmarks: the Mint Museum addition; the award-winning Charlotte-Mecklenburg Government Center; 6100 Fairview, SouthPark's tallest building; Thalhimers department store at SouthPark Mall—the newest addition to the mall that Metric's sister company J.A. Jones Construction built in 1970; and the shopping center at University Place.

Metric's commitment to the "quality in construction" tenet and to the quality of life in Charlotte has been blended in three projects: the International Concourse D, Charlotte's gateway to the world, at the Charlotte/Douglas International Airport; Calvary Church, the city's largest, in south Charlotte; and the Piper Glen Clubhouse facility at Charlotte's only Tournament Player's Club golf course.

The Jones Group also builds durable roads. The 51-year-old Rea Construction Company, a Jones Group subsidiary headquartered in Charlotte, recently received the National

Designed by J.N. Pease Associates, the Charlotte-Mecklenburg Government Center is one of the many Charlotte-area projects that Jones Group, Inc., has constructed. Photo by Gordon Schenk

The Mint Museum, a Metric Constructors, Inc., contribution to the quality of life in Charlotte.

With a national as well as local reputation for quality-focused on-time construction and cost-cutting, innovative building techniques, Jones Group, Inc., built the Fort Drum Cogeneration plant in Fort Drum, New York. Photo by Peter R. Barber

The professionals at Jones pride themselves on finding creative, cost-saving answers to problems on the construction project.

One entire Jones Group subsidiary is devoted to innovation. The J.A. Jones Applied Research Company operates the Electric Power Research Institute (EPRI) Nondestructive Evaluation (NDE) Center in Charlotte to develop research and development programs for improving electric power production, distribution, and utilization.

Today the Jones Group companies build cogeneration and waste-to-energy facilities, hotels and airport terminals, breweries and food-processing plants, high-tech university laboratories and classrooms, hospitals and long-term health facilities, power plants and dams, as well as some of the world's tallest structures. Quality construction, tight cost and time schedules, and innovative approaches to solving construction project problems are what the Jones Group companies excel in, and the dedicated professionals who work for Jones Group, Inc., will continue to meet these tough construction challenges in Charlotte and throughout the world.

Parking garages and International Concourse D under construction at Charlotte Douglas International Airport by Metric Constructors, Inc., a Charlotte-based subsidiary of Jones Group, Inc.

Asphalt Pavement Association Proof of Quality Award for a segment of Charlotte's Sharon Amity Road. Rea uses the latest in equipment and environmental standards in road construction, resurfacing (including asphalt recycling), and bridge construction throughout the Carolinas and Virginia.

Not only would Charlotteans know the Jones Group companies' projects at home, but throughout North Carolina, the nation, and the world. Among the recent projects are the Philip Morris manufacturing facility in Cabarrus County, North Carolina; the restoration of the East and West facades of the U.S. Capitol and the award-winning East Wing of the National Gallery in Washington,

D.C.; and the headquarters of AT&T in New York, Xerox and Union Carbide in Connecticut, and Transco in Houston. In Chicago, Jones erected the world's tallest concrete building, and more than 40 Jones-built structures grace the Atlanta skyline, including the Marriott Marquis Hotel, the Georgia Pacific headquarters, and the tallest hotel, Peachtree Plaza.

Jones Group's subsidiary J.A. Jones Construction Company has built projects in more than 60 countries. These projects range from constructing or upfitting American embassies and consulates for the U.S. State Department to providing project management on the $330-million Raffles City in Singapore.

If quality is Jones Group's first name, then innovation is its second.

MARSH ASSOCIATES, INC.

the help of excellent FHA financing, Marsh began building apartments, many of which the company still owns and operates in the Sedgefield and Camp Green areas. Marsh's projects at the time also included the Sedgefield Shopping Center on South Boulevard, Charlotte's first suburban shopping center, with Harris-Teeter as the lead tenant.

It was also at about this time that Lex Marsh made several significant contributions to the real estate

LEFT: Chairman of the board Lex Marsh reviews a layout of a new shopping center with David Francis, president, and John S. Johnston, vice-chairman.

BELOW: Executive vice-president Linda Theisen-Barnhill discusses a new mortgage product with loan originators, Sarah Wannamaker, Diane Stancombe, and Cathy Gardner.

Over the past 60 years in Charlotte, the name "Marsh" has come to be synonymous with apartments, real estate, and mortgage lending.

Lex Marsh, the company's founder and current chairman of the board, was born in Marshville, North Carolina, in 1900 and moved with his family to Charlotte when he was nine years old. At the time the Marsh family owned several tracts of farmland in Mecklenburg County, including the area known today as Sedgefield.

Marsh joined the Army when he was 18 and was ordered to Europe. As it happened, however, Marsh never left the country, because World War I ended just before his regiment was scheduled to sail. Returning to North Carolina and Wake Forest University Law School, Marsh earned a law degree at age 20 and became the state's youngest licensed attorney at 21.

It was during the Roaring Twenties that Marsh first went into real estate, selling lots on Biltmore Drive for about $2,500. Midway through the project, however, the Great Depression struck, and those same lots went for $250, if a buyer could be found.

In the early 1940s a friend in the Federal Housing Administration advised Marsh to get approval as an FHA mortgage banker to help bring badly needed capital into the area. "I had never thought about being a mortgage banker," says Marsh, "but six months later I was in the business in a big way."

After World War II, and with

and mortgage lending industries in Charlotte. He founded the multiple listing service for the Board of Realtors, and he organized and served as the first president of both the Home Builders' Association of Charlotte and the Charlotte Mortgage Bankers' Associations.

Over the years the Marsh organization built several single-family subdivisions containing thousands of lots and homes for Charlotte's growing population, including Forest Pawtuckett, Sedgefield, and Windsor Park.

In the early 1960s Marsh brought two young men into his company who would revitalize the operation and help lead it to substantial growth over the next quarter-century. First to join Marsh was John Sikes Johnston, a Charlotte native with family real estate ties and a law degree earned in preparation for a career in real estate. Next came David L. Francis, a loan officer with the Jefferson Pilot Corporation who was brought in to develop the mortgage banking and commercial real estate divisions.

Under the new Marsh team, apartment construction began anew in the late 1960s. Projects such as Ashbrook, Salem Village, Wembley Arms, Carmel-on-Providence, Pawtucket-on-the-Green, and Elmhurst were built. With more than

Jane McArver, property manager, and Trish Smith, resident manager, review construction progress at Strawberry Hill—a 567-unit apartment complex.

Christmas at the Strawberry Hill Apartments, Marsh Associates' flagship project.

1,500 units, Marsh is today the largest apartment owner-operator in Charlotte.

In the late 1960s the Marsh organization moved its operation from the Wilder Building at South Tryon and Second Street to the current Park Road location. It was at about this time that the firm's mortgage operation literally exploded, with loan servicing growing more than tenfold over the next decade. The Marsh team's reasoning that real estate brokers would appreciate the free park-

ing and convenient access the new suburban location offered proved to be correct. Within five years virtually every mortgage lender in Charlotte had followed suit and joined Marsh Associates in the suburbs.

Work was started in 1976 on what is today the Marsh flagship project, the Strawberry Hill Apartments complex of 567 units. Strawberry Hill was developed from five separate purchases, including the tract of land that was Lex Marsh's homeplace until 1970. His house eventually was converted into the elegant clubhouse now enjoyed by Strawberry Hill residents.

It's also in Strawberry Hill that the fifth Marsh neighborhood shopping center will be located. An innovative, carefully planned group of specialty shops and support services, the shopping center will be built completely within the complex, so resi-

dents can do their shopping without ever having to get into their automobiles.

Over the years Marsh established several companies to handle the various aspects of his business. To bring the organization under a single umbrella, Marsh Associates, Inc., was formed in 1979—its mission to originate and service mortgage loans and to develop and manage the company's various properties and investments, a multimillion-dollar enterprise.

David Francis, president of Marsh Associates; John Sikes Johnston, vice-chairman; and Lex Marsh, chairman, compose a team that has had—and continues to have—a significant and lasting impact on the life of this city.

From his vantage point of more than six decades in Charlotte real estate, Lex Marsh has this advice for a new generation of Charlotteans: "When you live in a city such as Charlotte, buy—but don't sell—real estate, and buy for the long pull—not for a quick profit."

249

CHILDRESS KLEIN PROPERTIES

Look at uptown Charlotte's most distinctive building, and you'll see the work of the partners who formed Childress Klein Properties. Their experience is clearly visible in the 42-story One First Union Center.

Their company develops, leases, and manages offices, industrial facilities, and shopping centers. Its assets are valued in excess of $750 million.

According to managing partner Fred Klein, "Our goal is to be one of the most focused, thoughtful, and dynamic developers in the area. We will maintain a hands-on approach to the market so we can respond quickly to fast-breaking opportunities."

Klein and Don Childress joined forces to apply their extensive experience and recognition as outstanding developers of commercial real estate. They have been involved in the development of some of the Southeast's most prestigious projects. In Charlotte, their landmark developments include LakePointe office park, the Arboretum retail center, and more than 7 million square feet of industrial space.

Childress Klein Properties also op-

RIGHT: The distinctive One First Union Center headquarters First Union National Bank. The 42-story landmark features polished granite, rich mahogany, and first-class amenities.

BELOW: LakePointe, Childress Klein's prestigious office park on the thriving Airport/Coliseum corridor, features Belk Stores' 580,000-square-foot headquarters.

erates regional offices in Atlanta and Richmond to assure close management of the major properties it developed in those cities.

The flagship of the company's assets is the One First Union Center in uptown Charlotte. Rising 600 feet above the corner of College and Third streets, it is part of a multiphase project including a luxury 411-room Omni Hotel and two additional future office towers.

At the center's opening, Ed Crutchfield, chairman of First Union Corporation, said, "We all owe a

great deal to Fred Klein, who has been one of the leading forces behind our new First Union building. He has left no stone unturned in making it the very best it can be. To me, One First Union Center is exciting and modern, yet steeped in the tradition of quality and service. It embodies our excitement as a company, a community, and a people."

In the thriving Airport-Coliseum corridor, Childress Klein is developing a premier corporate environment at the 265-acre LakePointe business center. Adjacent to the Charlotte Coliseum and the 370-acre York Road Park are LakePointe houses, among others, the headquarters of Belk Stores, the district office of Southern Bell, and major offices of Digital Equipment, General Electric, and NCR Corporation. Its wooded grounds, which include lakes, streams, and fountains, offer businesses an appealing natural location.

The firm also developed Pine Brook, an 850,000-square-foot planned business park just off I-77 on Arrowood Road. It includes research and development facilities for such companies as Eastman Kodak and Mercedes Benz/Freightliner. Moreover, it is developing Brookwood, a 150-acre office/industrial park off Westinghouse Boulevard, continuing its strong commitment to industrial development.

Childress Klein Properties has developed several retail properties in the Charlotte metro area. The Arboretum, a 350,000-square-foot shopping center, is part of a major mixed-use complex at the intersection of Highway 51 and Providence Road. It fea-

Childress Klein Properties partners are (standing, from left) Harry Clements, Chip Mark, Tad Leithead, and Landon Wyatt. Seated (from left) are Jim Patterson, Don Childress, Fred Klein, John Decker, David Miller, Gordon Buchmiller, Charles MacFarlane, and George Cornelson.

tures a mix of fashion and specialty shops and neighborhood services. The Arboretum has been designed to appeal to the tastes of the nearby upscale neighborhoods. Its traditional architecture has the flair of a European village market, accented with fountains, benches, and gazebos.

The Arboretum will expand upon the Childress Klein retail successes created at Tower Place Festival, Franklin Square, and Reddman Square.

For the future, partners Don Childress and Fred Klein have positioned their company as a prime developer of fine commercial properties in rapidly growing areas. They have prepared the firm for greater expansion into Charlotte's burgeoning Airport/Coliseum area.

They chose to locate their company in Charlotte because of the city's thriving diversified economy, resources, and high-growth potential. They say that as the Southeast's banking capital, Charlotte offers the firm access to major lending resources. The cooperative relationship between civic and business leaders and the ease of access to this transportation hub for the region also make the

Pine Brook, a 110-acre business park on Arrowood Road off I-77, displays Childress Klein's commitment to integrating quality architecture in a beautifully landscaped environment.

city the right choice for Childress Klein Properties.

In support of that choice, Childress Klein has become an active supporter of the city's charitable and cultural institutions. Its partners have involved themselves in community affairs and the activities of many corporate boards.

"We believe Charlotte is the right place for our company," says Klein. "Its exciting history and prospects for growth make it the perfect base for Childress Klein Properties. We intend to make Charlotte's success part of our own."

Tower Place Festival, repeatedly named as "Charlotte's Best Shopping Center," is located in dynamic South Charlotte.

ROWE CORPORATION

The Rowe Corporation headquarters building in Charlotte.

In 1921 Ralph Hubbard Bouligny used his savings to purchase the electrical construction department of the Charlotte firm he worked for, Tucker-Laxton Construction Company. He renamed it R.H. Bouligny, Inc., and began securing contracts to construct distribution systems and power plants in the South and Midwest.

His success and that of the leaders who came after him have produced the Rowe Corporation, a major international firm of nine diverse companies, seven of which are major operating companies, with more than 1,000 employees that serve customers worldwide.

The original company still operates today in the field in which it began. R.H. Bouligny, Inc., is a general contractor that specializes in heavy construction and maintenance of electric utility transmission systems, substations, and overhead and underground power distribution systems. Its methods, however, have undergone substantial changes.

In the early years Bouligny's construction crews had to use mules and oxen to transport heavy utility poles to rural installation sites. Today they take advantage of helicopters as well as a construction equipment fleet of more than 900 vehicles that are maintained at Bouligny's Charlotte equipment and engine-rebuild facilities. While the firm still operates its headquarters in Charlotte, it also uses division offices in Wytheville, Virginia, and Pensacola, Florida, as well as field offices in Huntington and Charleston, West Virginia, and Panama City, Florida.

In 1942 R.H. Bouligny, Inc., created a manufacturing division to act as a World War II defense contractor. That division became the Bouligny Company, a wholly owned engineering and manufacturing subsidiary that serves the international man-made fiber industry.

It provides entire plants, production systems, and major components for the manufacture of nylon, polyester and polypropylene staple fiber and filament yarns, slit tape, and monofilament systems plus winding for carbon and other high-temperature fibers.

The company's recent contracts have included several yarn production plants in the Peoples Republic of China plus plant upgrades for major U.S. fiber producers.

In 1982 the Bouligny Company expanded its customer and development services through construction of the Oliver Rowe Technical Center. The center uses several different man-made fiber systems to duplicate a wide variety of process conditions so as to test new concepts and equipment designs. In addition, it provides facilities for training customers' personnel on the types of equipment that will be installed in their plants.

Another Rowe company, Power Equipment Company of Charlotte, also began as an in-house facility of R.H. Bouligny. In 1953 it became a third division and today is a separate entity, offering sales and service for various types of truck-mounted equipment and accessories.

A fourth division, Powell Manufacturing Company, headquartered in

The Bouligny Company's machine shop is equipped with the most modern computer numerically controlled (CNC) machining equipment available.

Bennettsville, South Carolina, was originally established in 1950 in Wilson, North Carolina, as a tobacco transplanter builder. Now it serves American and overseas tobacco growers with its transplanters, high-clearance self-propelled sprayers, and tobacco harvesting and curing equipment, which is marketed as "Total Tobacco Mechanization." It also serves the general farming community with its Cole line of equipment for seed planting, conservation tillage, and fertilization.

Powell also manufactures the RO-KOR tree digger, which was developed and introduced to the landscaping industry in 1979. Today the ROKOR name is nationally known for its wide range of reliable tree-digging equipment, which is used by private firms as well as institutions and governmental entities.

In 1967 Bennettsville Advertising Company was formed to provide media-buying services, distribute business forms, and act as a leasing agent of Powell equipment.

In 1971 the Wood-Hopkins Contracting Company, an 80-year-old firm in Jacksonville, Florida, was acquired. The corporation has transformed this heavy-hauling and house-moving business into a marine engineering and construction firm. Today it builds large high-rise structures and demonstrates its expertise in pile driving, bridges, piers, docks, warehouses, and ship-loading facilities.

The next two companies were acquired in 1983. Implement Sales Company of Atlanta acts as a southeastern wholesale representative for manufacturers of many types of agricultural equipment. Catalytic Generators of Norfolk, Virginia, leases and sells ethylene gas generators that use a special patented concentrate to promote the ripening of fruits, vegetables, and tobacco under controlled conditions. Its equipment is particularly useful to distributors and

Powell tobacco combines can harvest and load up to three acres of tobacco per hour, reducing farmer manpower needs and improving efficiency while maintaining leaf quality.

A lineman awaits arrival of overhead ground wire on a power transmission line tension stringing project. R.H. Bouligny utilizes innovative equipment such as this finger line trailer, developed and built by the company.

handlers of fruits and vegetables and to tobacco growers for whom it hastens uniform ripening.

A subsidiary of Catalytic Generators, Ag Sales and Service exports agricultural equipment and supplies to users worldwide. It also provides technical assistance, service, and consultation to farmers overseas.

LaBarge Company of California was purchased in 1987 by Catalytic Generators. LaBarge offers a unique patented quick-ripe system that can ripen fruits and vegetables in a fraction of the time required by older methods.

Until 1971 all the member companies were divisions and wholly owned subsidiaries of R.H. Bouligny, Inc., which acted both as a parent company and as an electrical contracting firm with its own customers. That year the company began examining ways in which its management could operate more efficiently and support the growth of this expanding network of companies.

When Ralph Hubbard Bouligny died that same year, his long-term associate and partner, Oliver R. Rowe, acquired full ownership of the company. Discussions with legal, financial, and consulting experts led, on January 1, 1972, to the formation of

a new parent company, Rowe Corporation, with Oliver R. Rowe as its first president.

Today that corporation, under the leadership of Oliver Reagan Rowe, Jr., provides organization planning, investment and banking services, human resources services, risk-management programs, and legal, tax, and business information services for its nine diversified member companies, including R.H. Bouligny, Inc. From the success of that first Charlotte-based company, there has grown a successful family of companies providing construction, industrial, and agricultural equipment and service worldwide.

W.R. BONSAL COMPANY

W.R. "Rocky" Bonsal III, current chairman and chief executive officer of this leading building materials company, is the third generation of his family to run the privately held corporation founded by W.R. Bonsal, Sr., and O.L. Cloud in 1895 and later headed by his father.

Based from the beginning in North Carolina, W.R. Bonsal Company began as a supplier and contractor to the railroad industry in the South. In its earlier days the operation was engaged primarily in selling bridge timbers, cross ties, and telephone and telegraph poles. By the

is also the site of the company's first packaging plant for its cement-based products, built in 1947. By 1952 the firm was manufacturing products in Florida and has since expanded operations to Georgia, South Carolina, Tennessee, and Ohio.

The W.R. Bonsal Company currently employs some 400 people in two divisions, including a staff of 44 at its Charlotte corporate headquarters, which also houses a research and development department charged with developing new products and monitoring the quality of finished goods, as well as the quality of

W.R. Bonsal Company started by selling cross ties and telegraph poles and then branched into railroad contracting.

The corporate headquarters of W.R. Bonsal Company in Charlotte.

early 1900s it had begun railroad contracting, constructing sections of the Seaboard, Durham and Southern, and Virginia railroad lines.

In 1907 W.R. Bonsal Company contracted to build a large power dam on the Yadkin River in Blewett Falls, North Carolina, and began mining sand and gravel aggregates on company property for use in the dam.

As a side venture the firm sold the aggregate commercially, an operation that continues today in the Lilesville, North Carolina, area. Lilesville

raw materials.

The Mining Division produces sand, used as fine aggregate in concrete, and gravel, used by the roofing industry, in the production of the silicon and ferro-silicon used in the manufacture of aluminum and steel, and as coarse aggregate for concrete.

The Building Products Division, comprising eight plants, manufactures and sells products for the construction industry. The SUREWALL™ Products & Systems brand is well known to professional builders nationwide and abroad for exterior insulating systems, impact-resistant stucco systems, and weatherproofing and wa-

terproofing systems. Bonsal tile-setting products, specialty concrete and masonry products, and floor-treatment products for both exterior and interior applications also are prized by the industrial market.

Charlotte do-it-yourselfers are familiar with such SAKRETE™-brand products as concrete, sand, mortar mix, and black-top patch; Bonsal products, including SURE-STONE™ patio stone and pavers; SURE-FIX-brand concrete and masonry repair products; and the recently introduced STRONGFAST™ concrete mix formulated for strength and quick setup.

By the late 1970s the organization had grown and needed to consolidate its corporate functions in a single facility. "We knew we wanted to remain in North Carolina, versus relocating to Atlanta. The company started out in Hamlet, then moved west to Lilesville in the 1960s. So, in 1981, we just continued our westward movement and chose Charlotte

Ron Barnhill, Joe Murdock, and John Thompson check the quality of gravel at the Mining Division in Lilesville, North Carolina.

for our new headquarters," says Rocky Bonsal.

Bonsal cites Charlotte's emergence as the economic center and transportation hub of the region as an important consideration. "We already had ties in the city—our bank and our lawyers were here—and now we're only 90 minutes by air from any of our plants."

Many Bonsal-made products were used in constructing the 19,500-square-foot, passive-solar headquarters building on Arrowridge Boulevard in southwest Charlotte. An 11-panel bas-relief sculpture in the lobby court is a much-admired feature of the building.

Created by Alice Proctor, a North Carolina sculptor, the panels tell the story of Moses from the time Pharaoh's daughter found the infant in the river to the moment God showed him the promised land from atop Mount Pisgah. A variety of materials, including clay, wood, cast brass, gold leaf, and gold and platinum lustres were used, and the artist added interesting textural accents with various finishes, such as earth stains, oxides, and different kinds of glaze. The bas-relief creates a beautiful environment for employees and visitors alike.

The W.R. Bonsal Company today commands a large share of the market for its products in the southeastern United States. Rocky Bonsal attributes this record in part to his

company's ability to keep pace with developing technology and to keep in tune with customer needs.

The firm's emphasis on quality products and services is one thing that has not changed over the years. In a booklet titled "The Bonsal Way" is a mission statement written by employees: "The mission of W.R. Bonsal Company is to be the best privately owned company in the East." Among the yardsticks listed for measuring progress toward that goal is "our citizenship." This means, among other endeavors, participating in the life of the communities where the firm's employees live and work. To Rocky Bonsal it means taking part in volunteer activities, such as serving on the board of directors of Alexander Children's Center, "So I

The collage of Bonsal history and products was presented to the company by its people at the opening of the new corporate office in 1981.

can put something back into the community."

To many Bonsal people it means participating in a broad range of civic, industry, and professional activities. And it means sharing through organizations such as the United Way. The company matches United Way contributions twice, a direct match of employee contributions that goes to the United Way and a second match that goes to the Donation Committee at each company location for distribution to worthy, non-United Way organizations and charitable causes.

The W.R. Bonsal Company is approaching its 100th anniversary, having evolved from the simple operation of an industrious entrepreneur into a prosperous regional company. As for the future, Rocky Bonsal envisions the firm serving the entire eastern United States by the turn of the century. "As our customers grow and expand their businesses into new areas, we expect to grow and expand our operations right along with them," he affirms.

JOHN CROSLAND COMPANY/CENTEX HOMES

In 1937, when others were beginning to build offices and skyscrapers in Charlotte, John Crosland, Sr., built his first home there, the first of thousands of homes in scores of Crosland neighborhoods throughout Metrolina and the Carolinas. It was the beginning of Crosland's reputation for building affordable quality houses and for standing behind every home he built.

That first home was part of Crosland's "beautiful Club Colony . . . just off Selwyn Avenue . . . priced just below $7,000." The community was outside the city limits, near the still unpaved Colony Road. In 1938 a Club Colony home was named Home of the Year in a Charlotte *Observer* column. The neighborhood was, and still is, a community where growing families are welcome.

The idea was to construct a comfortable home in a good location, make it liveable and attractive, help the buyer find the best available financing, and provide excellent service after the sale. That mission is still central to the company today, when it operates as a division of Centex Homes, a national home-builder headquartered in Dallas, Texas. Today John Crosland Company sells more than 500 new homes each year in more than 20 Charlotte-area neighborhoods.

For 30 years John Crosland, Sr., continued to build single-family homes in neighborhoods throughout Charlotte. In the mid-1960s, when John Crosland, Jr., took over the John Crosland Company, the firm also began building its renowned quality into condominiums and town houses. During the next 20 years John Crosland, Jr., led the company during a period of unprecedented growth, both in and out of the Charlotte area. In the 1980s it expanded into neighborhoods in Columbia, Charleston, and Myrtle Beach, South Carolina; Raleigh and Wilmington, North Carolina; and Atlanta, Georgia.

John Crosland, Jr., had grown up in the home-building business and had formed his own small building company right after graduation from Davidson College. After he joined the John Crosland Company in 1953, he continually worked with government and within the industry to find ways to keep new homes affordable.

He became president of the Char-

TOP LEFT: A best-selling condominium community built by the John Crosland Company. Courtesy, Rick Alexander, photographer

LEFT: A best-selling John Crosland home that features an exciting open floor plan, four bedrooms, and room for a new growing family.

lotte Home Builders' Association in 1959 and the North Carolina Home Builders' Association in 1968. He served as vice-chairman of the mortgage finance committee and as an active member of other industry organizations. He also chaired a number of community organizations,

including the North Carolina Housing Finance Agency, Charlotte/ Mecklenburg Housing Cost Task Force, the Council of State Housing Agencies, and the Charlotte Habitat for Humanity, which sought to provide housing for low-income families.

His success made *Professional Builder* magazine name John Crosland, Jr., 1985 Builder of the Year. The honor came just one year after the magazine awarded the Smarter House for the Money Award to Crosland's Granville Place. This affordable entry-level house was designed to appeal to first-time home buyers. It was part of a company-wide effort to increase market share by structuring its efforts toward market segmentation.

TOP LEFT: A traditional living room in a move-up John Crosland home. Courtesy, Rick Alexander, photographer

BOTTOM LEFT: A best-selling traditional John Crosland home. Courtesy, Rick Alexander, photographer

BELOW: A traditional first-time John Crosland home. Courtesy, Rick Alexander, photographer

But entry-level homes were not the only goal of the company. Over the years Crosland has been able to shift its home-building emphasis to appeal to those shifting segments—from the first buyers to those who were ready to move up, to empty nesters, and to retirees. When it discovered the need for detached homes with low-maintenance yards, for instance, it began building high-density detached homes on 6,000-square-foot lots.

In 1986 the Crosland community of three-, four- and five-bedroom single-family homes at Mallard Trace was chosen as the site for the Home Builders' Association (HBA) second annual HomeArama. The association made the selection on the basis of the developer's ability to provide a site with beauty, accessibility, price, visibility, lot availability, and available financing packages. At Mallard Trace, the rolling, wooded terrain provided an appropriate setting for the homes, which were sold for $100,000 to $150,000.

While the homes in each Cros-

A traditional move-up home for the particular John Crosland purchaser. Courtesy, Rick Alexander, photographer

and stability while it expanded geographically.

In 1987 that combination of growth and stability led the John Crosland Company to become a division of Centex Homes, of Dallas, Texas. Since 1952 Centex had also been building homes in metropolitan areas in Florida, Texas, California, Minnesota, Illinois, and other states. It provided Crosland with the additional resources available to a company of its size, while allowing John Crosland to maintain its identity in the Carolinas.

Through CTX Mortgage Company, the mortgage financing division of Centex Homes, Crosland can offer competitive financing for its home buyers. Centex also offers home-

ABOVE: A typical open, airy interior of a John Crosland home. Courtesy, Rick Alexander, photographer

RIGHT: Many exciting new John Crosland homes feature Palladian windows, luxurious master bath, volume ceilings, and an open, airy floor plan. Courtesy, Rick Alexander, photographer

land neighborhood were designed and priced to appeal to a variety of specific market segments, the company maintained a single brand and image in advertising and public communications. All its homes were advertised and sold under the John Crosland name.

Throughout its period of heavy growth, the company's management was an important part in determining its direction. A strong team guided its strategies and maintained control of financial matters. Division managers were required to prepare three annual budgets: one they considered realistic, one optimistic, and one pessimistic. As a result, the company retained its financial strength

owners' insurance to buyers of John Crosland homes.

At the same time, John Crosland Company continues to provide buyers with one of the most complete warranty packages available on a new home. It begins with a thorough inspection by the buyer and the building superintendent before the buyer moves in. Any details that do not meet the company's high standards of quality are corrected before move-in.

Then, on the day of closing, the buyer is given two warranty cards for the 60-day and one-year warranty periods that cover the house. For the first 60 days, the buyer lists problems and details not noticed in the pre-move inspection and reports them to the company for adjustments covered by the warranty. After that period, problems can be reported under the one-year warranty. Buyers are also protected by manufacturers' warranties on appliances, water heaters, and heating and air-conditioning units.

Moreover, each John Crosland home is covered by a Homeowners Warranty Corporation (HOW) warranty for any major structural defects during the first 10 years of ownership. In fact, in 1988 John Crosland Company/Centex Homes became one of a very small number of

builders to receive the Citation of Quality from HOW for outstanding customer service on its 5,654 homes enrolled in the program. At the time, only 10 of the 12,000 HOW builders nationwide were presented with these citations.

That is why a typical John Crosland home owner has said, "There is no way I can say enough good things about the John Crosland Company. The homes are well built, excellently designed, and energy efficient. If there are any problems, they come out and fix them. They work with you fully."

Realtors who have participated in Crosland's co-brokerage programs for home sales praise the firm's attention to detail and reputation for service. They say the resale values of the homes are frequently high.

By 1988 those homes included condominiums such as Devonshire Court and Creswick priced from $40,000 and homes priced from under $70,000 to $200,000. The company's newest floor plans once again were in response to the demands of the buyers. They included spacious rooms, more elaborate kitchens and

This home in Club Colony won the Home of the Year Award in 1938. John Crosland homes and neighborhoods stand the test of time. Courtesy, Rick Alexander, photographer

A new transitional John Crosland home for the move-up purchaser features a traditional exterior, soaring ceilings, luxurious master bath, special appointments, and plenty of room for a growing family. Courtesy, Rick Alexander, photographer

baths, and garages. Homes increased the sense of space with cathedral and trey ceilings, bay and Palladian windows, and decks and patios. In addition, several Crosland neighborhoods feature tennis courts and swimming pools with cabanas.

Crosland Communities include homes ranging from $60,000 in Lynton Place; $70,000 in Bradfield Farms and Danby; $80,000 in Callaway Plantation, Cedarfield, and Wellington; to $90,000 in Cheverton. Prices start at the $100,000 range in Braddock Green, Wellington, Landen Meadows, Turnberry, Touchstone, Mallard Trace, Bridgeport, and Wyndmere.

In each community, homes are designed and built in the John Crosland Company tradition—providing quality and comfort in a good location, with attractive financing, and the best service available for the new home owner.

D.L. PHILLIPS INVESTMENT BUILDERS, INC.

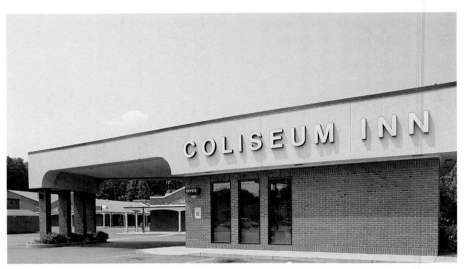

In the aftermath of the Great Depression, Dwight Ledwell Phillips took a prescient look into the future and decided his own future lay in buying and developing land. Today, more than 50 years later, brick, concrete, and steel—in their varied configurations as family homes, apartments, motels, restaurants, banks, and office buildings—testify to his talent and energy and to the practicality of his vision.

D.L. Phillips Investment Builders dates from 1939, when Phillips bought his first property for development, two old houses on Commonwealth Avenue. Soon he was buying and developing property all over Charlotte. During World War II Phillips expanded his operations to include building military housing in Georgia and in North Carolina at Cherry Point and Jacksonville.

Phillips, who had the ability to size up a large tract of raw land and understand the possibilities it offered, ran his company with a sure hand until his death on Christmas Eve in 1973. He was succeeded as president by his son-in-law, Tom Phillips, who joined the firm in 1955 and continues successfully directing and guiding the company's numerous holdings and operations.

Included in the firm's long list of projects, each of which it developed, owns, and operates, are the Roseland Apartments; Fern Forest Apartments in Gastonia; The Coliseum Inn, an 180-room motor inn; and the CenterSouth development in the 400-acre Phillips Office Park. The company has extensive holdings in Durham and Jacksonville, North Carolina, and Charleston, West Virginia.

On a still larger scale are such landmarks as the Charlotte Merchandise Mart, which opened in 1961. More than 400,000 people visit the Mart each year, adding some $80 million to the Charlotte economy. Every conceivable kind of trade, business, and industry show, plus shows to benefit various charities and the annual Christmas show, are held at the Mart. By early 1990 a new 138,000-square-foot-addition will expand the Mart's service capabilities.

Tom Phillips recalls that Dwight Phillips' philosophy always had been "to give something back." It's a philosophy that Tom Phillips has kept alive. To him, giving something back means meeting the construction needs of the city and the area while preserving and respecting the land, from something as simple as making sure a venerable old tree is left undisturbed by construction, to a project as complex as the company's development of Governor's Island at Lake Norman. Although the Governor's Island project was not especially large, it presented a unique challenge in that the developers were working with a rare piece of land, unspoiled and uncommonly beautiful, on the last lake to be built on the Catawba River.

Giving something back also means active participation in the affairs of the community. Dwight Phillips was instrumental in building Calvary and Sharon United Methodist churches, where he was a member, and he donated land to a number of other denominations as well, contributed land to the University of North Carolina at Charlotte, and served on the boards of several colleges. He also found time to be involved in politics. "If you want good government," he said, "you've got to work for it."

Tom Phillips has continued in that tradition, making time for political involvement, and serving as a member of the chamber of commerce's Advisory Council and as a board member of the UNC-Charlotte Athletic Foundation. He also serves on the business advisory council of Queens College.

Two D.L. Phillips Investment Builders, Inc., projects—(top) the landmark Charlotte Merchandise Mart, which opened in 1961, and (bottom) the Coliseum Inn, an 180-room motor inn.

The D.L. Phillips Investment Builders, Inc., headquarters at 2121 East Independence Boulevard.

C h a p t e r

11

Quality of Life

Medical and educational institutions contribute to the quality of life of Charlotte area residents.

Presbyterian Hospital, 264-265

The Orthopaedic Hospital of Charlotte, 266

Providence Day School, 267

Charlotte Memorial Hospital and Medical Center, 268-269

Page 261: photo by Mark Fortenberry; right: photo by Diane Davis/Transparencies

PRESBYTERIAN HOSPITAL

Since accepting its first patient on January 1, 1903, Presbyterian Hospital has grown steadily to meet the changing health care needs of the Charlotte community. While it has built a reputation for excellence in personal patient care, it is also recognized as a progressive, innovative health care center.

The hospital is the flagship of the Presbyterian Health Services Corp., a diversified multi-institutional system established in 1983 to serve Charlotte-Mecklenburg and surrounding counties.

What began as a 20-bed hospital

cancer, and psychiatry.

In 1917 it purchased the campus and buildings of Elizabeth College at 200 Hawthorne Lane. After a series of renovations and additions, that campus today is the center of a complete complex of buildings. Since 1974 alone a $100-million renovation and expansion program has created 16 new buildings or major additions. The majority of patient rooms are private, and new or newly renovated.

Nearly 800 physicians and surgeons serve on Presbyterian's medical staff. More than 3,000 full- and

thesia. In 1974 it introduced joint replacement surgery. Those innovations were just the beginning of the comprehensive, progressive health care services the hospital now provides.

As a modern medical center, Presbyterian offers a broad array of sophisticated diagnostic and therapeutic services. Specialized pathology and clinical laboratory capabilities include therapeutic drug monitoring, emergency toxicology, virology services, flow cytometry, and one of the largest surgical pathology services in the Carolinas.

State-of-the art radiology capabilities include CT and MRI scanning, diagnostic ultrasound, digital vascular imaging, and low-cost, self-referral mammography.

The Cancer Center is the first in the state designated as a community hosital compensation cancer program by the American College of Surgeons Commission on Cancer. The Harris Hospice Unit is one of only two inpatient hospice units in North Carolina and the only one in Charlotte.

The Presbyterian Family Maternity Center uses the most advanced methods to continue the hospital's long-standing reputation as a national leader in maternity and infant care. In addition to introducing the city's first birthing rooms in 1979, the hospital offers a family-centered approach to childbirth. It offers a variety of classes in childbirth preparation and infant care for expectant mothers, as well as classes and tours for grandparents and siblings.

In the hospital's Hemby Intensive Care Nursery, which opened in 1973, four experienced neonatologists and nurses provide expert care for infants born with medical problems. The Belk Heart Center, established in 1985, continues its rapid growth.

In recent years an even wider variety of services has been added. Presbyterian HomeCare, Presbyterian HomeHelpers, and Presbyterian Medical Equipment and Services

The Presbyterian Hospital campus at 200 Hawthorne Lane in the heart of the Elizabeth neighborhood is a Charlotte landmark, recognized for the beauty of its rose garden and its manicured grounds.

in a rented uptown building is now a private, not-for-profit, comprehensive health care center with 642 beds and 64 bassinets. Its broad range of inpatient and outpatient services include such specialties as a maternity center and intensive care nursery, same-day surgery services, and centers for care of the heart,

part-time hospital employees work with them.

Throughout its history the hospital has introduced the most advanced medical technology in the care of patients. In the 1950s it was the first Charlotte hospital to use surgical recovery rooms. Late in that decade it opened the city's first radiation therapy unit for cancer treatment.

During the 1960s Presbyterian was the first to bring Charlotte a psychiatric unit, intensive care, self-care patient services, and same-day surgery under local and general anes-

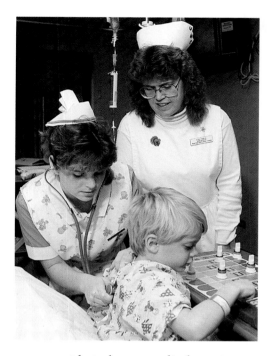

The widely regarded Presbyterian Hospital School of Nursing's 33-month curriculum places a premium on clinical experience with patients.

provide in-home medical services and equipment. Presbyterian Health-Plus creates programs that promote

The Belk Heart Center has become one of the finest facilities for cardiac care in the Charlotte-Mecklenburg area since its opening in late 1985.

corporate and community health. Company Care provides a comprehensive occupational health management program.

In the SameDay Surgery Center at Presbyterian, Stone Institute of the Carolinas, Inc., operates the area's only lithotripter for treating kidney stones without surgery.

The newest member of Presbyterian Health Services Corp., the 68-bed Presbyterian Specialty Hospital, specializes in eye, ear, nose, throat, oral, plastic, cosmetic, and orthopedic surgery. It also houses the Pain Therapy Center of Charlotte, which uses a multi-

disciplinary approach to treat chronic pain.

Presbyterian's School of Nursing, which began in 1903 with three students, is the largest hospital-based program in the Carolinas. It is fully accredited by the National League for Nursing and the North Carolina Board of Nursing.

In addition, Presbyterian has one of the state's most active volunteer programs through the Presbyterian Hospital Auxiliary and the city's old-

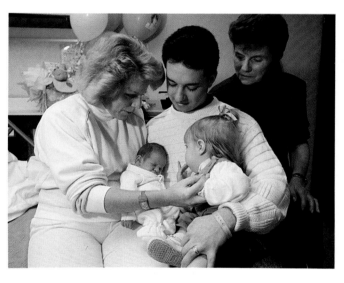

Presbyterian's Family Maternity Center—one of the nation's busiest—encourages full family participation in the birth experience, from young siblings to grandmothers and grandfathers.

est hospital-based chaplaincy. A majority of its trustees are selected from the membership of Presbyterian churches in Mecklenburg County that are members of the Mecklenburg Presbytery.

As a member of the SunHealth network, a partnership of not-for-profit health care organizations in 15 states, Presbyterian shares in a collective effort to improve and strengthen health care at all levels.

Now in its ninth decade as part of growing Charlotte-Mecklenburg, Presbyterian Hospital continues to uphold its commitment to bringing innovative, personal health care to the region's citizens.

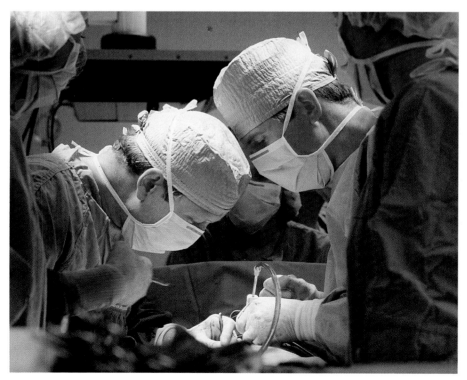

THE ORTHOPAEDIC HOSPITAL OF CHARLOTTE

It has not taken long for The Orthopaedic Hospital of Charlotte to grow from a city specialty hospital into a regional center for the treatment of musculoskeletal problems.

As one of only six orthopaedic specialty hospitals in the country, The Orthopaedic Hospital of Charlotte is especially recognized in such areas of excellence as reconstructive joint surgery, sports medicine, and pain management. In fact, the physicians there perform the largest number of total joint procedures in the Carolinas.

The hospital is one of very few places in the country to provide several highly specialized procedures for the repair of back and joint problems. Its metabolic bone laboratory is internationally known for diagnosing diseases of the bone. Its exclusive CT scanner provides the most advanced method of creating three-dimensional images of bones.

Patients come to Orthopaedic Hospital for care by more than 50 board-certified orthopaedic surgeons and a hospital staff of highly trained nurses, therapists, and other professionals. A unique, nurse-developed system of care accountability, emphasizing decisions with and for the patient by the bedside nurse, fosters a recovery environment that individualizes care and supports the patient's efforts to return to active living in the shortest-possible time.

During the 1980s the hospital has rapidly expanded. It originally opened in 1976 in response to the unmet surgical capabilities required by Charlotte's 27 orthopaedic surgeons. Today, as part of one of the country's largest Employee Stock Ownership Plan (ESOP) companies with 95 employee-owned Health-Trust hospitals nationwide, the hospital finds an increasing variety of ways to serve patients from throughout the Southeast.

When, for example, medical research began discovering new ways to manage pain, Orthopaedic Hospital was the first to offer those methods to the Charlotte community. In

A front view of The Orthopaedic Hospital of Charlotte. Photo by Jessie McLaurin

The Orthopaedic Hospital of Charlotte's bedside nursing individualizes care and supports the patient's efforts to return to active living. Photo by Jessie McLaurin

1986 the hospital's Pain Management Center opened to help people control and decrease persistent pain from a wide variety of causes, often without using drugs. The center's broad interdisciplinary approach treats pain that comes from sources as different as surgery, stress, arthritis, and cancer.

As more people have become active in sports, the hospital has offered outstanding expertise in the treatment of sports medicine. There surgeons have the most sophisticated equipment and expert staff to provide the best treatment for sports-related injuries. This excellence has allowed Orthopaedic Hospital to become the official hospital of the Char-

lotte Hornets NBA team, as well as the medical facility of choice for several other local sports franchises. In addition, the hospital has opened a unique Work Evaluation and Rehabilitation Center (WERC) program that helps workers return to their jobs after an illness or injury. The center evaluates the worker's rehabilitation status in relation to the requirements of his or her job. Then therapists create a personalized program of therapy that specifically prepares the patient to withstand those work-related activities.

As a private hospital, it supports the community through federal, state, and local taxes, as well as jobs for its employees/owners. Since 1986 it has provided rent-free office space on its campus for Arthritis Patient Services, a division of Community Health Services. It developed the popular Spring Thaw Foot Race to benefit area charities for the handicapped. And its employees regularly participate in many community service projects.

As the city grows, The Orthopaedic Hospital of Charlotte looks forward to growing too—to become the nation's most extensive provider of orthopaedic services.

PROVIDENCE DAY SCHOOL

On a 28-acre campus just 15 minutes from uptown Charlotte, Providence Day School gives its 800 students a traditional college-preparatory education while it helps them develop the skills necessary for a successful life. In classes from Transitional Kindergarten through grade 12, the school provides a safe, caring environment in which children can learn and grow.

The results of its efforts are visible in the awards that both the school and its students have received. In 1987 it was the only school in the Charlotte/Mecklenburg area to have been cited for excellence by both the U.S. Department of Education and the National Council of Teachers of English.

Graduates are winners of a long list of prestigious scholarships, including the John Motley Morehead, National Merit, Benjamin Duke, Vanderbilt, Furman University Freshman, and Georgetown University scholarships. All of the school's graduates go on to college, attending institutions from Duke and UNC-Chapel Hill to Tulane, Yale, and UCLA.

College credit is granted to 70 percent of the students who take Advanced Placement tests. In September 1988 one of its students was inter-

In 1987 Providence Day School was the only school in Charlotte/Mecklenburg to be cited for excellence by both the U.S. Department of Education and the National Council of Teachers of English.

viewed about his work with binary stars by ABC News for a television special called "Beyond The Shuttle."

Such achievements are clearly related to the education and accomplishments of the school's faculty, which averages eight years of teaching experience. More than half of these outstanding teachers have earned advanced degrees.

Each student's work is guided by his or her own faculty adviser. Moreover, senior students are placed in a two-week internship program in a career area of interest.

The school's facilities include two libraries, laboratories for science and computers, and a new 37,000-square-foot fine arts building that houses a 500-seat auditorium.

Academic achievement, however, is just one of the school's goals for students. About 90 percent of students also participate in at least one extracurricular activity. Their choices may include participation in areas of the arts and music such as drama, band, the yearbook, and hand bells. Or they may play a variety of sports on

the school's six tennis courts, two gymnasiums, football/soccer field, track, and baseball and softball fields. School teams have recently won state championships in football, baseball, and basketball.

The combination of these opportunities for physical and cultural development with a challenging academic curriculum provides day students with a truly exceptional education.

"When students leave Providence Day School, they are enriched as individuals, academically confident

"When students leave Providence Day School they are enriched as individuals, academically confident to face the challenges of additional educational opportunities and fulfilled as whole persons," says headmaster Eugene A. Bratek.

to face the challenges of additional educational opportunities and fulfilled as whole persons," says headmaster Eugene A. Bratek. "They have formed personal bonds with students and faculty—the result of the commitment of everyone in the Providence Day family to enable each student to become a successful and happy adult."

CHARLOTTE MEMORIAL HOSPITAL AND MEDICAL CENTER

Each year 17 specially designed health facilities of the Charlotte-Mecklenburg Hospital Authority provide treatment for 300,000 people, from tiny premature babies to aging senior citizens. It is the fifth-largest not-for-profit health care system of its kind in the United States.

At its center is Charlotte Memorial Hospital and Medical Center, which opened in 1940 under a state charter. Its state-of-the-art equipment, internationally recognized research programs, and teaching programs for resident physicians in nine specialties attract patients worldwide.

"The resources of the Charlotte-Mecklenburg Hospital Authority are formidable," says R. Stuart Dickson, chairman. "We have assembled some of the best medical minds in the country."

Among the best known of Charlotte Memorial's specializations is its treatment and research into heart problems. The Carolinas Heart Institute at the hospital treats more heart patients each year than any other medical center in the Carolinas. It performs more than 5,000 catheterization procedures and 2,000 open-heart surgeries annually. In 1984 it became the region's first facility to perform heart transplants.

The institute's five-story facility on the campus of Charlotte Memo-

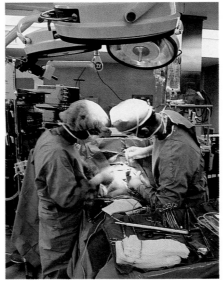

rial Hospital and Medical Center includes six specially designed operating rooms, two of which are equipped for laser surgery; a video conference room with high-resolution video monitors showing live pictures of surgery; 14 cardiovascular recovery stations; and 20 coronary intensive care rooms.

Much of the institute's expertise is derived from its 40-year association with the privately owned Heineman Medical Research Laboratory, an internationally known pioneer in the study of cardiological disorders. In addition, the hospital's teaching program provides a working link with the University of North Carolina School of Medicine.

These extraordinary resources make Charlotte Memorial a key member of the Carolinas Heart Emergency Network, which acts to dramat-

TOP: *The Charlotte Memorial Hospital and Medical Center—17 specially designed health facilities to serve the Charlotte-Mecklenburg Hospital Authority.*

LEFT: *Charlotte Memorial's specialization is the treatment and research into heart problems. The Carolinas Heart Institute at the hospital treats more heart patients each year than any other medical center in the Carolinas.*

BELOW: *Emergency flight service helps patients with life-threatening injuries reach the hospital center. The B-200 Super King Air cruises at up to 320 miles per hour. Equipped as a mini-intensive care unit, it carries trauma victims as well as other critically ill patients.*

ically improve the treatment of heart attack victims. Through this system, doctors at more than 20 hospitals across the Carolinas can begin clot-dissolving drug therapy and then, if necessary, rapidly transport the patient to the Carolinas Heart Institute for angioplasty. Such immediate intervention to clear blocked arteries can decrease heart damage and increase the patient's chance of survival.

Within its new maternity wing, the medical center also operates a Level III neonatal intensive care unit. There it offers the highest-possible

After the intensive care environment, the recovery process continues at Charlotte Rehabilitation Hospital, specializing in the care of stroke, heart attack, and accident victims.

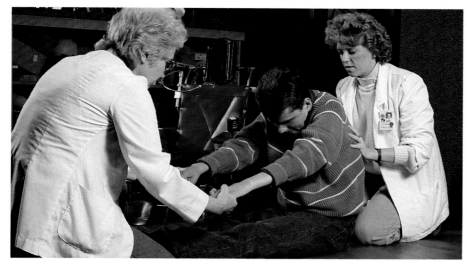

level of infant critical care, including use of the only extracorporeal membrane oxygenation unit in the state. Each year it gives more than 800 babies a better chance of survival under the care of five neonatologists. Babies weighing less than two pounds have a 70-percent chance of survival. Those between two and three pounds have a 90-percent chance.

As the regional trauma center, Charlotte Memorial offers immediate intensive treatment for accident victims. Its emergency flight service helps patients with life-threatening injuries reach the center as quickly as possible while under the care of a specially trained trauma flight team. Us-

ing a Bell LongRanger II, a jet-turbine-powered helicopter that can cruise at up to 140 miles per hour, the team reaches critically injured or ill people even at the immediate scene of an accident.

In addition, the hospital aids patients at farther distances through the use of its fixed-wing aircraft, a B-200 Super King Air, that cruises at up to 320 miles per hour. Equipped as a mini-intensive care unit, it carries trauma victims as well as other critically ill patients, high-risk mothers and infants, stabilized patients who need swift transportation to another facility for treatment, and seriously ill patients who require specialized treatment outside their own

communities.

In 1988 Charlotte Memorial opened the Hemby Pediatric Trauma Institute to treat children with critical injuries. It uses child-size intensive care equipment, 24-hour pediatric intensive care units, and pediatric specialists that may not be available at other general medical care facilities. Moreover, it sponsors educational programs to further knowledge about the prevention and treatment of pediatric traumas.

Such specialized care is just a part of the Charlotte-Mecklenberg Hospital Authority's rapidly expanding health care network. Its new University Memorial Hospital in northern Mecklenburg County, for ex-

The Maternity Center at Charlotte Memorial Hospital and Medical Center offers private labor, delivery, and recovery rooms. The hospital is the Regional Perinatal Center, with the largest neonatal intensive care unit in the Carolinas.

ample, provides 130 private rooms, a 24-hour emergency department, an Intensive-Coronary Care Unit, and an advanced Sleep Center for the treatment of serious sleep disorders.

In 1988 it opened the Carolinas' first Comprehensive Epilepsy Center to seek total control of this illness for the 100,000 people in the Carolinas who suffer from epilepsy. It is constructing a major medical care complex at the intersection of Highway 51 and Providence Road in the Arboretum Professional Park. Moreover, by 1993 a new bed tower on the campus of Memorial's Medical Center will replace old semiprivate rooms with 280 private ones.

The hospital's physicians are actively participating in research for new treatments. They are pioneering the use of indirect laser treatment to clear blocked peripheral arteries. And the center is the fourth in the nation chosen to cooperate with the National Institute of Health in testing the anti-clotting drug TPA for acute stroke victims.

According to Harry A. Nurkin, president and chief executive officer of the Charlotte-Mecklenburg Hospital Authority, "We are proud of our history and achievements. They provide a deep reservoir of experience as we move toward the next century, sharing our technology, ideas, and visions in making life better for more and more people."

12

The Marketplace

Charlotte's retail establishments, service industries, and products are enjoyed by residents and visitors to the area.

Belk Department Stores, 272

Piedmont Plastics, Inc., 273

Ivey's, 274-275

Carolina Tractor & Equipment Co., 276-277

Adam's Mark Hotel, 278-281

WeCare Distributors, Inc., 282-283

Lance, Inc., 284-285

Distribution Technology Inc., 286-287

United Data Systems, 288

The Marker, 289

Photo by Mark Fortenberry

BELK DEPARTMENT STORES

Twenty-five-year-old William Henry Belk could hardly have imagined that the small bargain store he opened in Monroe, North Carolina, on May 29, 1888, would be the start of an organization that today encompasses nearly 340 Belk and Legget department stores in 14 states across the Southeast.

It was in this first store, which was called the New York Racket, that the company began its successful tradition of offering customers quality merchandise, friendly and efficient service, and a "satisfaction guaranteed" policy.

In 1891 William Henry Belk was joined in the business by his brother, Dr. John Montgomery Belk, who had been a practicing physician. This marked the beginning of a remarkable 37-year partnership that resulted in the formation and opening of stores throughout the Carolinas and the Southeast.

William Henry Belk left Monroe in 1895 to open and manage the company's fourth store on the first block of East Trade Street in Charlotte. The store succeeded, and, after numerous expansions and remodelings, it eventually became the company's flagship store and one of the South's largest, with nearly a half-million square feet of space.

Charlotte's SouthPark Mall Belk store, one of 13 stores operated in the Carolinas by Belk Brothers Company, is a complete fashion department store. With 240,000 square feet of shopping space on four levels, the store's interior, which was remodeled in 1986, offers shoppers the feeling of a series of specialty shops.

In 1970 a second Belk store opened in the city's booming southeast section at SouthPark Mall, and a third store opened five years later in the northeast part of the city at Eastland Mall. The uptown store closed in 1988 to make way for a major new office/hotel complex and performing arts center. Proceeds from the sale of the store property, totaling approximately $3.15 million, were donated by Belk to benefit the new arts center.

Another new 160,000-square-foot Belk store, which will serve the Charlotte-area market from Carolina Place Mall in Pineville, is scheduled to open in 1991.

Belk's long-standing goal has been to be the leading fashion retailer in every market it serves by listening to customers and responding to their changing needs for merchandise and service. Today it is the nation's largest family- and management-owned department store organization, employing more than 35,000 people in markets from Delaware to Florida and from the Carolinas to Texas. Its stores offer the top national brand fashions, as well as the company's exclusive private brands.

Uniting all Belk and Leggett stores and groups is a support organization called Belk Stores Services, Inc. (BSS), which has offices in Charlotte and New York City. Since the 1920s BSS has provided leadership and direction to Belk and Leggett stores on all aspects of retail operations.

A modern 562,000-square-foot office building and show center opened in the fall of 1988 to house Belk Stores Services' 1,200 Charlotte employees and to host the 20 private merchandise shows held by the company each year. John M. Belk, who served as Charlotte's mayor from 1969 to 1977, and his brother, Thomas M. Belk, serve as chairman and president, respectively, of BSS and of most of the individual Belk stores.

Belk Stores Services, Inc., provides merchandising services and many other support services to the nearly 340 Belk Leggett stores.

PIEDMONT PLASTICS, INC.

The 55,000-square-foot Piedmont Plastics headquarters facility in Charlotte is one of five, with four others located in Raleigh, Atlanta, Greenville, and Nashville.

In 1968, when Charlotte was obviously emerging as an industrial and transportation center, the founders of Piedmont Plastics, Inc., chose the city as the right place to establish a premier provider of plastics for the region. There they found fast, easy access to cities in both the Carolinas.

In its first 20 years the company has grown to offer customers the largest inventory of plastics in the Southeast. Its products range from decorative and mar-resistant glazing materials, used as replacements for glass, to specifically designed engineering materials for use in mechanical applications such as gears and bearings.

Its 55,000-square-foot headquarters facility in Charlotte, and four others in Raleigh, Atlanta, Greenville, and Nashville, are linked together 24 hours per day by a sophisticated computer system. When a customer places an order not in-store at one location, the computer can be used to locate the item in the next closest location and ship it from that point. Before shipment, plastic sheets and rods are cut to the exact size ordered. That kind of service is what keeps customers coming back.

To provide the most current technical service, the firm continually looks for new products to meet the needs of its wide variety of customers. In addition, it constantly provides information about the appearance and performance of products it sells. As a matter of course, it is aware of the physical attributes of its products such as a plastic's strength, corrosion resistance, hardness, or light-diffusing qualities.

Moreover, a staff of sales specialists can provide technical assistance and help a customer choose the right plastics for a specific task. They inform customers about new plastics on the market and help customers find cost-effective ways to use them.

President Henry G. Booth, Jr., and his partner Hugh Lewis, who manage the 35,000-square-foot facility in Atlanta, went to work for the company in the early 1970s. They bought it from its founders and changed its focus from fabrication of plastic parts to distribution of plastics from many different manufacturers. In 1984 they formed a subsidiary, Piedmont Polymers, which distributes adhesives.

As a result, they now sell more than $15 million worth of plastics annually to thousands of companies—more than 5,000 from the Charlotte office alone. Piedmont customers range from major manufacturers and *Fortune* 500 companies to small entrepreneurs. Its products are used by companies as wide ranging as manufacturers of machinery and textiles to yacht builders and glaziers. "Our objective is to have the kind of plastic the customer wants in the size he wants, and to ship it when the customer wants it," says Booth.

That goal of quickly bringing customers an increasing number of plastics should keep Piedmont Plastics, Inc., growing in the future.

Piedmont Plastics, Inc., remains a leader in providing plastics to the Southeast through its continuing efforts to provide the most advanced and efficient service to its customers. This sophisticated computer system links all five of the company's headquarters facilities together 24 hours per day.

IVEY'S

For 23 Ivey's department stores in the Carolinas and Florida, Charlotte is the center of action. In uptown Charlotte, the stores' executive and corporate offices direct their merchandising, sales promotion, operations, and credit activities. A few miles away at SouthPark mall, the organization's flagship store offers its most expansive line of merchandise and most glamorous environment.

stores in the Carolinas and 10 in Florida.

In the market area of each Ivey's store, only select Ivey's brings customers fashions by Night Boutique; Gem, Arpel, and Bijan fragrances; and Hoya crystal. Each store is also the exclusive source of Ivey's own private-label merchandise and Moon's Surf Shop active wear for young men. Moreover, Ivey's stores

Nearby a distribution and data center provide operational support for the region.

In fact, Charlotte has been central to the organization's future since Joseph Benjamin Ivey opened his first store in the city in 1900. He believed his stores should reflect his personal regard for quality in people, ethics and ideals, and the community. Within 10 years that philosophy led to the store's expansion into Florida.

Today, as a division of BATUS, Inc., Ivey's continues to uphold that philosophy in its offerings of fashionable, high-quality merchandise and exclusive brands, and its support of cultural activities in its communities. It brings its own distinctive style to discriminating shoppers through 13

Exciting and informative events prevail at Ivey's. Here a cooking demonstration is taking place at the Main Ingredient.

try to assure a selection of fine quality clothing in a wide range of sizes. Its women's departments, for example, extend from Club Petite (sized for women under five feet four inches tall) to The Woman (sized for full-figured women).

Ivey's stores also serve customers with such services as its own credit card and centralized Bridal Registry. At the Bridal Registry, a bride's gift preferences and the gifts that have been purchased for her are kept on file at every store to prevent duplication.

At many Ivey's stores a trained professional helps men and women

plan their wardrobe and select clothes for business, social, and weekend occasions.

Every month Ivey's loyal customers send in more than 4,000 suggestion cards, all of which are read and carefully considered by Ivey's management. Many of those suggestions are implemented as part of Ivey's effort to make each store meet the needs of its particular group of customers.

At the Charlotte uptown store, for example, Ivey's serves busy professionals with such additions as clothing for career women in its Executive Club department and free delivery of purchases to uptown offices.

During a 15-month renovation of the Southpark store, ending in 1988, Ivey's added 60,000 square feet on the third floor to the original 120,000 square feet. The entire store was updated with bright colors, marble floors on each level, and opulent furnishings and accessories. The result is an Ivey's that is considered a prototype for the stores of the future.

Its upscale merchandise is now en-

ABOVE: Ivey's SouthPark crystal gallery displays some of the finest crystal from Baccarat, Lalique, Orrefors, and more.

ABOVE RIGHT: The men's clothing department is a fine example of the warmth and ambience a shopper will find at Ivey's.

hanced by dramatic surroundings that include bright lighting in every department, deep green and mahogany wall treatments in the men's departments, hardwood floors in the men's Ralph Lauren 8% shop and rich burgundy trim in the cosmetics areas. Special lighting treatments in the same departments involve the use of skylights and ceiling-mounted halogen spotlights.

The store's expansion increased the size of virtually every department. The cosmetics showcase space more than doubled, from 300 to 700 linear feet. Women's apparel went from 40,000 to 65,000 square feet in 12 different departments on the second floor, and men's apparel went from 14,000 to 24,000 square feet.

Its Crystal Gallery—which offers such desired names as St. Louis, Baccarat, Lalique, Waterford, Hoya, and Orrefors—features a $45,000 Lalique glass table at its center. Among the more than 40 china patterns at the store are six different lines from Limoges, France.

Ivey's Eastland is currently undergoing a reallocation of space in order to enhance and update several departments. This, as well as other facial uplifts, will bring the 101,000-square-foot store in line with the mall itself, which is experiencing a major redecoration and modernization throughout the summer and early fall.

However, Ivey's dedication to the fine taste of customers has also been expressed in its support of the culture of its communities. The company's contributions to such artistic organizations as the Charlotte Symphony, the Mint Museum of Art, and Spirit Square in Charlotte, as well as the symphonic, theatrical, and arts organizations of other cities

have won Ivey's public recognition, including the North Carolina Governor's Business Award and the Charlotte Vanguard Award for public service.

Nine decades after Joseph Benjamin Ivey began his mission to bring quality to people in Charlotte, Ivey's continues to pursue that mission from the Carolinas to Florida.

Friendly and knowledgeable sales associates make shopping a pleasant experience at Ivey's.

CAROLINA TRACTOR & EQUIPMENT CO.

Since L.M. Weisiger first established a dealership for Caterpillar Tractor in Asheville in 1928, the company has changed its name and moved its headquarters twice. But the family philosophy that originally made the firm successful is still helping it grow.

In fact, every employee of Carolina Tractor & Equipment Co. is given a small card that states the firm's values and mission. It says, "We are committed: To placing the customer first. To conducting business with integrity. To showing respect for the individual."

Those values guide each employee's mission: "To provide positive and good career opportunities for our co-workers. To provide maximum value in all products and services for our customers. To maximize the market potential and profit opportunity in our existing Caterpillar territory."

Operating with that mission, the company now occupies 150,000 square feet of office, warehouse, and service facilities and more than 300,000 square feet of paved or reinforced storage area on Charlotte's northern edge. Under the leadership

of Edward I. Weisiger, son of the founder, Carolina Tractor has tripled its sales since the headquarters moved to Charlotte in 1971. In 1988 its business totaled more than $100 million.

In 46 North Carolina counties, Carolina Tractor is the exclusive distributor of Caterpillar construction and material-handling equipment. In 14 South Carolina counties, it is the exclusive distributor of Caterpillar forklifts. It operates branches in Greensboro, Asheville, and Hickory, North Carolina, and Greenville, South Carolina.

That is a long way from the days when L.M. Weisiger, one of the first graduates of the Uni-

versity of South Carolina School of Engineering, left his job as a state highway engineer and, in 1926, helped form an organization to build the concrete roads that would carry the rising number of newly popular automobiles through North Carolina and Virginia.

In 1928 Weisiger was building a road at Fletcher in the North Carolina mountains when two representatives of the recently formed Caterpillar Tractor Co. approached him about establishing a dealership. They knew his experience would help him sell and service the belt-treaded tractors that were replacing the draft horse on roads, farmlands,

ABOVE: In the 1940s Carolina Tractor & Equipment Co. was headquartered in Salisbury, North Carolina, and operated from this facility.

LEFT: Carolina Tractor & Equipment Co. moved its corporate headquarters from Salisbury to Charlotte in 1971.

and logging operations. They could not have guessed, however, that his flexibility in meeting the needs of a changing economy would help him create and guide a major company.

Just two years later Weisiger bought a majority interest in Carolina Tractor & Equipment Co., which had been formed in 1926. He closed the Asheville operation and merged it with his new one in Salisbury, which had become a rail and market center for the state. But the hard years of the Depression were just beginning.

Buyers for large equipment were

scarce. The firm survived with five employees selling products that ranged from road machinery to dairy supplies and from bottle caps to washing powder that was mixed in a galvanized tub at company headquarters.

A decade later the corporation faced a different problem. It had buyers, but World War II limited the equipment that could be sold for non-military uses. To support the war effort, the company's service department worked hard to keep old farm tractors and other equipment running. At the same time Carolina Tractor built a service facility at New Bern to maintain equipment used at coastal military bases.

In 1951, when North Carolina was split into two Caterpillar dealerships, the company maintained its presence in the western half of the state, and once again Weisiger opened a branch in Asheville. Five years later his son Edward, who had earned a degree in mechanical engineering from North Carolina State University and served as an Army vehicle maintenance officer, joined the firm as a sales trainee. Within a year he opened the Charlotte branch, where he was manager until returning to the Salisbury headquarters as vice-president and general manager in 1958. Seven years later he became the company's president.

When the commercial vitality of Charlotte became apparent, Carolina Tractor moved to the fast-growing city and expanded its line of equipment to meet the needs of the area. Today it sells, leases, and rents everything from heavy construction equipment and forklifts to diesel truck engines and electric generating sets.

It has contributed to creating the highways, residential developments, and commercial buildings that have been an important part of the city's growth. It has provided the equipment to build Charlotte's new Douglas International Airport, as well as emergency power generators for the city's major hospitals and high-rise buildings. Its products have been the

source of backup power for the computer centers at Duke Power Company and First Union National Bank in Charlotte and for U.S. Air in Winston-Salem.

More than one-half of the company's 450 employees work in the Charlotte area. Roughly 60 percent of them provide service on the equipment the firm sells, leases, or rents.

ABOVE: *Caterpillar lift trucks were added to the line in 1968 and have become an important part of the company's business.*

RIGHT: *Thirteen field service trucks operate in the Charlotte area. Equipped with booms and air compressors, they are fully stocked with diagnostic tools.*

The Charlotte stockroom alone holds more than 38,000 different parts—all efficiently managed by a computerized system. In fact, Carolina Tractor guarantees that it can ship 98 percent of the parts ordered within 48 hours. It even runs a nightly shuttle to the Caterpillar central depot in Atlanta for extra stock.

Edward Weisiger has been an active member of the Charlotte community, serving on the boards of the Charlotte Chamber of Commerce and the YMCA and on the Southern Regional Board of Wachovia Bank.

He has been chairman of the board of trustees for North Carolina State University from 1987 to 1989. In the early 1980s he helped build the Brown-Weisiger athletic facility, dedicated to his father, at North Carolina State.

Weisiger has been joined by his son, Edward I. Weisiger, Jr., who is manager of the Engine Division. The

company's executive vice-president and general manager is John Hendrix. Together they work to maintain the family tradition in a growing city.

"We're fortunate to have a great opportunity in a good area and have good people working with us," says Edward I. Weisiger, Sr. "We want to maximize those advantages in sales and service to our customers."

277

ADAM'S MARK HOTEL

Just south of uptown Charlotte's central business district, the Adam's Mark Hotel gleams white in the Carolina sun, its trademark red "splash" logo visible from several major approaches to the city. To the north the hotel offers guests an unobstructed view of the ever-changing Charlotte skyline, and to the south lies the "greenscape" of the city's famous canopy of trees.

Adam's Mark has long been a jewel in the Queen City's crown, a valued community resource playing host to two separate but quite compatible constituencies. On one hand it is the hotel that provides complete services for meetings of all sizes for the full spectrum of business, industry, and private organizations. And on the other hand it is the hotel that caters to guests who wish to enjoy its gracious atmosphere and famous amenities.

In either case Adam's Mark guests expect—and receive—luxury accommodations and efficient service, delivered with professional skill and polish by a staff of roughly 400 well-trained employees. Although it is the largest hotel between Washington, D.C., and Atlanta, guests at Charlotte's luxury-class, 600-room hotel

The Adam's Mark Hotel, located just south of uptown Charlotte, provides luxury accommodations and a friendly professional staff for visitors and Charlotte residents alike.

never feel lost in the shuffle; the attention they receive is warm, personal, and always timely.

The Charlotte facility is one of seven Adam's Mark Hotels owned and operated by the St. Louis-based HBE Corporation. Fred S. Kummer, president and founder of HBE, grew up in New York City, where his father was a vice-president of the Sheraton Corporation. Kummer, who started his own career as a one-man general contractor, has over the years built his business to its current standing as a diversified corporation and one of the 10 largest building contractors in the United States.

In 1967 Kummer formed Hospital Building and Equipment (HBE), now recognized as the world's largest designer-builder of health care facilities.

HBE Corporation currently employs approximately 3,200 workers nationwide. In recent years McGraw-Hill's *Engineering News-Record* magazine has ranked it 42nd among the top 400 general contracting firms and eighth in the top 50 building con-

A nighttime view of the convention entrance to the Adam's Mark Hotel.

tractors in this country.

Other HBE divisions are involved in providing plan-design-build services to financial institutions; attending to the needs of a growing elderly and retired population in retirement communities; developing, leasing, and managing Class A office buildings in major cities; and leasing medical, graphic arts, industrial, and agricultural equipment and truck trailers.

Another major project, Adam's Rib Recreation Area, is in the master-planning stages as a world-class, year-round resort that will include ski runs on Adam and Eve mountains. It comprises 3,000 of the 5,600 acres surrounding Adam Mountain in Eagle County, Colorado. Currently operated as Adam's Rib Ranch, HBE grazes 2,000 head of

Hereford cattle on the property.

Although the Charlotte hotel was the first in Kummer's national chain, it was not the first Adam's Mark, a distinction that belongs to Houston. It was, however, under Kummer's ownership that the 17-story North Tower Extension was completed in 1984. That same year the hotel was renamed Adam's Mark, joining the other HBE Corporation Adam's Mark Hotels in Clearwater Beach, Houston, Indianapolis, Kansas City, Philadelphia, and St. Louis.

The Adam's Mark Hotel division is, of course, only part of a large corporation, but the personal touch of Fred Kummer and his wife, June, a landscape architect, is visible in the ho-

tels and throughout HBE headquarters. Both Kummers are avid contemporary art collectors, as visitors to the Charlotte Adam's Mark can testify. The hotel's public areas are graced with arresting examples of their taste.

It is perhaps appropriate to begin a description of the services and amenities of this particular Adam's Mark with a discussion of the Conference Center, what might be considered the hotel's more serious, or business-oriented, side.

In a city that boasts excellent meeting facilities, this conference center is nonetheless a standout, particularly since the addition of the North Tower Extension. In 27,000 square feet of flexible meeting and banquet

The Adam's Mark Hotel has excellent dining facilities for both formal and informal occasions.

space—from the Carolina and Mecklenburg ballrooms, each accommodating more than 1,000, to the Governor's Ballroom and its 400-person capacity or the Cardinal Ballroom designed for 200, to some 37 parlors and meeting suites for smaller groups of 10 or 12—the Conference Center accommodates them all. Whatever the group's special needs— conference, classroom, or theater-style seating as well as food service, audiovisual equipment, lighting, electrical outlets, and special lighting systems—the staff at Adam's Mark makes it happen.

In tribute both to the center and its capabilities, numerous organizations regularly schedule their most important events at Adam's Mark. The annual Fourth of July Light Show is launched from its parking deck. Adam's Mark also is the locale of the annual Carolina Opera Ball and the March of Dimes Gourmet Gala, and in recent years the Printing Industry of the Carolinas has held its annual Excellence-In-Printing Award presentations there.

On a perhaps lighter side, but one that perfectly complements Conference Center activities, are the excellent restaurants and live entertainment that are uniquely special at Adam's Mark hotels.

Topping the list of fine restaurants in Charlotte is The Marker, known for many years to Charlotteans and visitors alike as *the* place to dine in this city. An elegant ambience and exquisitely prepared American regional cuisine are what make it so. Less formal, but equal to The

ABOVE: *Live entertainment is only one of the many special amenities that make the 600-room hotel an enjoyable place to stay.*

RIGHT: *Part of the North Tower extension was the addition of 27,000 square feet of meeting space. The Carolina Ballroom is just one of these meeting facilities—accommodating more than 1,000 people.*

Marker in quality and service, is Appleby's. Designed for lighter, more rapid-paced dining, this charming spot is open most hours of the day.

For high-energy nightlife, look to Players, which features live entertainment every night of the week, as well as specially scheduled events to add a little extra pizazz, such as a recent Beatlemania Month, which included a John Lennon—Strawberry Fields Forever Night, and regular ladies' nights. A dance floor, backgammon tables, spectacular lighting effects, and large-screen music videos complete the Players entertainment package. Or, for a more relaxing atmosphere after a long day of meet-

ings or an evening at the theater, there is the quiet Marker Lounge—another favorite spot of both Charlotte residents and visitors to the city, where they are entertained by the Beth Chorneau Trio playing jazz music.

And "just for the health of it," Adam's Mark has a complete health club as a complimentary service for its guests. Located on the second floor of the North Tower Extension, the club offers Nautilus equipment, Life Cycles and Rowers, whirlpool and saunas, and indoor and outdoor swimming pools.

Jim Alsdorf, general manager of the hotel, has worked in the hospitality industry for more than 17 years—including eight years with the Hyatt Corporation and five years with the Sheraton Hotel Corporation—prior to joining the Adam's Mark chain in 1983. He is in charge of the overall operation, which in terms of complexity and scale might rival managing a small town or community.

Adam's Mark offers several attrac-

The Marker Lounge is a favorite after-dark spot for local jazz and good conversation.

tive programs for its guests. For the corporate traveler, for example, there is the Preferred Member Program. Among its features are guaranteed preferred member rates and priority handling of reservations and checkout, as well as priority on blocks of rooms for special events or meetings.

For frequent guests there is the Gold Mark Club, with its own set of membership amenities and privileges, including money-saving room rates and other discounts.

Another popular feature that lures guests from throughout the Southeast to Adam's Mark is the Remarkable Weekend, which comes in three distinctive editions: the Bed and Breakfast, Enchanted, and Romantic Weekends. Because the hotel is in close proximity to such Charlotte attractions as the Mint Museum, Discovery Place, Spirit Square, historic Fourth Ward, and the Charlotte Coliseum, visitors can take in the sights and still be pampered, well-cared-for guests for a luxurious weekend at Adam's Mark.

The management of Adam's Mark is ever vigilant in its search for ways in which it might provide extra sparkle to the hotel's already splendid amenities, something to delight hotel guests and members of the community. A recent example is the year-

long, exclusive relationship established with the noted Firestone Vineyards in California's Santa Ynez Valley. Brooks Firestone, founder and owner of the vineyards, had selected the Charlotte Adam's Mark to be the sole U.S. retailer for his red and white table wines, the first time in the city's history that such an arrangement had been made with a California vintner. The year was a great success, with Firestone making several visits to the city to conduct training seminars and to teach the food and beverage staff the fine points of storing and serving his wines. As for the hotel's dinner guests, their first preference was for the white table wine, with the chardonnay, cabernet, and sauvignon blanc following close behind in their favor.

Over the years many famous people have stopped for the night in Charlotte at the Adam's Mark, famous people with famous names and faces—Senator Robert Dole and Transportation Secretary Elizabeth Dole, Senator Jesse Helms, Vice-President Dan Quayle, North Carolina Governor James Martin, Richard Petty, the Reverend Pat Robertson, Mikhail Baryshnikov, General Alexander Haig, Michael Jordan, Daryl Waltrip, and Luciano Pavorotti. Each received star treatment, which is to say, exactly the same Old South hospitality and caring service that each business, professional, and private guest of this Charlotte landmark receives every day of the year.

WECARE DISTRIBUTORS, INC.

In March 1982 Rose Marie and Pete Monroe began working toward their dream of building the finest skin care company in the world. Rose Marie created her skin care products, The Rose Marie Collection, using the expertise of Dr. William Wellman, a noted cosmetic chemist, to incorporate oil of mink into creams and lotions for moisturizing and conditioning the skin. Their objective was to involve independent people in having a business of their own without having to make a large investment.

WeCare has expanded its operations through thousands of its independent distributors throughout the United States and into foreign markets. WeCare chose Charlotte as its headquarters because of the atmosphere of its business community and its transportation facilities. The beautiful city of Charlotte mirrors the beauty of The Rose Marie Collection.

WeCare's distributors can offer its customers 50 different skin care products in The Rose Marie Collection, from moisturizing creams and foundation makeup for women to shave cream and cologne for men. Every year WeCare adds two to four more items to its line. Most of the company's creams, moisturizers, and foundations still include the oil of mink on which the original products were based.

"We use oil of mink because it is the oil most characteristically similar to the body's natural oil. It can be quickly absorbed by the skin without feeling greasy, easily mixed with other beneficial skin care ingredients, and stored a long time without becoming rancid," says Rose Marie.

WeCare distributors are trained to show customers how each of the products can be used in an overall program of skin care, whether for maintenance or for therapy of problems. Those distributors are the key to WeCare's success.

They are people who believe in The Rose Marie Collection and feel that they are helping customers, not

Some of the products from The Rose Marie Collection skin care line.

simply selling products. Moreover, the WeCare distribution program is designed to make each person feel a part of the whole team.

Distributor sales are consistently rewarded with recognition and money. Each month 50 to 200 distributors arrive in Charlotte from throughout the United States, Canada, the Bahamas, and the Caribbean islands to participate in four- and five-day Leadership Conferences. Annual conventions, which have drawn 2,000 distributors to Charlotte for training, motivational talks, and awards, stimulate the feeling of friendship that the company cultivates.

A monthly magazine *Realities*, features letters, photos, and success stories from dozens of distributors. Some have only recently begun selling WeCare products; others have reached their goals for success as re-

gional and national distributors.

These people are led by an executive staff that believes families and married couples should share in the success of selling WeCare. Rose Marie and Pete Monroe together serve as chairman of the board.

At the top, Rose Marie and Pete Monroe are WeCare's dreamers and motivators. Their message to distributors was expressed in a 1988 letter that said: "Winners are people who make a difference in everything they do and everywhere they go . . . Why do we believe we will have the number-one skin care company? Because we have a company full of winners—You! Go For It! Strive for excellence in all areas of your life, and you will win!"

WeCare Distributors at a Celebration Convention in Charlotte.

Christmas presents. Moreover, the company is involved in the Big Oak Ranch for abused boys in Glencoe, Alabama, and it has donated more than $140,000 to build a similar 90-acre ranch for girls in Springville, Alabama.

WeCare combines concerns for the well-being of children with devotion to its distributors and the belief that its products are the best available. WeCare's corporate philosophy stresses excellence in products and service combined with the principle of placing one's faith first, family second, and vocation third.

When asked about the future, Rose Marie and Pete Monroe answer with assurance, "What lies ahead? Success as the number-one skin care company. Why? Because we have the number-one product, the number-one opportunity, and, more important, the number-one distributors."

Rose Marie and Pete Monroe, founders and owners of WeCare Distributors, Inc.

That goal of excellence extends beyond selling the firm's products to include supporting charitable causes.

WeCare galvanizes the efforts of its distributors to help teenagers avoid drugs and to award college scholarships through an essay contest on avoiding drug use. In 1988 it awarded 132 scholarships ranging from $500 to $2,500, bringing the total given since 1984 to $143,000. That same year it began sponsoring The Acorn Festival, a leadership conference for teenagers that also rewards outstanding teachers who participate.

WeCare and its distributors have also contributed more than $75,000 to local charities in the Charlotte area and $50,000 to national projects, including the Phoenix House, a home for drug abusers in New York. Among its gifts is more than $100,000 worth of WeCare products to be used by these charities as

LANCE, INC.

From a street corner in New Orleans to the top of a Colorado ski trail, there is a Lance snack machine just about anywhere anyone could decide to get something to eat. The machines are found at more than 70,000 different places in 36 states from the Atlantic to the Rocky Mountains.

What is more, the company can virtually assure that every cracker, cookie, cake, nut, chip, or piece of candy is fresh. They ought to be; once each week every one of Lance's 2,500 sales representatives gets a new supply, delivered straight from the Lance bakery on one of Lance's own trucks. And once each week he takes them to every one of his customers.

ABOVE: An aerial view of Lance headquarters and bakery in Charlotte.

LEFT: Pictured here is (seated) A.F. "Pete" Sloan, chairman of the board, and (standing) J.W. "Bill" Disher, president.

An early photo of the Lance plant at 1300 South Boulevard in Charlotte. Photo circa 1940

In fact, says company president J.W. "Bill" Disher, there is a good chance those snacks are still warm from the oven when they are loaded on the truck. If a state (such as California) is too far from the manufacturing plant to assure weekly delivery, Lance snacks are not sold there.

That distribution system, as well as the commitment to giving customers consistent freshness, taste, and quality have made Lance, Inc., one of North Carolina's top 10 industrial companies. In addition, the system has helped the firm earn an enviable record; since it was founded in 1913, the operation has not recorded a single year of loss.

Lance's history of success began when Charlotte food broker Phillip

L. Lance was left with 500 pounds of raw peanuts after a customer cancelled an order. He and his son-in-law, Salem A. Van Every, roasted them in kitchen ovens and sold them in small bags.

Soon they had a mechanical roaster and were giving out samples of their peanut butter on crackers. The result was the first commercial peanut butter sandwich. During World War I the company was famous for its sales of the sandwiches—and its new peanut brittle candy—wrapped in glassine paper and packed in shirt boxes that were saved by local merchants.

By 1938, 12 years after Lance died in an automobile accident, Salem Van Every led the company into making its own crackers. Five years

later his 29-year-old son, Phillip, assumed the leadership when his father died of a massive coronary.

During the next 30 years Phil reorganized the firm's system of sales and distribution on a district basis and instituted automation throughout the plant. While he was doing it, he also found time to be Charlotte's mayor for two terms.

Today A.F. "Pete" Sloan, Lance's chairman of the board, actively participates in the Charlotte community while he helps Lance increase its market share. And the Lance Foundation is noted for its funding of a wide variety of the area's charitable, educational, and cultural institutions.

The Charlotte plant now covers one million square feet of a 275-acre complex. According to Disher, Charlotte makes a good spot for the company's largest manufacturing facility. Roughly 60 percent of the nation's population lies within a 600-mile radius. Another Lance plant in Greenville, Texas, makes fresh snacks available to western states east of the Rockies.

Each month the two bakeries transform some 5 million pounds of flour, one million pounds of shorten-

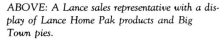

A Lance sales van outside of company headquarters.

ABOVE: A Lance sales representative with a display of Lance Home Pak products and Big Town pies.

LEFT: A Lance floor display filled with single-serve snacks, typically found in convenience store accounts.

ing, 2 million pounds of peanuts, and 600,000 pounds of sugar into the snack products for which Lance has become famous.

They are products that underwent an invisible, but major, change in 1988. After two years of research and testing, Lance eliminated the use of lard and oils high in saturated fats. It began producing 64 products that were low in saturated fats and either low in or free of cholesterol. The process involved much more than a simple substitution of vegetable oils for animal fats and tropical oils.

"We wanted to respond to an increasing awareness of health issues," explains Bill Disher. "But we know people buy our products because they like the taste. That meant we had to formulate, test, reformulate, and re-test . . . until we could produce low-cholesterol cookies, crackers, cakes, etc., with exactly the same taste and texture that had been so successful for years."

When the new formulations were introduced on the market, Lance began labeling its products for cholesterol and sodium content. Public response to the new nutritional content was good, and sales soon responded.

Also in 1988 the company introduced another change. It began selling family-size bags in convenience and grocery stores.

For years its profits were derived from single-serve packages sold over the counter and through vending machines, and from institutional items such as crackers sold to restaurants and institutions. The vending-machine distribution method aimed to make snacks immediately available to people anywhere they worked or played.

However, Lance recognized that the major market for food is the grocery store. The new four-ounce and 6.5-ounce bags of potato chips, pretzels, corn chips, popcorn, and pork skins were designed to put Lance snack foods into the home.

Once again, the 5,500 Lance, Inc., employees are bringing more fresh snacks to more people within their area of distribution.

Lance soup and salad crackers, the company's "bread basket" institutional items.

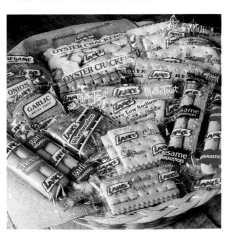

DISTRIBUTION TECHNOLOGY INC.

A group of local investors, believing in Charlotte's potential for growth, got together in 1970 to form Distribution Systems Inc., a closely held North Carolina private stock corporation.

Their intent was to develop public warehousing distribution facilities that would provide handling, storage, and administrative services to area business and industry. Operations got under way in a 100,000-square-foot warehouse in Chemway Industrial Park.

To run the organization, the owners called on R.J. "Rock" Miralia, then group vice-president of R.T. Systems Inc., a Chicago-based distribution and transportation firm. Says Miralia, "I was anxious to accept the job because of the quality and financial management experience of the original investors." Two of those individuals are today chairmen of major banks: Hugh McColl of NCNB and Luther Hodges of National Bank of Washington. "Alex Porter, who is a principal of the New York investment firm of Porter-Felleman, was another key person in the company's initial development," Miralia recalls, "and he continues to serve as a corporate director."

In late 1973 the owners of the company, which by then had been renamed Distribution Technology, agreed to a leveraged buyout by Miralia, company officers, and certain directors. In the years since the

buyout, says Miralia, now the company's chairman and president, "Our efforts are directed to identifying Charlotte as a major southeastern distribution center. We place a lot of emphasis on organizational development and on providing a broad range of physical distribution services to the marketplace."

Miralia says that Charlotte's position as a major transportation hub, as well as its large number of trucking carriers providing direct-line service, two great railroad carriers, and the vitality of the city's growth have created an ever-increasing demand for Distribution Technology's services.

The company's organization and operations have significantly changed and broadened over the past 15 years, aided substantially by the latest and best electronic technology. "We have evolved from a public warehousing operation into a third-party logistical organization providing a full range of physical distribution and management services to the marketplace from locations throughout the southeastern United States," Miralia says.

Distribution Technology is the parent corporation of several divisions. Piedmont Distribution Centers (PDC), for example, began operations in the mid-1970s and is the public warehousing division. PDC operates exclusively in Charlotte and provides warehousing and distribution services from centers in various Charlotte industrial parks. Currently, 850,000 square feet of warehouse space support the requirements of grocery, chemical, textile, and general commodity clients in the southeastern region.

In support of the city's efforts to attract international firms to Charlotte, Distribution Technology spearheaded a venture, which included the North Carolina Commerce Depart-

ment, the Charlotte Chamber of Commerce, and a number of public-spirited citizens, to apply to Washington for approval of a North Carolina Foreign Trade Zone (FTZ).

"Dick Primm, a vice-president of Distribution Technology, was the quarterback in this development," Miralia says. Primm today is director of FTZ 57, the first such zone in North Carolina. "The purpose of the FTZ," Miralia continues, "is to stimulate and expedite international commerce by allowing foreign goods to come into the country duty free and quota free for an unlimited amount of time. This means that although the zone is supervised by U.S. Customs, it's considered to be outside U.S. territory." Foreign goods brought into the zone can be stored, used in a manufacturing process, combined with other foreign or domestic

A view of Piedmont Distribution Center's 390,000-square-foot grocery products warehouse. Located in Arrowood Industrial Park, the facility was designed with room for expansion of 600,000 square feet on adjacent land. Photo by John Garner Agency

materials, exhibited, or reexported without payment of duty, which must be paid only when goods leave the FTZ and enter the United States for domestic consumption.

Initially, two of the company's warehouses were designated as FTZ sites. In late 1978 Distribution Technology reached an agreement with Wachovia Bank's South Point Industrial Park to establish 50 acres of that prime location as Charlotte's Foreign Trade Zone Park.

Other Distribution Technology divisions are PDC Trucking—operating in North and South Carolina, Virginia, Georgia, and Tennessee as a licensed common carrier; IFB Transportation Systems—a traffic and distribution firm licensed and regulated by the Interstate Commerce Commission and representing a number of major shippers and carriers; Contract Warehousing and Manufacturing Services—dedicated facilities, operations, labor, and management services for clients with large, specialized warehousing requirements; and Record Storage Systems—providing secure, humidity- and temperature-controlled storage for office files and magnetic media.

Distribution Technology has more than 400 employees in its various divisions, serves more than 100 corporate clients, is a common carrier and transportation broker, ships some 1.6 billion pounds of product annually, and has 1.5 million square feet of warehouse and manufacturing space in its varied enterprises.

Visualizing what 1.6 billion pounds of product represents might be difficult, says Miralia, so he provides this framework: "We ship the equivalent of 40,000 fully loaded tractor-trailers every year. Our true activity, of course, is double that amount because we first receive the products, which are placed in our storage facilities, and then we ship them out at the rate of 800 truckloads weekly."

Rock Miralia and the other Distribution Technology Inc. founders recognized early on Charlotte's great potential as a financial, services, and distribution center. Says Miralia, "We remain committed to investing in this growth and to providing support to area businesses as a major player in southeastern distribution services."

A view of the interior truck docks and staging area. Eighty-seven truck docks are utilized to accommodate the significant inbound and outbound activity. Photo by John Garner Agency

UNITED DATA SYSTEMS

Utilizing the skills and knowledge of computer consultants, marketing experts, and data-processing managers, United Data Systems helps companies of all sizes use computers efficiently.

Using the widely varied talents and experience of a professional team at company headquarters in Charlotte, North Carolina, United Data Systems helps companies of all sizes use computers efficiently. Its clients range from a small veterinary office to a large manufacturer of textiles. Their needs run from accounting to a complete inventory control/financial management program.

United Data Systems combines the skills of computer consultants, marketing professionals, and data-processing managers to meet those needs and guarantee that customers will be satisfied.

"Our marketing representatives can help customers find solutions because they are very knowledgeable about both the hardware and the software," says Joe Ganzler, marketing director. "We sell computer hardware and software packages, develop

custom software, and modify a customer's existing software for PCs and for IBM Systems 36, 38, and AS-400."

United Data has developed several software packages for the specific needs of the apparel and manufacturing industries. One of these, for the apparel industry, is a complete system for order entry through shipping, inventory control, basic accounting, and invoicing. It can keep track of the many variables such a company requires: all the sizes, colors, fabrics, and styles it must manage efficiently to be profitable. It codes various types of fabric and main-

tains a constant inventory of supplies on hand.

United Data's software for manufacturers lets them use a PC to keep track of materials and parts easily and efficiently.

On the other hand, if United Data has not developed such a software package or system to help a customer and cannot find an existing one on the market, it can create one. According to manager Teresa Hoffman, the company has the expertise to set up the kind of system the client needs. In fact, the firm offers a 100-percent satisfaction guarantee on its services. It is confident that the experience and knowledge of United Data's people can solve virtually any customer problem.

"We find what a client needs. We don't just sell a customer something because it's what we have," says United Data president Jackie McEntire. "We are working with a very dedicated group of talented people to guarantee our clients 100-percent satisfaction with our operation."

With that guarantee, United Data Systems expects to use its Charlotte headquarters to expand into other southeastern cities with computer solutions for other growing companies.

United Data Systems guarantees 100-percent satisfaction for its customers, providing the best in computer knowledge and services.

THE MARKER

The Marker Restaurant has long been the place for elegant dining in Charlotte, whether a special occasion, entertaining an important client, or simply to enjoy superb food and service in a beautifully appointed room.

This crown jewel of the Adam's Mark Hotel is perhaps most renowned for its tableside food preparation, always carried out with a bit of fanfare and flourish, and its opulent Sunday brunch with delicacies to suit every taste and fancy.

The Marker specializes in American regional foods. The lunch menu carries such items as blue crab, corn chowder and lobster bisque soups, club and prime rib sandwiches, a variety of salads and succulent dishes such as Carolina brook trout and roast Concord duck. Pastries and desserts are devilish and made fresh daily by the Marker pastry chef.

Dinner is an absolute dining delight, with soups, salads, hot appetizers, cold appetizers, and a variety of entrees that appeal to the most discriminating—grilled swordfish steak, charbroiled salmon bouillon, veal chops, prime rib, and double lamb chops. The menu is simple, but difficult to choose from. The wine list is also most impressive with an excellent overall selection of French, Italian and California vintages. The Marker also is rather unique in that the table water is bottled spring water and served in a tall glass with a slice of lemon, and a number of the entrees are prepared with ingredients low in sodium and fat—a strong appeal for the diet conscious.

The ambience of The Marker is striking and provides three distinctive areas for one's dining pleasure. The main level is split into two sections. One side is done in various beige and whites, with mirrored columns, sweeping arches, and high ceilings. The other is abundant in earth tones, complete with rich dark paneling, stone walls, and two large fireplaces. All of the tables are supplied with large, nicely spaced, comfort-

ably padded armchairs.

A smaller section is raised above the main level and reflects the simple style of a small European cafe. The perception is made more complete by live jazz music from the Davenport Trio, featuring the sultry sounds of Beth Chorneau.

A small dining area is also available that will comfortably seat 15 to 20 people in privacy—perfect for an important family gathering or a small business meeting dinner.

Elegant, but unobtrusive; extraordinary service; fine food and wines—all apt descriptions of one of Queen City's premier establishments, The Marker Restaurant in The Adam's Mark Hotel.

Specializing in American regional cuisine, elegant dining, and excellent service, The Marker distinguishes itself as one of Charlotte's most cosmopolitan eateries.

Patrons

The following individuals, companies, and organizations have made a valuable commitment to the quality of this publication. Windsor Publications and the Charlotte Chamber of Commerce gratefully acknowledge their participation in *Charlotte: City at the Crossroads*.

Adam's Mark Hotel*
Aetna Life & Casualty*
James M. Alexander Realty, Inc.*
Barnhardt Manufacturing Company*
Belk Department Stores*
Bell, Seltzer, Park and Gibson*
W.R. Bonsal Company*
Broadway & Seymour*
Cansler, Lockhart, Burtis & Evans*
Carolina Tractor & Equipment Co.*
Charlotte Memorial Hospital and
    Medical Center*
Charlotte Pipe and Foundry Company*
Childress Klein Properties*
Cogentrix, Inc.*
John Crosland Company/Centex
    Homes*
Crosland Erwin Associates*
Deloitte Haskins & Sells*
Dexter Plastics*
Distribution Technology Inc.*
Duke Power Company*
E.I. du Pont de Nemours and
    Company*
Epley Associates, Inc.*
First Union Corporation*
Frito-Lay, Inc.*
The FWA Group*
Hoechst Celanese Corporation*
Homelite/Textron*
ICI Americas Inc.*
Interstate/Johnson Lane*
Ivey's*
Johnson & Higgins Carolinas, Inc.*
Jones Group, Inc.*
KPMG Peat Marwick*

Lance, Inc.*
Little & Co.*
The Marker*
Marsh Associates, Inc.*
Merrill Lynch Realty, Inc.*
NCNB Corporation*
Okuma of America*
The Orthopaedic Hospital of
    Charlotte*
Parker, Poe, Thompson, Bernstein,
    Gage & Preston*
Pepsi-Cola Bottling Company of
    Charlotte*
Philip Morris U.S.A., Cabarrus
    Manufacturing Center*
D.L. Phillips Investment Builders,
    Inc.*
Piedmont Plastics, Inc.*
The Pneumafil Group*
Presbyterian Hospital*
Price Waterhouse*
Providence Day School*
Robison & McAulay*
Rowe Corporation*
Royal Insurance*
Sandoz Chemicals Corporation*
Southern Bell: A BellSouth Company*
United Data Systems*
USAir*
Verbatim Corporation*
Waters Incorporated*
WeCare Distributors, Inc.*
Westinghouse Electric Corporation*
WMIX Radio*
WPCQ Channel 36*
WSOC-FM 103*
WSOC-TV*

* Participants in Part Two: *Charlotte: City at the Crossroads*. The stories of these companies and organizations appear in chapters 7 through 12, beginning on page 158.

Bibliography

NOTES

Thanks to the following for the use of their files
    and publications:

The *Business Journal*

Charlotte Chamber of Commerce

Charlotte Convention & Visitors Bureau

Charlotte-Douglas International Airport

Charlotte-Mecklenburg Historic Properties
    Commission

Charlotte-Mecklenburg Planning Commission

Charlotte-Mecklenburg Public Library

Charlotte-Mecklenburg Schools

The *Charlotte Observer*

City of Charlotte

Mecklenburg County

Update Magazine

Blythe, LeGette and Charles Raven Brockman.
*Hornets' Nest: The Story of Charlotte and
Mecklenburg County*. Charlotte: McNally
of Charlotte, 1961.

Claiborne, Jack. *The Charlotte Observer: Its Time
and Place, 1869-1986*. Chapel Hill, N.C.:
The University of North Carolina Press,
1986.

Gaillard, Frye. *The Dream Long Deferred*. Chapel
Hill, N.C.: The University of North Carolina Press, 1988.

Kratt, Mary Norton. *Charlotte: Spirit of the New
South*. Tulsa, Okla.: Continential Heritage
Press, Inc., 1980.

Morrill, Dan L. "Edward Dilworth Latta and the
Charlotte Consolidated Construction
Company (1890-1925): Builders of a New
South City." *The North Carolina Historical
Review*, July 1985.

Quirk, Bea. "Charlotte Report." *Pace Magazine*,
June 1986.

————. "The Charlotte Area Report,"
Pace Magazine, December 1988.

————, and Sally J. Craig. "Development
in Charlotte." *Pace Magazine*, August 1987.

————, and Carol Timblin. *The Insiders'
Guide to Charlotte*. Manteo, N.C.:
Storie/McOwen Publishers, Inc., 1987.

WTVI/Charlotte-Mecklenburg Public Broadcast
Authority. *From Uncle Tom to Jim Crow*.
Charlotte: 1984. Videorecording.

————. *Trading Path to Transit Mall*. Charlotte: 1985. Videorecording.

Index